Live and Die Like a Man

Live and Die Like a Man

Gender Dynamics in Urban Egypt

Farha Ghannam

Stanford University Press

Stanford, California

Stanford University Press
Stanford, California

©2013 by the Board of Trustees of the Leland Stanford Junior University.
All rights reserved.

Printed in the United States of America on acid-free, archival-quality paper

Library of Congress Cataloging-in-Publication Data

Ghannam, Farha, 1963- author.
  Live and die like a man : gender dynamics in urban Egypt / Farha Ghannam.
    pages cm
  Includes bibliographical references and index.
  ISBN 978-0-8047-8328-6 (cloth : alk. paper)--
  ISBN 978-0-8047-8329-3 (pbk. : alk. paper)
    1. Masculinity--Egypt. 2. Men--Socialization--Egypt. 3. Sex role--Egypt.
  4. Social norms--Egypt. 5. Egypt--Social conditions--1981- I. Title.
  HQ1090.7.E3
  [G43 2013]
  305.310962--dc23   2013021485

  ISBN 978-0-8047-8791-8 (electronic)

Typeset by Bruce Lundquist in 11/13.5 Adobe Garamond

Contents

Illustrations

Acknowledgments

THIS BOOK is the product of many years of work and the support of many people, all of whom have contributed to my way of thinking and writing. First and foremost, I would like to thank my friends and interlocutors in al-Zawiya al-Hamra. I very much appreciate the hospitality, friendship, and generosity of spirit that they have extended to me (and to my family members) over the past two decades. I am grateful for the warmth, care, great meals, and many hours of conversation and interaction that enriched my understanding of life in their neighborhood and Cairo more broadly. Regretfully, to protect their privacy, I am not able to name each and every one of them.

Many of my colleagues and friends have been a tremendous help in shaping my thinking about gender and embodiment, generously reading parts or full drafts of the whole manuscript, and offering endless types of support. In particular, I am deeply indebted to Liz Braun, Maya Nadkarni, and Christy Schuetze, the core of my writing anthropology group at Swarthmore College for the past three years, who read all of the chapters and offered me wonderful comments and support. I would also like to thank Sa'ed Atshan, Jennie Keith, and Steve Piker for reading full drafts of the manuscript and offering very helpful comments. Ann Lesch, who was the Dean of Humanities and Social Sciences at the American University in Cairo, was a terrific support throughout my research. Many thanks to Fida Adely, Soraya Altorki, Miguel Diaz-Barriga, Maha Eladawy, Julia Elyachar, Lizzy Falconi, Noha Gaballah and her family, Sherine Hamdy, Connie Hungerford, Montasser Kamal, Karima Khalil, Moukhtar Kocache, Nadine Kolowrat, Rose Maio, Shana Minkin, Emilio Spadola, Gregory Starrett, Robin Wagner-Pacifici, Sarah Willie-LeBreton, and Jessica Winegar. Special thanks to Sierra Eckert, a remarkable student and research assistant. I would also like to recognize the help of Jane Abell, Ben Bernard-Herman, Lindsay Dolan, Zeinab Farahat, Lissie Jaquette, Karem Said, Humzah Soofi, and Allison Stuewe.

I have presented parts of this book at Stanford, Georgetown, George Mason, MIT, Bryn Mawr, Swarthmore, Colgate, Princeton, the American University in Cairo, and the University of Texas at Austin. The audiences of these different schools have provided excellent feedback that helped me think about the gendering process. A grant from the Ford Foundation's office in Cairo allowed me to spend the year of 2006–2007 doing fieldwork for this book. Swarthmore College has generously provided financial support during different parts of this project, including a Lang Faculty Fellowship, which enabled me to dedicate the time to complete the writing. Kate Wahl has been a terrific editor. I appreciate her enthusiasm, support, and understanding. Her comments as well as the feedback of the reviewers she selected for the manuscript have very much enriched the book. I am also thankful to Richard Gunde, Frances Malcolm, and Mariana Raykov for their help in seeing this project come to fruition.

My dear sister, Abla Ghannam, has helped me in numerous ways over the past ten years and I am grateful for her generosity, thoughtfulness, and love. My husband, Hans Lofgren, has read all the chapters of this book and shared with me invaluable feedback. I very much appreciate his love and support for the past twenty years. Our awesome daughter, Lena, has been the joy of my life since she was born twelve years ago. Her visits with me to al-Zawiya, the questions she asked, the observations she made, and the impact of her wonderful presence on my relationships with others and my status as a mother helped my research a great deal. I am especially grateful for her amazing ability to understand the endless hours I had to spend doing fieldwork and then writing. Lanloun, I love you very much and thank you for your help.

Hopefully, I did not forget to mention any of the people who were generous with their time and energy. To any friends and colleagues whom I failed to mention by name, I hope you still know that I very much appreciate your support and will be mortified when I discover that I forgot to mention your name.

Live and Die Like a Man

Introduction
Masculinity in Urban Egypt

ON JANUARY 25, 2011, thousands of Egyptian men and women began the now famous Egyptian revolution.[1] For eighteen days the number of protestors dramatically increased throughout Egypt, putting tremendous pressure on the political system and ultimately forcing President Mubarak's resignation on February 11, 2011. The revolution was impressive in several ways: the speed of the change, the quality of the resistance, the interplay between bodies and spaces, and the role of virtual and physical space in enabling and sustaining effective peaceful opposition. One of the most important aspects of the protests is that they were largely organized, publicized, and enacted by young men and women. Asma Mahfouz, a 26-year-old woman, has been widely credited by many for sparking the protests. On January 18, she posted a video urging Egyptian youth to participate in the protests planned for January 25.[2] Asma forcefully declared that she was going to protest in Midan al-Tahrir on that day and asked others to join her. She used the masculine noun to direct her speech to men: "Anyone who sees himself as a man, should go out to protest. . . . Whoever says that women should not go down [to Tahrir Square] because they could be maltreated (*byitbahdiluh*), or because it is improper (*ma ysahhish*) . . . , should show some honor (*nakhwa*) and manhood (*ruguula*) and go out to protest. . . . If you are a man (*raagil*), you should go out to protect me (*tihmeeni*) and protect any girl who is out to protest."

This appeal to the man, who defines himself as a man, who could protect female protesters, as well as the sense of partnership and interdependence that Asma emphasized, resonated in a powerful way with my anthropological research on masculinity and embodiment in Egypt. Asma's words and the praise in various media for the "real men" who initiated and sustained the protests clearly paralleled the ways that people spoke of the "real man" (*raagil bi saheeh*) in al-Zawiya al-Hamra, a low-income neighborhood in northern Cairo, where I have been working since 1993.[3] My ethnographic work in Cairo helped me understand the mobilization of millions of men and women who continued to protest before and after Mubarak's political demise. The dispositions that structured their conduct; the courage, solidarity, and determination they have shown; and the way their bodies became vehicles for political protest were informed by dynamics I have studied in Cairo for nearly two decades.

This book was conceived and researched largely before the January 25 Revolution. However, much of it was written during and after the massive nonviolent movement that has begun to change the face of the political system not only in Egypt but in other Arab countries as well. My references to these events throughout the book reflect their strong influence on how we think about contemporary Egypt and analyze its current socioeconomic and political structures and imagine its future. At the same time, against the backdrop of these events, it is productive to think of what my ethnography reveals about the social and economic frustrations that shape men's lives, particularly unemployment and low-paying jobs, political marginalization, inefficiency of government services and bureaucracies, and brutality of the police. More important, my analysis helps us understand some of the cultural meanings that informed the reactions of men and women to the changing events and how "structures of feeling" have been shaped by the interplay between local cultural meanings and values and broader national struggles and events. The phrase "structures of feeling" was advanced by Raymond Williams to capture the interplay between the social and personal, objective and subjective, fixed and active, explicit and implicit, and thought and feeling.[4] He chose the word *feeling* to "emphasize a distinction from more formal concepts of 'world-view' and 'ideology'" and to highlight the need to account not only for formally held and systematic beliefs but also for "meanings and values as they are actively lived and felt, and the relations between these and formal or systematic beliefs."[5] This notion is particularly helpful in accounting for how emerging ideas and feelings are being articulated within existing systems of meanings. The story that emerges, I hope, helps us understand the massive mobilization of millions of Egyptians and the unexpected magnitude of the changes that ensued.[6]

Whenever possible, I draw attention to some parallels, overlaps, tensions, and contradictions between local values and broader political and national projects, events, and discourses during and since the Egyptian revolution. However, this book is first and foremost a study of masculinity (*ruguula*) and embodiment in al-Zawiya al-Hamra. It aims to give the reader a sense of the meaning of manhood and the multiple agents who invest time and energy in the making of men. Acquiring a masculine identity is not simply an individual endeavor but is deeply connected to the recognition granted by others.[7] While this identity is embodied by the individual actor, this book shows that masculinity is a collective project that is negotiated through interactions between the private and the public, men and women, young and old, parents and children, neighbors and strangers, friends and foes, community members and outsiders.[8]

In order to give the reader a sense of how men and women in Egypt "do gender,"[9] this book draws on the daily practices and life stories of men and women in al-Zawiya al-Hamra whom I have known for almost twenty years. Since I first visited the area in 1993, I have gotten to know several families very well, keeping in touch with them over the years. In addition to fieldwork for two years between 1993–1994, eight months in 1997, and one year in 2006–2007, I have visited the area almost every summer since 1993. The latest visit was in the summer of 2012. My longstanding relationship with several families in the area allowed me to see babies born, infants become teenagers, children become adults, and older people age and retire. Some of my close interlocutors got married, some became sick, and some died. While both emotionally challenging and exhilarating, tracing their life trajectories allowed me to see how, under different circumstances (such as sickness, unemployment, debt, migration, marriage, and fatherhood), they struggled to meet the expectations of their families and materialize the social norms that defined them as men (and women).

Gender and Embodiment

This book is an argument against the "over-embodiment," especially in Western media, of the women and "disembodiment," both in the media and scholarly work, of the men of the Middle East. By "disembodiment" I mean the tendency to equate men with mind ('*aql*), culture, reason, honor, and public life, while offering little (if any) discussion of emotions, feelings, or bodily matters.[10] In contrast, women are often equated with body, nature, passion, secrecy, shame, and the private domain. Until recently, we have read about women mainly in the context of bodily functions and practices such as veiling, segregation, birthing, and sexual control.[11] In addition to the excessive focus on the *hijab* (women's head cover), a telling example is the attention directed to female circumcision. While this practice has been the focus of much attention, evoking "images of child abuse and torture" and "neocolonial visions of culturally disrespectful Eurocentric paternalism," little scholarly attention has been directed to male genital cutting.[12] In the process, the literature (without necessarily intending) continues to contribute to the over-embodiment of women and the disembodiment of men.

This is such a hegemonic view in Middle Eastern studies that I am struck by my own inability to think of the male body as a subject of analysis until recently. Since I started my research in al-Zawiya, I have heard young men talk with admiration about the strength and abilities of Arnold Schwarzenegger (loved and referred to simply as "Arnold") in *The Terminator* or *True Lies*, as well as the ever-whitening skin of Michael Jackson. I have seen young men obsess over their hair, skin, ironed clothes, and matching colors. I have seen older men work very hard and wear out their bodies in their endeavor to secure the income their families so desperately need. I have seen men age, get sick, and become immobile. All of this would seem to merit reasoned attention. And yet I was absorbed by a discourse that emphasized the physicality of the woman and ignored the materiality of the male body. Interestingly enough, I came to see "the male body" and its social and political significance only after being "distracted" by a religious audio tape, circulated in Cairo in the late 1990s, that focused on young men, their sexual desires, and how these can be managed and controlled.[13]

Concurrently, I have seen Middle Eastern and Muslim men dehumanized in American media, including, especially after September 11, a strong tendency toward depicting Arab, Muslim, and Middle Eastern men (often lumped together and assumed to be the same) as terrorists, suicide bombers, and oppressors of women.[14] Just think of how often we read statements like "women and children were among the victims" in reports of events in Iraq, Palestine, or Afghanistan. Here the assumption is that only women and children are innocent and deserve our sympathy while men are guilty and deserve being brutalized, tortured, or killed. The images of Middle Eastern men in the media frequently depict humiliation at the hands of American or Israeli soldiers as well as groups of angry men chanting against the West or attacking "innocent" Westerners and their allies.[15] In short, these men are portrayed either as a threat to be crushed or enemies to be subjugated and controlled.

This book aims to contribute to current studies of gender by engaging the male body as a social product and a producer of social life, as a biological entity that is elaborated by specific economic, social, political, cultural, and religious forces. The study of gender in the Middle East has shifted greatly over the past thirty years. Roughly speaking, up to the early 1980s, most studies were about men. These included studies of the market, religious orders, tribal systems, and much more.[16] Men were largely presented, however, as a generic agendered group. While their words and views were the focus of many studies, their gendered identities were not problematized, leaving masculinity unmarked, under-studied, and under-theorized. Since the early 1970s, feminists have offered compelling critiques of the tendency to universalize the views of men to the whole society and pointed to the need for the study of women, their practices, identities, spaces, and worldviews.[17] Over the past three decades, an impressive number of studies have complicated the meaning of femininity as well as the diverse socioeconomic and cultural roles of women.[18]

Only recently, however, have scholars begun to unpack the category of men, by, inter alia, looking at how they are affected by infertility and reproductive technologies, family planning, violence, military service, and neoliberal governmentality.[19] Although over the past ten years there have been a growing number of studies that explore the sociocultural constructions of the male body and masculinity in the United States and Europe,[20] no similar rigorous investigation of embodiment and masculinity has occurred in the Middle East. Even though several feminists have questioned the association that patriarchy creates between the woman and the body in the Middle East,[21] they have paid little attention to how it also distances men from their bodies. Thus, one gains the mistaken impression that the male body is not subject to social regulations, meanings, and expectations. Hardly any studies tell us about how Middle Eastern men groom themselves, feel about being single, getting old, sick, bald, or overweight. What is the relationship between embodiment and masculinity? How does the intersection between work demands and gender norms shape the male body, its health and death? How do men negotiate different social expectations that aim to define their bodies and masculine selves? What do men and women think constitutes a real man?[22] Although we often assume that we know the answers to these questions, they have rarely been addressed in scholarly work on the Middle East.

This book explores these questions by looking at the daily presentations of the body and analyzing how masculinity is embodied in different contexts. It shifts the analysis to gender dynamics and seeks to highlight the labor, time, and energy continuously invested in the construction of notions of masculinity (and femininity). It aims to recuperate the concept of gender, which is too often reduced to women in studies of the Middle East, by directing our attention to how manhood is socially produced and how a major part of this production is shaped by collective work and the joint effort of men and women. The discussion strives to account for the ever changing socioeconomic and political circumstances that shape gender dynamics as well as the productive interactions and links—and also the separations and divisions—that structure the daily lives of men and women.

Each chapter addresses some aspects of what I call a "masculine trajectory." I use this phrase to refer to the process of becoming a man. It aims to account for the important structures, especially gender and class, that intersect in powerful ways to shape men's conduct and identifications. It extends over a man's life span, but it is not a linear, predetermined, or clearly defined process. It intends to capture the shifting norms that inform the making of men but cannot be neatly mapped into a set of transitions or age-based passages. A "masculine trajectory," thus, departs from the "life cycle" concept, which assumes a fixed and repetitive socialization of individuals into clearly defined roles that support existing social structures.[23] Instead, "masculine trajectories" are characterized by contradictory, dynamic states: achievements and failures, stability and fluidity, clarity and ambiguity, coherence and contradiction, recognition and misrecognition. A masculine trajectory may be oriented in its path, often following expected and collectively defined social expectations (such as getting married and fathering children), but it may also be fashioned by emerging and unexpected encounters (such as a demonstration in the street or a major economic change as well as mundane activities like a ride in the bus, an encounter with a police officer, or a trip to another neighborhood). It is elaborated through the interplay between the individual and the collective, the internalized and the externalized, the embodied and the discursive, and the conduct and the context. But above all, I use the phrase "masculine trajectory" to depict a continuous quest for a sense of (illusive) coherence that has to be cultivated and sustained in different spatial and temporal contexts to garner the social recognition central to the verification of one's standing as a real man. I also use it to show the centrality of the deeds of individuals and their daily conduct while, at the same time, accounting for the collective expectations, power structures, and social norms that configure their lives and deaths.

The notion of masculine trajectory both builds on and departs from the common notion of "hegemonic masculinity," which has been used by different scholars to describe "the pattern of practice . . . that allow[s] men's dominance over women to continue."[24] My work draws on the productive aspects of this concept, especially in placing power at the center of my analysis, showing the interplay between persuasion and force, and emphasizing the contested nature of masculinity. The concept's vague, ambiguous, and elusive nature, however, has led scholars to struggle with several issues, especially how to define "what is actually to count as hegemonic masculinity."[25] Although the notion was originally intended to depict a configuration of gender practices and relationships, over time it has become part of a set of static typologies that are not able to account for the changing embodiment of manhood and the shifting norms that inform the meaning of manhood over a masculine trajectory.[26] It often "obscures the very relationality, fluidity, and dynamism that it was developed to explain."[27] Instead of classifying and categorizing different masculinities, I aim in this book to look at daily practices, moments of recognition, legitimization, and authorization as well as the interplay between individual actors and "the judges of normality,"[28] the conduct and the context, and the norm and its actualization. Instead of thinking about hegemonic masculinity and how it relates to complicit or marginalized masculinities, my goal is to look at what hegemonic norms define as the category called "men" and how these norms are materialized in various places and times.

It is useful here to consider the concept of "intersectionality," coined by Kimberle Crenshaw in 1989. This notion aimed to illustrate how different social structures (especially class, gender, and race) interact and overlap in shaping subjectivities.[29] It was initially used to call attention to differences among women, but it can also be useful in studying men as a diverse group, whose bodies, subjectivities, and practices are shaped by the strong intersection between patriarchal structures and capitalist systems of production. In particular, my ethnography argues that the overlapping between class and gender is central to any adequate conceptualization of how masculinity is materialized, supported, challenged, and reinforced. However, it is important to take note of "the legacies of the concept, emerging out of Black feminist critique of the lack of race in feminist theorizing" in the United States.[30] The coming chapters refer to "colorism," yet I would like to caution against using American racial categories and histories to understand the preference for lighter skin in some circles in Egypt.

As in other parts of the world,[31] people in al-Zawiya show a preference for fair skin and view it as an important part of beauty, attractiveness, and desirability, especially when evaluating a potential wife. Nevertheless, seeing colorism as either a sign of self-hating or Egyptian racism does not capture the strong historical (including colonial legacies) and contemporary local, regional, and global forces (such as media representations and a booming market for products that promise to whiten one's skin) that shape preferences for lighter skin. Neither view can account for how discussions of skin color are often codes for class and regional differences (such as Upper versus Lower Egypt). The origin of this preference and the contemporary forces that support and reinforce it are beyond the scope of this book, but a couple of comments are in order to avoid hasty conclusions about colorism in Egypt. First, "unlike race, which is based on the idea of mutually exclusive categories, skin color is arrayed along a continuum that crosscuts racial categories."[32] Rather than an opposition between black and white, in al-Zawiya there is a wider range of skin colors, which are evaluated differently.[33] Some of the shades people mention include *abyad* (white), *abyad bisafaar* (yellowish white), *abyad bihamaar* (reddish white), *faatih* (pale or light), *amhaawi* (wheat-colored, light brown), *khamri* (tawny brown), *asmar* (dark skin), and *iswid* (black). Second, people's judgments of these shades differ from one context to the other and often crisscross with other aspects of a person's bodily features, dispositions, and ethical standings. Skin color alone did not make or break marriages, restrict job opportunities, or limit friendships. I do not want to underestimate the desires, resources, and energy that many, especially young women, invest in trying to achieve a lighter shade, but it is important to note that the color of the skin is only one factor, among others, that people draw on to judge and evaluate others. In short, race in Egypt is not the same structuring historical force that we see in other countries, especially the United States. Instead, this book privileges the intersection between gender and class as especially meaningful in understanding how desires are cultivated, bodies are disciplined, and identities are constructed.

Religion is another important structuring force that intersects with class, gender, age, and spatial location to shape dress codes, rituals, and many aspects of daily life in al-Zawiya. In light of the great emphasis on the study of Islam and its impact on different facets of life in the Middle East in general and Egypt in particular, two points are important to make. First, religion structures the conduct of residents of al-Zawiya in diverse ways. For some men Islam is a central force that guides their understanding of piety and molds their daily practices; for many others it is only one force that has to compete with others (such as social conventions and global flows of ideas, products, and images), which shape their views and feelings about what is proper, fashionable, and desirable. Second, there is no direct and linear relationship between religion and masculine identification. Some men may pray regularly, frequent the mosque, and abide by most normative religious instructions. Yet, they may not have a strong standing as real men in the community (because they are not assertive, brave, or generous). Other men may not pray regularly, never attend the mosque, and sometimes violate religious teachings (for example, drinking alcohol, using drugs, and gambling) but still enjoy social recognition and distinction for being real men. Performing one's religious duties contributes positively to one's reputation, but it is not sufficient to produce a "proper man" as understood in al-Zawiya. A real man may not necessarily be a pious man and the converse may also be true. Thus, while it is significant to investigate the place of religious values, meanings, and teachings in the making of proper men, it is equally important to explore the broader socioeconomic and political forces that structure the articulation of these values in daily life as well as the complex set of social norms that influence masculine trajectories and that might overlap, contradict, and challenge religious discourses.

The intersection between gender, class, and religion is contextualized by urban forces and Cairo's spatial and social landscape. From the very beginning, I found the urban milieu to be significant when thinking about masculinity and how it is materialized in daily life.[34] The diverse actors, institutions, and discourses that shape subjectivities in the city are markedly different from what anthropologists have described in rural and tribal contexts, where the principles that structure manhood seem to be clearly articulated and communicated to boys.[35] In a megacity like Cairo, such assumptions cannot be sustained due to the great diversity in the discourses, norms, and audiences that define the meaning of ruguula. As will become clear in the coming chapters, city life profoundly influences masculine trajectories. The social standing of men strongly depends on their ability to master the city's transportation system, maneuver its spaces, make use of its different economic opportunities, manage its disciplinary powers, and avoid its risks. At the same time, "the rules of the game" are much more diffused in urban centers and men may be judged by a wide variety of criteria and several audiences.[36] The "judges of normality" are present in different areas, venues, and spaces. Encounters at homes, workshops, streets, schools, markets, and police stations have important implications for "doing gender." Available resources and systems such as medical services, surveillance techniques, entertainment facilities, and service industries (for example, gyms and barbershops) all impact masculine trajectories. Although the city offers different spaces for young men to escape the disciplinary power of their families, they remain subjected to others' gazes and come under the power of others, especially the state, who seek to regulate their movements, practices, and identities. They also must negotiate the unexpected nature of urban life and the possibilities it offers. Numerous fleeting images and encounters characterize city life: a stroll on the Nile Corniche, a conversation on the bus, a poster in the barbershop, a disagreement with a seller, a slap from a police officer, or a religious audiotape in a taxicab. Such encounters may have strong implications for the hairstyles men choose, the clothes they wear, the routes they take, the spaces they frequent, the memories they formulate, and, ultimately, the kinds of cultural and social capital they accumulate. Such mobilities and the possibilities they generate are meaningful in shaping a man's reputation, how he views himself, and how others view him. They offer new potentialities for reimagining one's gendered identity, generate a sense of uncertainty about the enactment of masculinity, and present challenges to how it should be negotiated and materialized in different spaces and for multiple audiences.

The Place and the People

Al-Zawiya, currently a densely populated urban area, was mainly agricultural land until the early 1960s. In 1993, it was still on the outskirts of Cairo. Since then, the rapid expansion of the city has made this neighborhood much more centrally located and connected to the rest of the Egyptian capital. In the early 1990s it was viewed by many of its residents as far removed from the center of Cairo, but today it is a highly desirable location and only lucky men and women manage to afford housing in this very crowded neighborhood. If you take a look at Google Maps, you will see that the neighborhood is only five miles northeast of Tahrir Square.[37] The route from the square to al-Zawiya looks clear and straightforward and the directions indicate that the drive between the two locations will be around 16 minutes. In reality, however, the movement between the two spaces is much more complicated. Depending on type of vehicle, time of day, and traffic, the trip could take anywhere from 30 minutes and two hours.

To get to the square and other important sites and attractions for shopping, work, and entertainment, such as the metro station, the Nile Corniche, al-Ataba, Bab ash-Sha'riya, and Abbasiyya, people in al-Zawiya use different modes of transportation depending on their budget and the purpose of their trip. Several different types of bus services connect to al-Zawiya, including the city bus (government-run, the cheapest but most crowded and least reliable means of transportation), mini-buses (a more recent, government-regulated but privately run alternative that is able to seat most of its passengers, but is more expensive and has fewer seats), and micro-buses (privately run vans that are reasonably priced but have limited seating and restricted routes). These means of transportation facilitate the engagement of men and women in economic activities, consumption practices, social networking, and leisure trips, and keep them connected to different parts of Cairo.

The population of al-Zawiya is diverse. There is a major social and spatial distinction in the neighborhood between those who live in privately owned and constructed houses and those who live in state-built public housing projects.[38] The geographical origins of individual families and the time of their migration to the area also create important distinctions. Families come from diverse places, including villages in Lower and Upper Egypt, other cities, and various neighborhoods in Cairo. In addition, it is estimated that around 10 percent of the population is Christian.[39] But perhaps the most significant distinction stems from the distribution of material and cultural capital.[40] My approach to these socioeconomic differences is informed by the work of Pierre Bourdieu. Drawing on Karl Marx and Max Weber, Bourdieu wrote that classes are constituted through the distribution and volume of material, social, and cultural resources.[41] He differentiated not only between classes (based on the volume of capital) but also between factions within each class (based on the composition of capital). Thus, we find significant differences between those who are rich in material capital but lack cultural capital and those who are rich in cultural capital but less so in material capital. These differences are significant because they form the foundation of a continuous struggle within classes over legitimacy and distinction. They are also meaningful for a deeper understanding of how class intersects with gender and age in the presentations and representations of masculinity.

In al-Zawiya, there are marked differences between families who have unstable or low incomes and those who enjoy relatively high and stable earnings. The low-income group consists mainly of families headed by members who have limited economic leverage because of their lack of education, training in a desirable occupation, and/or high levels of unemployment. In contrast, skilled workers (*ustas*, or masters of their trades, such as plasterers, tailors, machinists, bakers, and house painters) tend to enjoy both higher incomes and greater social distinction.[42] Other men, those with a high school or higher education, often manage to hold more than one job, which enables them to earn steady and reasonable incomes. For example, a post-secondary degree may allow a man to work in a job (for example, in a government agency) that yields a low to moderate salary but significant non-wage benefits, such as health insurance and a pension, while holding a second job, which usually involves manual work, that could be less stable but pays a higher wage. Combinations may include teacher/painter, low-ranking-government employee/tailor, teacher/driver, factory worker/office messenger, or technician/*makwagi* (master of ironing clothes). Alternatively, some men have managed to land one of the high-paying jobs created by the opening of Egypt to international investors, such as in the garment industry that produces for multinational corporations like Calvin Klein and Victoria's Secret or in tourism-related services. The luckiest men, as seen by people in al-Zawiya, are those who manage to find temporary jobs in oil-producing countries like Saudi Arabia, Kuwait, and (until recently) Libya. These jobs allow the migrants to save enough money to support their families, buy or renovate apartments, and start small income-generating projects.

Many women also work outside the home before they get married. They usually aim to secure their share of the trousseau and most leave their jobs after their engagement or upon their marriage. This act confirms that their husbands are good providers and therefore do not need them to work. But women are also realistic about the job market, which only offers them low-paying jobs with long hours and involves dealing with the inefficient public transportation system, the lack of affordable and adequate child-care services, and the social expectations that women remain the main caregivers for their families and housekeepers in their homes. When they evaluate all of these aspects, women often conclude that it makes more sense for them not to work outside the home after marriage. Widows and divorced women may take up paid employment but often have to do work from or around the house in occupations such as bead work or selling vegetables, clothes, or cooked food. These last options are also available to married women whose husbands are not able to earn enough to sustain their families. Selling domestic goods and offering localized services enable women to continue their role as caregivers and homemakers while allowing them to contribute significantly to their families' income. More importantly, it enables the family to uphold the norms that equate men with working and providing and that stigmatize the work of married women outside the home.

Cultural capital, especially in the form of high school diplomas and college degrees, is important for most families in al-Zawiya. Since President Nasser started his policies in the late 1950s, which promoted education as a universal right for all Egyptians, education became a central part of most people's views of social mobility and a better future for their children. The promise is still alive, but major problems in public schooling make the task of good education more and more the responsibility of individual families. Currently, education is one of the most significant class markers and is a major site for the reproduction of inequalities in Egypt. Most low- and middle-income families have to depend on public schools; the rich, on the other hand, are able to send their children to Cairo's expensive private schools, including British, American, and German schools. The typical family in al-Zawiya allocates a large share of its income and time to educating its children and ensuring that they accumulate the cultural capital necessary for economic success and social mobility. Public schools, largely seen as ineffective, are supplemented by a relatively costly informal tutoring system, paid for by the parents. Women, especially mothers, tend to spend a great deal of energy in arranging, managing, scheduling, and making it financially viable for their children to be part of a group of youngsters receiving good private lessons. These lessons are offered by individual teachers and are held in the homes of one of the students. They tend to be costly and are indulged in only by families with a relatively high and stable income. Several local mosques also offer cheaper alternatives to these arrangements, but parents often feel that private lessons offered at home, though more expensive, are more attentive to the educational needs of their children. The level of education and cultural capital becomes fundamental to how different socioeconomic fractions are formed in al-Zawiya. Having a college degree certainly provides distinction and social recognition, but it is not always accompanied by material capital. Thus, savvy families work to equip their children with some type of vocation (*san'a*) and send them to train with a master (*usta*) during the summer break. They aspire for their children to combine skilled manual labor, to make sure they earn enough income, with a white-collar job (*wazeefa*), which secures future pensions and some social distinction.

It is important to note that while my approach to class inequalities is informed by Bourdieu's work, my analysis aims to avoid some of the determinism that characterizes his approach.[43] At the same time, although having much to offer about the embodied nature of social inequalities, Bourdieu's work remained largely focused on explaining the reproduction of social divisions at the macro level. He paid little attention to how situated individuals experience and reimagine class and gender divisions in daily life and how their experiences may change over time. In addition, in Bourdieu's work, class and gender came often divorced from each other. Thus, while his work on the Kabyle and masculine domination privileges gender, his work on distinction and taste tends to privilege class and considers gender a "secondary" criterion.[44] My analysis aims to show how inseparable class and gender are and how their intersection shapes bodies and selves all the way through.

The Changing Scene

Sights, sounds, and smells are rich and complex in al-Zawiya. The scenes in the area tell stories of daily struggles and intense social interaction. You see men and women as they partake in economic and social activities on the sides of the streets, under housing blocks, in front of buildings, and around every corner. Their activities reveal the resourcefulness, creativity, and abilities of children and adults to find new ways to socialize, fend for themselves and their families, and enjoy some laughter in the middle of hardships and daily struggles. Signs on streets, decorations on buildings, blankets on laundry lines, writings and images on walls, and the clothes people wear all communicate messages and meanings about recent events (such as a wedding or a birth), religious piety, new ways of taking care of one's body, and socioeconomic status. Strong smells also guide your way around the area and alert you to different aspects of its activities and landscape. From the delicious scents of fried fish, *ta'miyya* (broad beans patties), freshly baked goods, and other cooked food to the stench of sewage leaks (an indication of the bad infrastructure that plagues many of Cairo's low-income neighborhoods) and trash that is collected only irregularly (another major problem in Cairo that neither the government nor private companies have been able to solve), the various smells indicate different facets of life in the area.

But it is sound that comes to my mind most vividly when I sit down to write about al-Zawiya. Over the past twenty years, I have spent many days in this area and I am always impressed by the life that never stops, day and night. It is never too late to hear children playing, crying, and talking, or men and women chatting, laughing, and quarreling. Sounds of ululating women celebrate happy events, shouts of men warn that a fight may be brewing, loud readings from the Quran mark the mourning of a recently

Residents of al-Zawiya gather to view a bridal trousseau a few days before the wedding celebration. All photographs are by the author.

deceased person, blasting music celebrates the engagement or marriage of a young couple, kissing or hissing sounds indicate a friend is calling, and piercing shrieks publicize an accident or a death. Depending on where you are staying, you may hear cars madly honking, workers banging, dogs barking, chickens and ducks clucking, or goats and sheep bleating. All day you hear the noises of sellers calling for people to buy their merchandise. Some come walking, some riding a bicycle, some pulling or pushing little carts, some with a wagon led by a donkey or a horse, and others drive around in small pickups. Products are often seasonal; depending on the time of year residents are offered foods (such as tomatoes, melons, molasses, ice cream, and various drinks) as well as household items (including soap, bleach, and dishwashing soap). Traders also come to buy things such as old bread, broken household appliances, and school textbooks. It took me a long time to distinguish a few of the audio signals of these sellers and buyers, and I am always impressed by how easily and quickly people (including young children) differentiated the various chants, rings, bangs, clicks, honks, and voices of the men and vehicles roaming the area to sell or buy things. These sounds, smells, and scenes and much more are an integral part of the urban identity of al-Zawiya and its daily life. Hearing the whistle of a friend, returning the gaze of a young woman, responding to the scream of a neighbor, reacting to the commotion of a fight, and navigating one's way among speeding cars and other pedestrians while moving in the neighborhood and the city at large are all central to how bodies are shaped and selves are articulated. These rich sensory experiences as well as the countless social interactions made possible by city life shape the daily life of men, women, and children and their locations in Cairo's social and spatial landscape. They also have been central to my understanding of the neighborhood, its spaces, daily life, and gender dynamics.

Al-Zawiya's spaces as well as its economic and social scenes have been impacted by the liberal economic policies started by Sadat in the 1970s and then pursued by Mubarak for thirty years. This period witnessed significant changes, such as the shrinking role of the state in offering basic services, an increase in socioeconomic inequalities, high rates of unemployment, a growing emphasis on consumption (especially of commodities, technologies, and media images), and massive urban expansion. This last change, in particular, has generated many problems, including an acute shortage of housing, high levels of pollution, and unbearable pressure on Cairo's deteriorating infrastructure (including an untenable traffic situation). The shift to neoliberal rationality and forms of governmentality has occurred alongside the consolidation of "the security state," which deploys violence and surveillance to tighten its control over the city and its residents, especially in low-income neighborhoods.[45]

In al-Zawiya these changes have been manifested and felt in a variety of ways. From unemployment, low wages, sharpening inequalities, and the consolidation of police surveillance in the area to an increasing emphasis on consumption and the spreading of new forms of media and means of communication, life in al-Zawiya has been shaped both by national policies and global flows of ideas, images, and products. New means of communication (such as satellite TV) have been offering new and quick ways for the circulation of information and have been profoundly transforming daily life and social interaction.

Perhaps nothing illustrates these changes as well as the telephone. In the early 1990s, when I started my fieldwork, there were few phones in the area. In some cases, when I needed to talk to a friend, I had to call the neighbor who had a phone and then stay on line until the neighbor brought my friend to the phone. Residents had to walk to local shops to make calls and pay for them on the spot. Since the late 1990s, as phone technology has advanced, phone access has rapidly expanded. In the past many families had to wait for up to twenty years before getting a landline; today almost all people in al-Zawiya have landlines and the majority of young men and women have mobile phones. Most recently, better-off families have replaced the landlines with individual mobiles for all of their members. These phones are increasingly becoming signs of distinction and visible markers of socioeconomic inequality. Those who can afford them buy the most fashionable and expensive cell phones, which they use to take photos and to download video clips and songs. They may designate specific ring tones (which range from prayers by famous preachers to popular songs) for their various friends and colleagues. Those who are not able to acquire the most fashionable phones still manage to get used or out-of-style mobiles that enable them to stay in touch with their family members, friends, and relatives in different parts of Cairo and beyond. Ringing others is becoming a quick, easy, and cheap way of connecting.

Labor migrants in oil-producing countries and relatives in different parts of Egypt frequently ring and hang up to simply communicate that they are fine or that they are thinking about the person they called. It is impolite to immediately answer a call. People usually let the phone ring several times and then press cancel. If the caller really wants to talk about something, he or she calls again. Mobile phones have been especially useful for workers, who can arrange work with clients and peers in different localities, and for women, who are able to move about the city while staying in touch with their family members. In fact, phone calls became part of my research both in Egypt and abroad. The phone became an important asset in my fieldwork in arranging visits to specific families beforehand, coordinating with my friends from al-Zawiya for trips to different parts of Cairo, and communicating urgent news and events (such as accidents, deaths, and funerals). It also became key for me while in the United States to keep connected to my closest friends in the neighborhood and stay updated on current events, such as the recent political protests and their effect on individuals and families in the area.

When the Egyptian government tried to quell the January 25, 2011, protests by disconnecting cell phone services, I spent a few agonizing days trying to get in touch with people in al-Zawiya.[46] As soon as the service was reinstated and the volume of calls subsided, relieving some of the pressure on phone lines, I managed not only to confirm the well-being and safety of my friends but also to follow up on some of the events in the area and hear about the changing feelings of the people about the protests, Mubarak's regime, and the future of Egypt. Over the phone, I heard from some of my close friends about their worries, hopes, and aspirations. I heard about how men quickly formed neighborhood groups to protect the area when the police withdrew from the streets and about how fear and panic were exacerbated by rumors, including stories about the "escape" of thousands of criminals and thugs (*baltagiyya*) from police custody.[47] Men took turns protecting the streets, directing traffic, and offering basic services. They armed themselves with knives, batons, hatchets, bottles, and hoses. They spent the night awake looking out for their families and neighbors. They cleaned local streets and, when prices increased drastically during the first few days of protests, they went to adjacent rural communities to look for cheaper vegetables. In many ways, they were materializing norms and values that already existed in their neighborhood, norms that associated masculinity with providing, defending, caring, and protecting.

Researching Urban Masculinities

My original fieldwork, which began in 1993, was shaped by my positionality as a newly married Muslim woman who was raised in an Arab country (Jordan), spoke Arabic (with a Levantine dialect), and was completing her studies in the United States.[48] Over time, my life (and that of all the people I know in al-Zawiya) changed. I finished my graduate studies and became "el-doctora," as most people I know insist on referring to me. I got a job teaching in the United States, an achievement highly regarded in the area. After much waiting, they warmly and lovingly greeted my only child, who visited them for the first time at the age of one.[49] They have followed her life over the past eleven years and eagerly anticipated her summer visits. Strong relationships were also cultivated between my close interlocutors and members of my extended family who visited from Jordan. Over the past two decades, I became an honorary family member of several families in al-Zawiya and they made me feel at home in every possible way. I became a daughter, an older sister, and an aunt for several people in the area, enjoying both the rights and obligations that come with this honorary membership. I delighted in hearing about and celebrating the successes of children at school, happily participated in weddings and engagement parties, excitedly visited new mothers and held newborn babies, and sadly mourned the death of some of my close interlocutors. The changing nature of the life for children, men, and women I know in the area taught me a great deal about the norms that structure gender distinctions and relationships. For example, some of the most startling points in my research were when baby boys whom I carried in my arms and toddlers who sat in my lap, and who greeted me (as is customarily done) for several years by offering their cheeks to be kissed, became teenagers. Between the ages of fourteen and sixteen there were awkward moments when boys (now young men) did not know whether they should continue to offer me their cheeks to be kissed or whether a handshake was enough. In some cases, people teased those who continued to expect to be kissed, and most of the teenagers eventually stopped doing so. Such encounters highlight the relationship between age and the norms that structure interaction between men and women as well as the changing expectations that young men have to negotiate over their masculine trajectories.

Over the years, I have had the chance to talk to young men and women about ideals of beauty, health, and attractiveness, as well as the social meanings of masculinity and femininity. I have documented the life stories of several of my close male interlocutors to explore how they feel about issues such as growing up, having children, getting married, finding a job, and growing old. These life stories have given me a sense of how masculinity, as a collective process of becoming, is embodied, enacted, and contextualized. Because many men have to work for long hours, it was important to coordinate my presence around their schedules. In order to ensure access to men, I stayed up very late, made sure I was present during the weekend, attended social events, and visited local workshops. While sharing a meal or drinking tea, Nescafé, or soft drinks, we would talk about their work in Cairo, travel abroad, marriage plans, uses of violence, relationship to their children and wives, understanding of masculinity, and the social and political changes in the area and Egypt at large. I also talked to children about their life and their views of school, street and family life, and gendered identities. In addition, I discussed with women their understandings of masculinity, views of the ideal man, reactions to the conduct of men around them, and what they expected from future husbands. Whenever possible, I attended engagement parties, weddings, and celebrations of birth. I paid particular attention to how men and women interacted with each other and presented their bodies in different contexts. The way they dressed, the colors they chose, and the styles of their hair or hair covers were especially important gender and class markers that indicated different aspects of how individuals view themselves and are viewed by others. In addition, I interviewed pharmacists, hairdressers, and barbers to learn about how bodily representations change over time.

Despite the value of such interviews and discussions, it was participant observation, anthropology's flagship methodology, that best captured the paradoxes generated by the discursive formation of gender and the daily enactment of femininities and masculinities.[50] For example, if you asked Hussam, a 30-year-old worker, about the importance of a man's appearances and how he grooms himself, he would immediately give the conventional answer: a man is not vain and does not pay attention to his appearances. A man (*er-raagil*) is measured by his ability to earn money and provide for his family. Yet, if you spent some time in Hussam's apartment and followed some of his daily practices and outings, you would notice the care he gives to his skin at home and at the barbershop, the attention he pays to his clothes and shoes, the money he spends on buying gels and oil for his hair, and his strong reactions to people's comments about his body size and facial hair. Participant observation allowed me to include but go beyond discursive statements made about gender constructions, how they related to the management and presentation of the body, and how they were worked and reworked over time and through space.

It was at moments when I just sat down quietly in a living room, listening to discussions between men and women about different aspects of life (including male/female relationships), that I learned most about gender distinctions. It was when watching satellite TV, listening to songs, screening videos of weddings or engagement parties, and viewing video clips on mobile phones that I gained a sense of the many forces that configure people's daily lives. It was during the sharing of meals, outings with friends, walks to neighborhood markets, crossings of local streets, and stops at grocery stores that aspects of the daily embodiment of gender became clearest to me. Through my own experiences and by tracing the practices of others, I came to see the significant aspects of the concept of embodiment both by going beyond the dichotomies that often are used in scholarly work (such as subject vs. object, mind vs. body, and individual vs. society) and by capturing the body as the locus of agency, the medium for social interaction, and the ground for the making of selves.[51]

This book explores how masculinity is embodied and emphasizes the need to analyze the dialogic relationship between the body and social context.[52] It shows that bodies "are both *objects* of social practice and *agents* in social practice" and that bodies are produced by and producers of social life.[53] Through our ability to labor, walk, talk, interact, and much more, we are active in the making of social life at the same time as social life makes us.

A Woman in the World of Men?

Why, some readers may ask, would a woman want to study men and masculinity? If men are from Mars and women are from Venus,[54] how would a female anthropologist be able to understand anything about men? Would not it make more sense for female scholars to focus on the study of women and leave the study of men to male researchers? Although such assumptions no longer retain much purchase in anthropology, they are still common in Western and Middle Eastern media and continue to shape the views of the public of the roles of men and women. So if you happened to have these concerns, I would like you to consider why you think you feel the way you do: Is it because you think masculinity is essentially biological and only a biologically defined man would be able to appreciate what masculinity is all about? Is it because you think masculinity is equated with sexuality and that men would not talk about sexual matters to a woman? Is it because you think that men and women are segregated in the Middle East and that female anthropologists would not have the opportunity to interact with men, who live in a different world from the world of women?

This book, I hope, will address some of the assumptions behind such questions. It is worth noting that women have studied men in different societies and that most pioneering studies of masculinity in the Middle East have been conducted and published by women.[55] As my ethnography will show, men and women in al-Zawiya are not segregated but interact daily, shaping each other's practices, subjectivities, and views. They are not from different planets but inhabit the same social and cultural space and share many norms and values. My discussion shows that masculinity is a social process that, though connected to biology, cannot be reduced to it.[56] It is a multifaceted project that can and should be viewed from different perspectives. Though sexuality is an important component of the story, it should not be equated with masculinity. I should mention here that when several of my colleagues in the United States and Egypt heard about my interest in embodiment and masculinity, they immediately assumed that I would be studying sexuality and sexual performance, relations, and identifications. This view is indeed represented in popular discourse (including Egyptian media) and scholarly work on masculinity and the body. So much attention has been paid to the sexual organs and sexual performance that we have ended up with little understanding of other facets of the embodiment of masculinity.[57]

My fieldwork has taught me that sexual competence is just one dimension and that it is not always central to how manhood is defined and presented in daily life in al-Zawiya. There are contexts when sexual abilities become central to the definition of a man, such as the groom's ability to deflower the bride on their wedding night and then impregnate her,[58] or when more than one woman competes for the attention of the man, seen in the cases where the wife believes that her husband is having an affair or the rare instances in which a husband has a second wife. However, rather than being simply linked to sexual performance, ruguula is a multidimensional, contextual, and contingent process. As the coming chapters show, daily assertions of ruguula are strongly linked to good grooming, nice manners, fashionable clothes, skill in navigating the city, assertiveness and courage, the ability to provide for one's family, and knowledge about when to use violence to defend self, family, and relatives. These are all enactments that are observed, evaluated, critiqued, and credited or discredited by others, including women.

My gender did of course shape my research experience and approach to masculinity. As I chose to adhere to social norms when it came to male/female interaction, I refrained from attending male-only spaces such as the male-designated part of mosques, local cafés, and alcohol and *bango*-smoking sessions.[59] I am fully aware, for example, that the coffeehouse (*'ahwa*) is an important space where men with different educations, professions, ages, and experiences could interact and negotiate the norms that guide their masculine trajectories.[60] There are some coffee shops in Cairo, especially in upper-class neighborhoods, that are frequented by men and women, but this is not accepted in al-Zawiya. Thus, I decided to abide by the norms that excluded women from the coffee shop and limited my understanding of those spaces to discussions with men. I am mindful of the limitations these choices imposed on my research. The point remains, nonetheless, that masculinity is not an entity or a whole that can be apprehended by an individual researcher, male or female. We need to approach any gender construction, including masculinity, from a multiplicity of locations and perspectives in the hope of weaving together different parts of the complex process of engendering.

My status as a married woman in her forties, a mother, and an anthropologist who has been working in al-Zawiya for a long time afforded me a specific vantage point from which I could view masculinity. In particular, it enabled me to see manhood not only as a public performance that is done by men for men,[61] but also as it is defined, formed, and reinforced in the personal domain of the family and through the interplay between the public and the private. Admittedly, "the focus on men brings possible danger in re-excluding women" from our analysis of gender.[62] My identification as a woman, however, made it impossible for me to exclude women's presence, words, and views. As a parent, I was also sensitive to children and their voices. These different identifications enabled me to offer a "thick description" of the important role of mothers in raising boys, the energy sisters and wives invested in the making of their brothers and husbands, the inequalities that structure men's lives as well as male/female interactions, and the social norms that shape the embodiment of masculinity over time and through space.[63]

Writing This Book

My motivation for this project came from my stance as a feminist, eager to understand and challenge patriarchy; as an anthropologist of Middle Eastern origin, eager to share rich knowledge of the region with a broader audience; and as a woman with firsthand experience of the impact of gender hierarchies, eager to engage critically with the region and question the inequalities that structure the life of its peoples. As part of my attempt to understand the different articulations of patriarchy and how men and women are entangled in its systems of inequality, I wanted to highlight the embodied aspects of manhood in order to move us beyond the assumption that equates the man with the mind and roots his domination in rational thinking and cultural superiority. I wanted to show how patriarchal and capitalist structures celebrate yet conquer, recognize yet dismiss, acknowledge yet downplay, build upon yet ignore, and display yet negate the materiality of the body in the construction of the ideal man. At the same time and in light of the ongoing vilification of Arab and Muslim men in the media, I considered it necessary to write about Egyptian men's daily struggles and how they work to materialize social norms that define them as men.

Writing a book about masculinity in Egypt has proven much more challenging than I originally anticipated. Contrary to what some might expect, my challenge has not been in gaining access to men and women in Cairo, but rather in translating my knowledge of being *there* to a text that can be read by people *here*. Clifford Geertz saw this translation as a challenge that faces all anthropologists;[64] I view it as especially pressing in the anthropology of the Middle East, a region that is often negatively viewed in the United States. Every chapter in this book was written with full recognition of the damaging assumptions that proliferate in the media, policy circles, and some scholarly work. When writing about masculinity and violence, for example, I had to negotiate my interest in a thick description of violence, which points to the inequalities and intimacies that structure the interaction between men and women, with dominant myths about the violent Middle Eastern man who controls his family with an iron fist and in particular "the discourses that portray working-class Arab men as inherently predatory."[65] When writing a chapter about embodiment, sickness, and death, I had to struggle against the "culture of death" discourse that generates a split between the life-loving culture of the West and the death-seeking culture of Islam.[66] How to write, I ask myself every day, in a way that is intellectually honest and politically responsible? How to write to humanize but not to romanticize or idealize?

There is no single perfect answer to these questions, but I have found it productive to tackle them by tracing specific masculine trajectories, following precise enactments, and offering thick contextualization of "visions and divisions" to help us analyze the inequalities that structure the interaction between male/female, male/male, young/old, government/citizen, individual/society, and local/global.[67] This strategy, I believe, allows us to appreciate the challenges, contradictions, and uncertainties rooted in the process of engendering. The following chapters present voices and experiences of men of different age groups and explore their diverse ways of being and doing, as well as the various competing discourses that constitute their identities, practices, and subjectivities.

To avoid the linearity embedded in the "life cycle" notion and to avoid imagining a masculine trajectory as a set of standardized shifts between different stages, the chapters are organized around themes rather than simply age. In Chapter 1, I explore the broad meaning of manhood and analyze how boys are taught about their classed and gendered location in the social space. Tracing some moments in the tender life of a young boy from the time when I met him when he was one year old until he turned eleven in the summer of 2012, I look at some of the expectations communicated to him and analyze some of the techniques his family used to cultivate a particular habitus that is generated by the intersection between class and gender. The discussion highlights the uncertainty embedded in the attempts at making him a man and the labor and time invested in engendering young boys. The chapter concludes by reflecting on some of the labels used in al-Zawiya to critique different modes of conduct and the social meanings people attach to various enactments of manhood and how they relate to the "ideal man." It emphasizes that a real man is not created by or through a simple binary opposition between male and female but through an elaborate process of differentiation between diverse ways of doing and being.

Chapter 2 explores how gendered subjectivities are formed through the embodiment of certain social norms and the repetition of specific acts that aim to produce and naturalize assumptions about masculinity and femininity. Through focusing on *er-ruguula mawqif*, or manhood as an attitude, a stand that one takes in daily life, I elaborate on this phrase by looking at the masculine trajectory of a 40-year-old man and his attempts to find a wife. Tracing different moments of this worker's life, the chapter analyzes the importance of work, engagement in community life, getting married, providing for a wife, and becoming a father in the construction of a masculine identification. Critically drawing on Pierre Bourdieu's notion of bodily hexis (the ways our bodies reflect our socioeconomic positionalities),[68] I look at how young men groom their bodies and present them to others in different contexts as well as the various interpretations people (including potential brides) make of specific bodily presentations and representations. The chapter shows the contextual nature of masculinity and how it shifts over time, and argues that the ability to respond properly in the right context (both spatially and temporally) plays a central role in the construction of the real man.

As a collective project, masculinity is produced through the work of many agents. Chapter 3 analyzes the active role women play in shaping masculine trajectories and shows how they contribute to the making of men. Looking at the life of a man in his early thirties and his attempts to marry the woman he loved and then exploring the role of husband-wife relationships in shaping masculine trajectories, the chapter captures the shifting meanings of manhood and the various discourses that men and women circulate to question, challenge, and reaffirm one's identity as a proper man. As a diversified group, positioned differently in relation to men, women play a multiplicity of important roles in the making of men. First, by conforming to the social norms that define their proper roles as doubtful daughters, obedient wives, and respectful sisters, women contribute greatly to the standing of their male relatives. Second, women offer material and emotional support and instruct male relatives in the proper way of becoming and being a man. Third, they monitor, judge, and exert pressure on sons, brothers, and husbands to ensure they abide by social norms. Fourth, whenever necessary, women step in to defend the reputation and public image of their male relatives in different contexts. The discussion shows that rather than through their separation and opposition, it is through the interaction between men and women that gendered identifications are produced and elaborated.

As argued by many scholars, there exists a strong relationship between masculinity and the use of violence across societies. Drawing on Victor Turner's notion of social dramas, Chapter 4 examines the structured and performative nature of violence. Contrary to popular belief, violence in domestic and public domains is not arbitrary. My ethnography shows that the ability of a man to selectively use violence—to know how and when to deploy it and when to avoid it—is an important part of how he is defined by others and he views himself. Through looking at the notions of *gada'* (the honest, brave, reliable, and capable man who uses violence only for proper purposes) and *baltagi* (the thug, bully, and self-centered man, who uses violence to serve his own interests), my discussion pays attention to instances in which certain types of violence are socially acceptable and even celebrated and others in which the use of physical force is socially stigmatized and rejected. It reflects on how categories used to differentiate, classify, and judge different forms of violence have shaped the views of men and women of the Egyptian revolution, especially during the first eighteen days of the protests that led to Mubarak's downfall. Finally, it relates the social meanings invested in different forms of violence to the hierarchies that structure the relationships between those who commit violence and those who are subjected to it.

Chapter 5 looks at sickness and death as effective points of entry to our conceptualization and understanding of the body because it forces us to see its limitations as a project, compels us to question the association we often make between the body and the self, and allows us to ponder the role of the materiality of the body in the making of proper men. In this chapter, I focus on the life and death of two men. The first is Abu Hosni, who died at the age of sixty-four after a long illness, and the second is Karim, a worker who died in Saudi Arabia when he was thirty-eight years old. Through these two losses, I explore the deep intersection between patriarchal structures and capitalist forces and how this intersection shapes the health and death of men. I pay particular attention to how religion offers meaningful discourses that inform the attempts of families and community members to depict the death of young men through the cherished notion of "good death" (*moota kwaisa*) or "good ending" (*husn el-khaatimah*). I then relate these notions to the death of hundreds of Egyptian young men during and after the January 25 protests at the hands of the police or unknown thugs. Unlike simplistic assumptions about fatalism, I argue that these narratives establish a strong relationship between the notion of good man and good death and relate the life of the deceased, his work, his rapport with family and neighbors, and his contribution to community life and resources to the notion of good ending and consequently his standing in the afterlife.

The book ends by highlighting the significance of thinking of masculinity as a collective project that is produced through the work of multiple agents and the interplay between fixed and changing meanings, well-defined and fluid norms, established and emerging feelings, and clear and ambiguous instructions. It explores some of the questions that the Egyptian revolution has been forcing us to consider about the future of gender distinctions in Egypt. In addition, it relates my discussion to broader studies of masculinity and then explores its contribution to studies of gender in the Middle East. Unlike the tendency in scholarly work and media representations to disembody men and over-embody women, the Conclusion emphasizes the need to think of both men and women as embodied actors who struggle, albeit in different ways, with specific power relationships, economic inequalities, social norms, political systems, and religious discourses.

1

Uncertain Trajectories
The Joys and Sorrows of Boyhood

Patriarchal assault on the emotional life of boys begins at the
moment of their birth.

bell hooks, *The Will to Change*

ACCORDING TO MONA, a single woman in her late twenties, there
are two kinds of men: a *raagil* and *illi bye'mil raagil* (one who pretends
to be a man). While the first term implies an "authentic," genuine manhood, the second implies more of a pretense, an act that is not real.
The difference, according to Mona, is that a raagil conducts himself in
a manner befitting a man all the time, while *illi bye'mil raagil* does not
consistently materialize the norms that define a man. Her examples focused on the way a man treats his wife. *Er-raagil* fears for his wife's safety
and reputation and thus establishes clear boundaries for her behavior,
explaining what is permitted and what is not and why. If she goes to
visit his mother, he ensures that she does not return to their home alone
at night; he instructs her not to leave until he comes to accompany
her home. He is tough, firm, and strict but clearly articulates his logic
and reasoning to his wife without resorting to violence. In contrast, *illi
bye'mil raagil* may do one thing in one context and then something contradictory in another. He would claim to care about his wife but would
say, "Let her go back home late. What's the problem? What could happen to her?" One of Mona's brothers, as she explains, falls into the second category; he makes a big deal out of trivial things (*haagaat hayfa*)
but ignores what is more important. Mona contrasts her brother with
a proper man, who is tough (*shideed*) but reasonable (*bi 'aql*), who is

strong (*qawi*) but tender (*hinayyin*), and who controls his wife but does not suffocate her.

Mona's description touches upon some key aspects that define the ideal man more broadly in her neighborhood: he is generous but careful with his money, controlling but affectionate, dominating but caring, concerned about himself but not vain, assertive but gentle, serious but fun-loving, absent but present. These expectations may seem contradictory and impossible to materialize in any meaningful sense, and, in a way, they are. However, upon closer inspection, one can see that they are context-bound. The materialization of a socially credible and recognized masculine identification depends, to a large extent, on a man's ability to enact the proper practices, stances, and feelings in the right context. This materialization is central to sustaining a "coherent" masculine trajectory and a credible definition of a real man. In this chapter, I use the word "materialization" because it captures the struggles, challenges, and physical and emotional pressures embedded in the processes of becoming a man. The alternative, more common term "performance" continues to evoke some of its daily connotations of deliberate, fake, temporary, and playful acts, which are not part of how masculinity is lived, practiced, and experienced in al-Zawiya.[1] My use of the word "materialization" aims to encompass both bodily gestures, movements, and representations as well as other discursive practices and stances enacted in daily life to assert one's standing as a man. It also aims to capture the interplay between the internalization of specific norms and their externalization in particular practices, bodily presentations, and social interactions.

A masculine identification is not fixed, complete, or fully established but has to be re-created and reasserted in different settings. It is always under the gaze of others, who may challenge, reaffirm, legitimize, or discredit its durability and "authenticity." This chapter aims to account for some facets of this interplay and seeks to give the reader a sense of how men internalize and externalize the discursive and embodied knowledge that they are imbued with from the moment of birth. To paraphrase Simone de Beauvoir, one is not born, but rather, becomes *a man*.[2] I start by looking at one young boy and how he is taught the meaning of boyhood, informed about manhood, instructed about his body, and introduced to his quarter and its various spaces. As mentioned in the Introduction, the "life cycle" notion has proved to be inadequate for capturing the multiple spatial and temporal contexts that shape shared projects of gendering. Thus, rather than looking at a linear or chronological history of the boy's life, this chapter traces certain themes and significant moments of his cultivation as a future working-class man. I then move to look at some of the words and labels used to evaluate and critique various aspects of the materialization of masculinity and the social values attached to them. My discussion highlights some of the hegemonic norms that families work to inculcate in young boys in hopes of producing real men, but I also account for the challenges, uncertainties, and struggles embedded in this process.

The Joy of Having a Boy

When Hiba became pregnant, she and her husband, Karim, were overjoyed. They had waited for that news for three years. The pregnancy was important to them, not only because children are highly valued and loved in Egyptian society and are central to confirming their parents' social status as a couple but also because Karim was a long-distance commuter. Just a few months after their wedding, he had to travel back to his work in Saudi Arabia and could spend only limited time in Egypt. Despite the time they spent together immediately after their wedding and a return trip by Karim nine months later, she did not get pregnant, and the expense of additional return trips continued to eat into their savings. After both of them consulted several doctors and received some treatments, they were delighted to learn that Hiba was finally pregnant. Their joy doubled as the newborn was not only healthy but also a boy. This was especially desirable because Hiba's husband was from Upper Egypt where, she explained, males are greatly valued and viewed as important sources of financial and moral support.[3]

While her husband was abroad, Hiba and her baby, Ahmed, received his financial support but lived with her family in al-Zawiya. When he was in Egypt, they spent most of the time (usually around two months) in their own apartment in Upper Egypt. Five years after Ahmed's birth tragedy struck when Karim, at the age of thirty-eight, died in Saudi Arabia (see Chapter 5 for details about his death). Hiba, who was only thirty-three at the time, and her two children (Ahmed, who was five, and his sister, who was five months) now permanently live with her family in al-Zawiya. She makes sure to visit her husband's family at least once a year to maintain social connections with her in-laws as well as to protect her children's rights to the apartment that their father built and the inheritance they could receive after the death of their grandfather.

I have been fortunate to follow Ahmed's life since he was one year old; he turned eleven in the summer of 2012. Given that my daughter was born just two months before him, it was especially interesting for me to observe his upbringing, including a strong emphasis on the teaching of a classed and gendered identity. I followed his life with the eyes of an anthropologist and the interest of a mother and found his boyhood profoundly informative. By watching Ahmed grow, I learned a tremendous amount about how gender norms are circulated, taught, and inculcated in young males and, as we will see later, embodied by men of all ages.

From the moment the doctor announced that the newborn was a boy, Ahmed's evolving identification had a pervasive gender component. Immediately after his birth, there was a process of negation. This, as defined by Connell,[4] denies similarities across genders and underscores differences between infant boys and girls.

Several concrete measures flagged his identification as a boy. First was his name. Ahmed was named after his paternal grandfather. Naming, as argued by Judith Butler, "is at once the setting of a boundary and also the repeated inculcation of a norm."[5] The name marked Ahmed as a boy and a future man who would maintain the continuity of his father's lineage. Second was his circumcision. In Cairo, most male infants are circumcised discreetly during the first week of their life,[6] but Ahmed, in Upper Egypt, was circumcised at the age of one. Hiba and her husband were respecting Ahmed's paternal grandfather's wish to abide by the traditions of his village, which marks the circumcision of boys with public celebrations and festivities. Third, there were the colors he wore, the bodily adornments he lacked,[7] and the celebration his family had when he reached the end of his first week.[8] But above all, there were the continuous discursive directives by various people who instructed him about his gendered identity. His mother, grandparents, uncles, and aunts always stressed his identity as a boy in their interactions with and treatment of him. As soon as Ahmed started talking, his family would instruct him to behave in certain ways in line with established gender expectations. They would say, "Don't cry. Boys don't cry," or "Don't be scared, you're a man." Other times, they would tell him, "Don't back off. Hit her, you're a boy," or "Go ahead and shake his hand, you're a man." Once, when he was six years old, Ahmed came back home in tears after picking up his uncle's clothes from the dry cleaner. He described how a big boy had teased him and asked the shop owner to call the police, accusing Ahmed of stealing the clothes. His uncle and aunt immediately told him to "be a man" (*khalleek raagil*) and to make sure to respond to any boy who insulted or attacked him. His uncle teasingly reminded him of how he keeps referring to himself as a man (*raagil*), implying the need to live by his words. When I commented that perhaps he should not retaliate because the other big boy may beat him up, his mother quickly retorted, "one time he'll be hit, another time he'll hit back. Over time, he'll learn how to handle himself." Such statements were coupled with specific forms of self-discipline (for example, how to control his emotions), of regulating his bodily gestures and movements (including how to walk, sit, and shake hands), and of educating him about the social expectations that define him as a boy and a future man.

Ahmed's tearful reaction to the possibility of calling the police to detain him was part of a broader outlook that shaped his views and feelings about the security forces and their role in his life. As a man, and as will be further discussed in the coming chapters, he would have to learn how to handle the police gaze and make sure to avoid interacting with security forces as much as possible. At the age of six, Ahmed told me about a dream where he saw a police officer grabbing him from the back of his neck and pulling him away. I asked him if he was afraid in the dream and he answered "no." "When you dream of the government [people in al-Zawiya often used the word *hukumah* (which means government) to also refer to the police, in the process equating the two], tell yourself that what you see isn't real so you don't feel scared," Ahmed explained to me, repeating his mother's advice about bad dreams. Over the years, he told me several stories, jokes, and rumors about the brutality of the police, the bravery of some of his relatives in tricking or standing up to corrupt policemen, and the changes in the status and authority of policemen after the January 25 Revolution. In the summer of 2012, he was proud to tell me how the authority of the police has been challenged in deep ways in his neighborhood. According to Ahmed, in the past police officers acted like they were the masters and the people their slaves. He argued that the revolution fundamentally undermined the power of the police and restricted their ability to use unlimited force in their daily interaction with people. Ahmed supported his point by describing how in the past people had to put up with being falsely accused, detained, and subjected to insults and beatings, but after the revolution, the police have to be careful about their conduct and might not even retaliate after hearing direct insults from an ordinary citizen.[9]

Learning to Be a Good Boy

A central part of Ahmed's training has been focused on acquiring knowledge of al-Zawiya, its streets, shops, mosques, and markets. Already at the age of four, Ahmed was going down from the fourth floor, where his family lived, to run errands for his relatives at different nearby shops and stands. At first, one of them would keep an eye on him from the balcony until he went and came back. He would buy matches, soft drinks, cheese, detergent, bleach, milk, yogurt, and more. He was eager to do these chores and his mother was proud of his abilities. If she needed several items or something he could not remember or pronounce, she would write a list to give to the seller, instructing Ahmed carefully about how to handle himself so as to not lose his money or spill what he would buy. Through these chores, he was being trained to negotiate his way around the neighborhood and how to navigate its many spaces. He was instructed to go only to the shops and stands around his family's building and was totally forbidden from crossing any main streets. When he went to kindergarten, either his mother or a neighbor helped him cross the street to and from school. Slowly, his ability to move around expanded and, by the age of seven, he was able to cross the busiest street in the area. After many years of visiting al-Zawiya, I can attest to the fact that this was no trivial accomplishment, seriously complicated by the many pedestrians and sellers who occupy the sides of the street as well as the speedy vehicles, which have caused several tragic accidents and deaths. A child usually learns how to cross with a relative, who instructs the child to look in both directions, wait for the moment when he could find a break in the line of vehicles, and then quickly but carefully cross to the other side. When no relatives are available, a child could ask an adult to help him cross. By the age of seven or eight, most children are able to cross by themselves. During the summer, with school out of session, Ahmed could go up and down the stairs to his apartment more than ten times a day—a major feat, given the hot weather. His chores were complicated by his family's limited income, lack of storage areas, and deep appreciation for fresh produce. These factors restricted their ability to stock up on household products and demanded Ahmed to make trip after trip to get small quantities of required cooking supplies and cleaning materials.

At the age of seven, Ahmed became the person designated to buy the bread for the family during the summer. This entailed waiting in line for several hours under the hot summer sun and enduring harassment from grown-ups who would not respect his turn in the line. He was introduced to this chore by his grandmother when he was around four. She would take him with her, tell him to stand in line, give him the money, instruct him how to handle the bread when it was given to him, and stand next to him to help.[10] He slowly started going by himself. Before Ahmed turned eight, he would wait in the women's line for bread; however, as he grew older, he began standing in the men's line, which he says is usually faster and more organized than the women's.[11] In the summer of 2012, Ahmed was proud and happy to tell me that he had good connections (the mother of one of his close friends) that enabled him to quickly get good-quality bread. However, his happiness did not last for long. His mother got furious when he came back one day with half-baked bread and instructed him to only get bread from another place that is much farther than the one he frequented. Usually, he would return to the apartment after this chore totally exhausted and sweaty but often, even before he rested and despite his protests, he would be sent down to buy something else.[12]

In the summer of 2011, Ahmed was instructed in finer points about interacting with merchants and sellers. His mother wanted him to properly use his arithmetical skills to make sure that he received the right change and kept track of the prices of each item he bought. She wanted him to compare prices, notice if the cost of an item changed over time, and make certain that he would buy the best and cheapest items. His mother emphasized the need for him to "look and pay attention" (*bus wi lahiz*), to make good decisions based on what he knows and what he sees in front of him, and to reject the attempts of sellers to either give him bad-quality items or substitutes for what he requested.

Like many other families, Hiba and her relatives were preparing Ahmed for a life that revolves around manual labor, endurance, and hardships. They were preparing him to negotiate his way around various spaces, interact with several audiences, and work hard to provide for his family, all of which are central to his masculine trajectory. In developing the skills necessary for his future life as a man, Ahmed was also internalizing a habitus that is both classed and gendered.[13] Through his many errands, waiting in lines and buying things from various sellers, Ahmed was learning "bodily" how to master his neighborhood and its different spaces.[14] He was also learning how to interact with its diverse social groups and how to negotiate various demands and expectations.

Children are an important part of the household and are responsible for daily chores such as buying bread.

He may have been sent down, for example, to buy bread from a particular bakery because his uncle's friend worked there and usually gave him good-quality bread. If he did not find the young man there, he would have to decide if he should still buy the bread from there and risk getting low-quality bread, which could anger his mother, or go to another place, which could take more time and effort.

In the summer of 2012, I was impressed by his increasing ability to find ways to appease his mother and reduce the amount of work he had to do or find ways to earn some extra money to spend on some of his favorite activities. The first day of Ramadan, Hiba told Ahmed to go to a nearby place to buy bread. Even though this place charges twice as much money for a loaf of bread, Hiba was willing to pay extra to avoid exhausting Ahmed during the first day of fasting.[15] Ahmed, however, decided to go to a farther place and paid half the money his mother gave him. Upon his return, he asked her about the quality of the bread and was very pleased when she praised him and the bread. He then announced that he only spent half of what she gave him and asked if he could keep the rest of the money to spend on a game of pool, a game he adored.[16] His mother was only too happy to grant his request, which she took as a sign of intelligence and prudence. By trial and error, he was learning how to make reasonable choices that would be practical for him and acceptable to others. In doing so, he was also learning about the importance of others in his life and the value of their judgments in his present and future standing as a man.

The Absent-Present Father

Unlike Ahmed, most children in al-Zawiya grow up with their fathers around. Fatherhood is a highly desirable status for a man. Getting pregnant as quickly as possible reflects positively on both the husband and the wife. Soon after marriage, family members, neighbors, and friends wait to hear about the pregnancy of the bride. The conception of a child is so valuable that a bride may plan her wedding night to coincide with her fertile period. Having children not only consolidates the marriage but also defines the couple socially as parents and shapes their interactions within their families and the community at large. Infertility, as documented by Marcia Inhorn,[17] is considered a major social problem that could potentially strain marriages and relationships with families and relatives and must be treated at all costs.[18]

For the most part, fathers are very attached to their children and greatly enjoy spending time with them. One often sees fathers proudly taking their little children (both male and female) with them to local coffeehouses or to the homes of friends and relatives. They may bring their male children with them to the mosque for Friday prayer. Tamer, a man in his early thirties, described the delight and pleasure he took in his baby. At the time we spoke, his son was six months old, and Tamer described feeling as though something "tickled" (*bizaghzagh*) his heart upon seeing his baby. He added that he spent most of his day looking forward to going back home to see him. If he arrived home when the baby was sleeping, he sat down to watch him for a while, resisting the temptation to wake him up and waiting impatiently until he saw him in the morning. Tamer was proud and happy when his wife described to us how the baby knew his father and reached out to him as soon as he saw him or that he cried and clung to him when he sensed that his father was about to leave. Yet Tamer had to work long hours and did not have the luxury of spending as much time as he would have liked with his baby. His main responsibility, securing as much money as possible for his young family, kept him away from his wife and son for most of the day and night.[19]

Like Tamer, many other fathers in al-Zawiya are also absent out of necessity. Only men who manage to work for fewer hours, in better-paying jobs, are able to be active on a regular basis in the daily life of their children. We see one example of this in a man who earned a post-secondary degree and landed a job in a post office in an upper-middle-class area. His income, which crucially included tips from delivering the mail, was sufficient to allow him to satisfy his children's schooling and other needs without having to take a second job. Other fathers do not have this possibility. Ali, for example, holds two jobs. He usually leaves home at seven in the morning to work as a low-ranking government functionary. At around two in the afternoon, he spends an hour and a half traveling to his other job as a tailor on the opposite side of Cairo. He returns home between one and two in the morning to quickly eat his supper and get a few hours of sleep. During the week, he hardly sees his son and two daughters. On his day off, Ali has time to catch up on his sleep, see some of his friends, and spend a little time with his children.[20]

In light of the forced absence of husbands like Ali, the wife becomes a key agent in running the daily affairs of the family and the production of gendered identities. Ali's wife, Laila, for example, is the one who takes care of their household and looks after most of their children's needs. Most important, she keeps track of their schoolwork, including setting up the private tutoring and coordinating with other families to make sure her children (especially her teenage son, who is in high school) get the attention they need at a reasonable cost. She also keeps an eye on their son and makes sure he interacts with "the right crowd" while managing his time to ensure he spends most of it studying rather than playing on the computer or visiting with his friends. She is the one who does the daily shopping for the family's food and carefully selects the best vegetables and meats for the least amount of money. In addition, she participates in savings associations to secure sums of money necessary for special events or investments. She tries to spare her husband most of the family's troubles and resorts to his direct authority only when there is a serious problem that demands his intervention. At the same time, like many other mothers, she protects her children (especially the son) from the father's anger by covering up mishaps or telling half-truths about inappropriate behavior.

Two important points need to be emphasized here. First, even when (or perhaps because) he is away, the father remains a point of reference that women use to boost their standing vis-à-vis their children.[21] The father's anger, retaliation, and disciplinary power are usually used as a threat to induce children to do what is expected of them. "Wait until your father is back and I'll tell him about what you've done" is a common threat from mothers in the area. Second, the absence of the father throughout the day does not mean that male children do not interact with men. Grandfathers, uncles, neighbors, teachers, sellers, and many other males are part of the daily life of boys and young men. They are important agents in the education of children (either directly through verbal instructions or indirectly by offering examples through their own actions) regarding gender distinctions and the embodiment of masculinity. Boys, for example, learn how to dance like men at weddings, which are usually public events, held in shared spaces and open for all to enjoy. At younger ages, boys tend to imitate the dancing of their mothers and female relatives but it is at weddings that they learn the distinctions between the bodily movements of men and women. Here, without necessarily being told, they begin to imitate the style and form of dancing of other boys and young men. When we attended a wedding in the summer of 2011, Ahmed was pleased to show me his new style of dance, which was markedly distinct from what he did the year before. He proudly imitated the dancing movements and styles of his older cousins and teenage neighbors, who dance in ways unlike women and older men. By the summer of 2012, he seemed to have forgotten all about other movements except those performed by older boys and young men. He was able to reproduce these movements with ease and confidence. Similarly, through visits to mosques, workshops, and local stores, young boys also learn how to walk, sit, and carry themselves like men by imitation and without any clear verbal instructions.[22] Therefore, it is important to see boys as engaged in a broader set of relationships that includes but extends beyond the figure of the biological father, even when he is alive.

Making Him a Man

Both Hiba and Ahmed miss his father a great deal, both for his emotional and financial support. For Hiba, the main thing she laments is the affection and tenderness (*hiniyya*) that Ahmed and his sister are missing because of the death of their father. She fondly remembers how delighted her husband was when he saw his son for the first time. The father was working abroad when Ahmed was born and had heard from his extended family that the boy was very dark (*iswid*), implying that he was not good-looking. When the father was united with the son, though, he was thrilled and emphasized that the baby was handsome. Hiba spoke often about the short periods her husband spent with them, the care and devotion he displayed toward his family, and the time he spent pampering his son.[23]

Fully aware of the magnitude of their loss, Hiba has been trying to offer her two children as much moral and material support as she can.[24] Hiba's investment in caring for and educating her children reflects her deep love for them and the fact that their success, especially Ahmed's, would reflect on her status as a good mother and could influence her own future financial and social well-being. Her pride is unlimited when she talks about Ahmed's writing skills and her daughter's intelligence. She praises her son for being generous, loving, and caring and repeatedly emphasizes that he is much better behaved than many other boys she knows. For example, he never accepts food, gifts, or money from others unless they insist and his mother gives him permission. Hiba expresses her appreciation for her son by buying him new clothes and, occasionally, toys and by attending to his daily needs. She often gives him a bit of money to buy treats once he has completed his chores and homework. She spends a lot of time talking to him about the need for him to behave well, take care of his studies, look after his younger sister, and be considerate of people around him.[25]

To ensure that her son is raised properly, Hiba also finds it necessary to physically discipline him when he makes mistakes or defies her instructions. Like most parents in other societies, including the United States, who believe that "corporal punishment works as a disciplinary technique,"[26] people in al-Zawiya use it to control, regulate, and shape the conduct of their children. As will be argued in Chapter 4, although excessive or frequent use of force is viewed negatively, most people believe that some type of physical discipline is central to the proper raising of children. Perhaps because of the absence of the authority of her husband that she could have appealed to when dealing with Ahmed, Hiba feels the need to be more of a disciplinarian with Ahmed than she had intended. She knows that she would be blamed directly if he was viewed as the product of women's upbringing (*tarbiyyet niswaan*), a notion that implies unsuccessful parenting and an undesirable outcome. Simultaneously, in making him a proper man, Hiba is also actualizing herself as a good mother. The social recognition that he would earn now and in the future would also be recognition of the efforts and sacrifices she is willing to make to raise Ahmed and his sister.

The process of making Ahmed a man has been fraught with tension and Hiba has had to negotiate changing expectations, ideals, and strategies in dealing with her son and the judges of normality, who evaluate, complement, criticize, and correct her conduct. I remember her strong criticism of her older sister, Mirvat, who raised her children, especially

the first three boys, with an iron fist.[27] Since Mirvat's husband was working all day long, she was the primary caregiver for their children. She
would beat them severely for little mistakes and they grew to fear and
dislike their mother. Hiba often took their side and scolded her sister for
the harsh way she disciplined them. Hiba commented with irony on how
things have changed and how she now found herself in a position where
she had to use physical force to discipline her own son.

Hiba repeatedly shared with me her feelings of guilt and uncertainty about her treatment of Ahmed. She has felt torn between two
opposing points of view that she frequently heard from people around
her: some thought she was too strict while others thought she was too
lenient. Some individuals might even change their judgments from one
day to another, additionally complicating Hiba's attempts to find a solid
ground where she could feel some sense of certainty about how to deal
with her son. Her mother objected several times to her frequent beating
of the boy and warned that that tendency could undermine his standing as a future man. Hiba's older brother often disapproved of what he
viewed as excessive beating of the child and had told her that she should
ease up on her attempts to restrict his access to outside spaces. Yet others
have told her that she should be stricter with the boy to make sure he
grows into a proper man. I was present one time when Hiba's sister-in-
law Samia visited to see how the children of her deceased brother were
doing. At that time, Samia regularly visited and made a point of pampering her nephew and niece. Conflict erupted when Ahmed kept insisting
on watching a children's program on TV while his mother, grandmother,
and two aunts (Mirvat happened to be visiting that day too) wanted to
watch a religious TV channel. Mirvat scolded the boy for being spoiled
and not listening to their words (*ma byisma'sh il-kalaam*), blaming his
mother for not being strict enough with him and his grandmother for
not allowing anyone to discipline him. After enduring Ahmed's whin-
ing for a while, Hiba became annoyed and slapped him. I worried that
Samia might take offense, especially given that an "orphan," according
to social and religious norms, is supposed to be treated very tenderly.[28]
To my surprise, the sister-in-law quickly supported Ahmed's mother and
urged her to keep the two children "under control" (*taht eedik*, literally
meaning "under your hand"). She told a story about one of her neighbors

whose husband also died young and left her with three young children. According to Samia, the neighbor's easy-going child-rearing caused all three children to become "bad kids," in contrast to her own children, who, she claimed, understood her desires and requests by a look (*basa*) and without her having to say anything explicitly.[29]

Like single mothers in the United States, who worry that "their parenting maybe damaging to their sons" and "fear their sons will be weak, will not be prepared to be real men, men other men will envy and look up to,"[30] Hiba is deeply concerned about the future of her son. Although she is eager to create a good child and a real man out of Ahmed, and although she considers physical punishment as part of this creation, until recently Hiba worried that her way of disciplining him could be turning him into a frightened little boy who would not be able to stand up for himself in front of others. She felt joyous when others (such as Ahmed's female teacher) approved of her style of parenting and reassured her that boys who are disciplined at a young age grow to become strong and assertive men. But she often felt saddened and frustrated when Ahmed immediately covered his face when she approached him, even when she did not plan to hit him. She felt even more annoyed when he started crying or whimpering as soon as he noticed that she was angry or frustrated. Such gestures, which indicate fear and intimidation, enraged his mother, who worried that his conduct outside would make him seem like a crybaby (*bi dima'ah*). She would like to see him control his emotions and show restraint and strength, not weakness, when confronted by her or by others. Everybody also discouraged him from crying when disappointed or frustrated and pressured him to show strength and control. He was slowly learning how to control his emotions and put on a brave face. In the summer of 2012, I rarely saw him cry and he quickly left the room when he started tearing up. His mother also insisted that he was old enough to fast the whole month of Ramadan and was encouraging him verbally and materially (be offering him special treats) to make sure he fulfilled his religious duty. While she tried to press on him the importance of praying, she was not successful in keeping track of the five prayers and he often skipped some or all of them altogether.

Parenting in this context entails negotiating different competing visions and expectations: strictness and flexibility, verbal instructions and bodily training, physical discipline, and material and emotional rewards are all required to cultivate a strong and assertive but obedient and well-behaved child. Teaching Ahmed about his future as a proper man is not linear, clearly defined, or easily materialized. It encompasses contradictory expectations, multiple agents, and diverse practices. His mother wants him to listen to her words, follow her instructions, and obey her wishes but she also wants him to be assertive when dealing with sellers, brave when challenged by other boys, and fearless when facing possible risks. These uncertainties and contradictions frame Hiba's daily efforts, which aim to regulate her son's whereabouts, keep track of his schoolwork, monitor his behavior, and shape the presentation of his body in daily life. Perhaps nothing reflects these efforts as much as the struggle between Ahmed and his mother over his access to public space, especially the street,[31] and the management of his bodily presentation, particularly his hair.

Spaces for Play

As is commonly the case between children and parents in al-Zawiya, one of the main points of contention between Ahmed and his mother is his access to the shared spaces around their residential buildings that are frequented by other young children. While she and other family members send him down in many trips to do chores for them, they negatively view and strongly discourage his playing in the shared spaces near their housing units. Ahmed's desire to go down and play with the other children often collides with his mother's wish to keep him at home, away from "ill-mannered" children and focused on his studies.[32] Hiba criticizes the bad language the other children use and worries that Ahmed will learn improper behavior from them. Also, fights erupt between the children and parents are sometimes drawn into these fights, something that Hiba tries to avoid as much as possible.[33] Instead of "wasting" his time playing outside, she thought her son would be better off spending his free time preparing for his studies or playing with his little sister. Like many other parents, Hiba strongly believes in the value of education and its role in social mobility and tries to channel her son's energy to the improvement of his performance at school. She thus keeps track of his studies, reviews his lessons, and plans for tutoring in topics she is unable to handle. In the summer, she wants him to get ready for the school year and, during the school year, she wants him to spend his spare time carefully reviewing his lessons, neatly completing his homework, and thoughtfully preparing for the coming lessons.

Ahmed, however, prefers to play with his peers. During the summer afternoons, when the weather cooled down, I could see him yearning to join the children playing in the neighborhood. They would be kicking an old soccer ball, playing with marbles, enjoying a game of cards, playing tag, or using available resources such as sticks and stones to keep themselves busy.[34] When Ahmed would see them, he would beg and plead with his mother to let him go down. Most often his mother refused until he was done with the additional assignments she gave him (such as memorizing some verses from the Quran) and sometimes she would beat him when he persisted in asking. I was always impressed by his persever- ance in asking, even after being beaten, or his ability to find others (like me, his grandmother, or any other visitor) who would intercede on his behalf. Most frequently, Hiba would give in and send him down with a firm promise that he would come back after a short while to complete his additional studies. He would disappear down and not return for hours or until his mother called several times. When he would come up from the street, he would have a big smile on his face and an even bigger appetite. He would eat and then nap, after which he would get up to socialize with us or, when he was allowed, to watch children's programs on television.[35] He would stay awake until two or three in the morning before falling asleep on the couch and then would be carried by his mother to bed.

As noted above, his older uncle criticized Ahmed's mother for her reluctance to send him down to play. He emphasized the importance of the "street" in teaching Ahmed how to manage his relationships with other children now and with men in the future. In many ways, the uncle was right. In the street, Ahmed was learning a great deal about how to manage other boys and how to acquire a sense of his place and "a sense of the place of others."[36] When downstairs, he would form alliances with other boys so that they could play together and defend each other in the future. One of his cousins, who is a few months older and much stronger, was instructed by his father to always watch out for Ahmed and step in to help him in case he got into fights with older boys. At the age of nine,

Children play in the shared spaces around the apartment buildings.

Ahmed proudly told me that he interfered to protect younger children when they were harassed by older or bigger boys. He was also cultivating relationships with other youngsters, who would help and support him when needed. In the summer of 2012, I was moved by the delegations of two or three boys who either came up the stairs or stopped his mother in the street to beg her to let Ahmed play with them. They would plead with her to allow Ahmed to join them for just a few minutes and then, when she occasionally relented, they would negotiate for a longer period. They would jump and squeal with delight before wrapping their arms around Ahmed, who would immediately agree to all the instructions and promises his mother loudly blurted out, and rushing away to play.

Ahmed also learned important aspects of social life from the street, such as how people are classified and the differences between boys and girls. Nicknames, for example, are important identity markers in al-Zawiya. Ahmed told me about one of his friends, who was nicknamed Namla (ant) because he was very speedy like an ant.[37] When I asked Ahmed about his nickname, he said that other children call him il-Mahrou' (the burned one) because of his dark skin. Ahmed gets angry when children call him by that name and responds with some insults.[38] Through these encounters, he is learning important lessons about how others view him and how he should react to the views and expectations of others. When Ahmed was six, I had a discussion with him about color and he was adamant that whiteness was beautiful and good while dark skin was ugly and bad (wihish). He saw himself as abyad and would ask his mother to scrub him hard while bathing him to make sure his skin became even lighter. In 2007, Hiba took Ahmed to a local studio to have his photos taken. She proudly showed me the pictures, commenting on how white Ahmed's face looked. Indeed, the photographer did whiten Ahmed's face drastically and the boy was so happy with his photos that he kept kissing them. At this age, he identified the color of people with his feelings about them.[39] Thus, he thought of the people he loved (like his mother, grandmother, cousins, or friends) as white and the people he disliked as dark. However, as a result of repeated teasing (including by his own relatives) about his skin color and many other interactions inside and outside his home, the way he sees himself and others has shifted over time.[40] At the age of nine, he talked about white and dark as attached to the categories girls and boys. He would say that girls are light skinned but boys are darker and would attach more positive qualities to darker boys (strength, for example) than he originally did.

The type of knowledge Ahmed is acquiring highlights the various uses and views of the street. Mastering it when running errands for relatives and neighbors is encouraged and is linked to the accumulation of important knowledge of the neighborhood and educating him about his future status as a working-class man. As a space of leisure and play, the street becomes more ambiguous and is seen as the site that could frustrate rather than enhance the attempts of families to create an educated and well-mannered young man. Yet, it is a space that is key to the formation of social capital and the constitution of important networks that could endure over a man's life span. This interplay and tension between the private domain of the family and the public domain of the street continues throughout a man's life, and managing the intersection as well as contradiction between these two overlapping domains is central to masculine trajectories, something that will be further elaborated upon in the coming chapters.

Hair Trouble

Another point of contention between Ahmed and his mother is his hair. As a visible gender marker, hair serves as a key "bodily idiom" in the distinction between boys and girls in Egypt.[41] While a girl's hair is worn long and is elaborately styled by mothers, a boy's hair is kept short and well trimmed. Ahmed's hair, which is not as soft or as straight as he would have liked, is highly influential in his daily outings and presentations of his body. He looks up to some of his older cousins and uncles and tries to imitate their hairstyles. When, at the age of seven, he discovered the magic of gel, he begged his uncles until one of them bought him a small jar. He started to secretly use his uncle's nice hair oil, so the uncle bought a cheaper kind for Ahmed. At times, he would go to the bathroom many times to soak his hair with water and comb it to the back. He would delight in oiling, gelling, and styling it. He would then move from mirror to mirror in the apartment to stare at his hair and repeatedly fix it. This act infuriated his mother who scolded him for his vanity by saying that even she (i.e., a woman who is expected to care about her looks) often ties her head cover without looking at herself in the mirror, so how could a boy like him spend so much time looking at himself (*ybuss 'ala nafsu*)? Hiba always carefully paid attention to his clothes and overall cleanliness, but did not want Ahmed to be overtly concerned with his looks. She disliked his attempt to comb his hair to the back and often forced him to style his hair the way she thought was proper, straight to the front, which showed good grooming. Things sometimes became tense when he went to the barbershop because his mother would either go with him to instruct the barber about the cut or clearly tell Ahmed to get a specific short haircut that he did not like. She always wanted a short and practical cut that was easily maintained and that lasted a long time. Occasionally, Ahmed would defy her and claim that the barber made a mistake and gave him a hairstyle other than the one Hiba had wanted.

The management of Ahmed's hair is part of the grooming that he, like other children, has been taught from an early age. Mothers, for example, spend hours preparing small children for a special occasion or trip to another neighborhood by bathing and dressing them in clean clothes and combing their hair. Little girls often scream and cry as their hair is elaborately styled. Girls with kinky hair particularly suffer as their mothers brush their hair until it looks silky and straight and then pull it into tight pigtails that are decorated with bands, ribbons, and barrettes. Children are instructed firmly and repeatedly about how to behave and the importance of keeping their clothes clean during an outing. Such preparations teach children about proper bodily presentation and emphasize its importance, even at the expense of personal comfort. Young boys and girls learn to endure the discomfort of tight shoes or heavy jackets in the summer when these items match the rest of their outfit or are the only nice clothes available. As children become young adults, they become increasingly active in the management and regulation of their bodily comportment and representations. They work to create an appearance that fits the social expectations of their neighbors, allows them to pass as "cool" among their peers, and signals their standing as good citizens, dependable workers, and trustworthy clients. Yet, this process is gendered and boys are taught to be discreet about the attention they pay to their bodily presentations and appearances.

The older Ahmed gets, the more skilled he has become in negotiating with others, especially his mother. He is learning how to manage his desires and bodily presentations in light of the expectations of others. When he was nine, he explained to me that when he heard the sound of his friends playing downstairs, he forgot about his mother's instructions, warnings, and anger and thought only of going down to play with them. Because he feared a beating from his mother, he used "tactics" such as lying, begging, pleading, or concealing to escape her gaze and its disciplining power.[42] For example, he might pretend not to hear her if she called for him while he was playing with his friends, walked very slowly when he was sent out for chores, took the opportunity to play with his friends when he was supposed to run errands for his family, or went down to play when his mother was on an outing. In these ways, Ahmed was testing and challenging the attempts of his family to restrict his mobility and regulate his bodily presentations.

At the same time, relatives were often aware of these tactics and would caution him against defying their expectations. They would also critically respond to the way he carried his body while doing his chores. One time, for example, his mother severely scolded him because she spotted him walking *misahhim* (looking preoccupied and absentminded), which is not befitting a man, who should be alert and aware of his surroundings. She also listened to reports from other children, relatives, and neighbors about his conduct in different places and either praised or scolded him, depending on the deed and the context. To ensure that he is interacting with the right crowd and that he is monitored by older children she approved of, Hiba enrolled Ahmed in a local club in the summer of 2011. While she primarily wanted him to play soccer, a sport that is loved by many boys and men in the area, she also wanted him to be monitored and protected by some of the older well-behaved children in the neighborhood. She was pleased when they reported good things about him but reproached him when they complained about him or reported misbehavior. Ahmed was being taught that he was operating under the judging eyes of others and that he should assume responsibility for his own behavior.

Who Is a Real Man?

The negation, which started at Ahmed's birth and tended to deny similarities and highlight (and even produce physical) variations between male and female infants, has become more and more elaborate over time, and Ahmed increasingly has become an active participant in defining himself as a boy and a future man. At an earlier age he played with little girls (such as his neighbors and cousins) and often declared, to the delight of his mother, that he would marry this or that little girl. But the older he has gotten, the more he has separated himself spatially, physically, and verbally from girls. When he was six, I asked him if he had any female friends at school, and he looked at me as if I did not know anything and firmly replied, "No, boys play with boys and girls play with girls." At the age of eight, he eagerly explained to me that boys are stronger than girls and are better at kicking when they fight with other children. He illustrated this claim by demonstrating three movements he learned from watching American wrestling on TV, a very popular show in al-Zawiya.[43] Despite his very skinny body,[44] he would try to impress me and others with his biceps and would ask me to press them to feel their strength. He wanted me to agree with him that he was stronger than my daughter (who was actually much stronger than he was thanks to good nutrition and gymnastics). For Ahmed, a clear opposition between boys and girls was becoming part of his common sense. At the same time, a process of "transcendence" ensures the transformation of the body and the production of corporeal qualities that materialize social expectations about physical distinctions between boys and girls and anchors them in seemingly purely natural differences.[45] Ahmed was aware of the need to cultivate a strong body, equated with working men, and felt the need to demonstrate that he had such a body even when in reality he did not. This awareness becomes especially intense among teenagers, who are increasingly using gyms and supplements to produce muscular bodies, widely promoted in the media as desirable and attractive.

Despite the work needed to produce a particular masculine body, people in al-Zawiya naturalize gender distinctions by absolute statements such as *"ir-raagil raagil, wis-sitt sitt"* (a man is a man and a woman is a woman). The categories man and woman are "social facts,"[46] thought to be rooted in biological variations and supported by religious discourses and social conventions. Gender distinctions are part of the doxic order of things and are taken for granted by both men and women.[47] Thus, in its attempt to produce a real man, Ahmed's family does not fear that he may be feminized or equated with qualities largely identified with girls or women. Rather, they would like to cultivate him as a "real man," a socially valued notion, compared to other socially stigmatized ways of doing and being a man. The notions of *raagil bi saheeh* or *raagil bi gadd* (a real or true man) and *gada'* refer to a man who excels in materializing social norms that define a proper man, including intelligence, valor, toughness, and decency. The adjective *gada'na* refers to a mix of gallantry and "nobility, audacity, responsibility, generosity, vigor, and manliness."[48] A gada' is a person "who does not swindle or cheat, isn't treacherous, and generally acts within the moral universe of Egyptian popular classes."[49] He "does not accept injustice or tyranny and usually stands for the weak against the strong."[50] Hiba has genuinely desired for her son to be gada' without oppressing others (*yiftiri 'ala hadd*). When at the age of seven he whispered to her that he did not want to walk in one of the roads that led to a specific store because some boys might beat him up, she said that he should be gada' and make sure to take that road. He should not let them intimidate him and should instead show his strength and bravery to them and to others.

It is important to note that not all men are *gid'aan* (plural of gada') and that not all gid'aan are men. A woman or a boy, who materializes key aspects of gada'na, could acquire this symbolic label. When Samah, a nurse in a local hospital, decided not to worry her family by not telling them that she was going to have an appendectomy until after the surgery, people around her thought she was *gad'a* (feminine of gada'). A woman who decided to spend the night with a sick female relative, risking the anger of her husband, was labeled as gad'a by other men, even though they generally thought that women should obey their husbands. A woman who is firm, savvy about traveling and managing money, and able to assert herself in front of men is referred to as gad'a. If she is hot-blooded (*dammaha hami*), fair (*haqaaniha*), and is a woman of her word (*kilmiteha wahda*), she may even earn the honorary phrase *sitt bi meet raagil* (a woman who equals a hundred men). It is important to note that such a depiction does not imply the sexual connotations that we often encounter in the study of female masculinity in the United States. As argued by Nakamura and Matsuo, "most of the scholarship on female masculinity in the United States has tied it intimately to lesbianism, with strong emphasis on the physical body and physical sex acts of those involved."[51] At the same time, in al-Zawiya a distinction is made between a woman who maintains a feminine identity (reflected in her clothing, marriage, mothering, and taking good care of her children and household), but through her conduct merits the positive label *sitt bi meet raagil*, and a woman who (often implicitly) rejects feminine ways of doing and being and who imitates the dress code or bodily presentations and gestures of men, and thus earns the negative label *mistargila*. While the first is a type of complement and celebrates a woman who excels in materializing some key norms linked to masculinity, *mistargila* is a critique of a female who is trying to publically embody men's ways of being. Hence, because the qualities that define a proper man could be detached from the male body and reattached to other bodies, materializing social norms over and over becomes an important part of the making of proper men.

While labels like "real man" and "gada'" are desired and aspired to, but there are other ways of being a man that are socially stigmatized and negatively viewed. People use words such as *khawal* (submissive), *hafa'* (insignificant), *kheekha* (weak or sissified), or *'ayyil* (childish) to describe a man who does not effectively materialize social norms that equate a real man with domination, assertiveness, and decisiveness. Other words may include *haayif* (trivial, a man who overlooks the important things and makes a big issue of trivial ones), *hafyya* (nobody, or insignificant), *khafeef* (not serious, talks too much), *mirakhrakh* (weak, soft, and spineless), and *tari* (soft, or weak). Some of these words might have sexual connotations. The word *khawal*, for example, a common insult directed at boys and men in al-Zawiya, indicates submission, including in sexual encounters. Singerman in her study of another neighborhood in Cairo noted that people use this word to "refer to homosexuals and use it as an insult against men when they want to challenge their masculinity, much as Americans use the term 'faggot.'"[52] In the nineteenth century, a *khawal* in Cairo was a male performer who danced and presented his body like a woman (for example, letting his hair grow long, plucking his facial hair, and using kohl and henna to adorn himself).[53] In the early twentieth century, the word referred to "the figure of cross-dressing male performer."[54] Currently, this word is often used in al-Zawiya to imply wrongdoing but is rarely used in its sexual meaning. However, all the words mentioned above are used in daily life to depict a certain social incompetence and an inability to materialize specific social norms in the right contexts (for example, being dominant in the right context but affectionate and easygoing in another). While the ideal man is the norm, these other, negative words highlight gaps, inabilities, and inconsistencies. Boys are taught to aspire to be real men and that to achieve that standing, they have to be educated, scrutinized, and corrected by others. The above words also illustrate the importance of social recognition in the making of a proper man.

It would be a mistake to assume that these negative characteristics are feminine in any sense. In fact, qualities of weakness, pettiness, and childishness are not attached to or desirable in women.[55] Rather, they are specifically used to describe those who fail to enact norms that define proper men.[56] We see here men defining themselves and being defined by others in contrast to other men who excel (or fall short) in materializing social norms. What is at stake is not the risk of feminization but of emasculation, of not being viewed as a real man. A proper man is not created by or through a simple binary opposition between male and female but through elaborate differentiation between modes of doing and being a man. This differentiation does not produce distinct masculinities but continues to reference and reinforce a socially defined set of norms that people draw on to critique, instruct, correct, and modify the conduct of those who are not seen as measuring up to these standards.

Ahmed is being taught not only to differentiate himself from girls but also to measure himself against other boys and men and to consider the importance of the gaze of others in judging his conduct. He is not trained to enact the autonomous independent ethos that many Americans may view as essential in the right way to raise children. In this, we do not see the opposition between individual and society that structures conceptions of individuality in the West and that regards agency "as the capacity to realize one's own interest against the weight of custom, tradition, transcendental will, or other obstacles (whether individual or collective)."[57] Instead, Ahmed is being taught to master and embody the social norms that guide his masculine trajectory and to appreciate the role of others in monitoring, evaluating, and legitimizing his conduct and granting (or denying) him the recognition that supports his standing as a man.

This process is similar to the Kabyle's constructions of masculinity and the sense of honor they try to cultivate among their male youth as discussed by Bourdieu.[58] Yet Bourdieu's analysis suggests a clear course of events, devoid of contradiction, uncertainty, and ambiguity. The men he describes are coherent, fully formed subjects who are perfectly in control of the rules of the game. A clear and enduring opposition between male and female, which is realized in bodily movements and postures, division of labor, and spatial structures, allows the production of feminine and masculine identities that are unambiguously defined, durable, and reproduced without much effort.[59] In contrast, Ahmed's boyhood shows that while there are specific norms that inform masculine trajectories and people's judgments of men's conduct in al-Zawiya, there is uncertainty about how to discipline and raise boys to become men and about how a man should conduct himself in different contexts in order maintain the sense of coherence and authenticity described by Mona at the beginning of the chapter. At the same time, the city is an important socioeconomic, cultural, and political spatial formation that opens possibilities for learning, forgetting, and relearning new ways of being and doing. The coming chapters look at different facets of this process and the complex negotiation embedded in it. They show that neither unlimited fluidity nor rigidity captures the struggles, tensions, and contestations embedded in the collective project of gendering.

2

Plans and Stands
The Challenge of Being Single at Forty

Endorsed rather than ordained, manhood remains forever in
doubt, requiring daily demonstration.

David Gilmore, *Manhood in the Making*

Male privilege is a trap, and it has its negative side in the permanent tension and contention, sometimes verging on the absurd,
imposed on every man by the duty to assert his manliness in all
circumstances.

Pierre Bourdieu, *Masculine Domination*

IF YOU HAD THE CHANCE to ask Samer when he was a single man
in his mid-thirties about the meaning of ruguula, he would have said
"er-ruguula mawqif" (manhood is a position, or a stand; plural *mawaaqif*)
and then list several mawaaqif when others judged his conduct as reflecting the standing of a man.[1] Most of the examples he would have offered would show his body as mediating his relationship with others. It
is by working, moving, taking risks, fighting, rescuing, and protecting
(especially women and children) that he asserts his agency as a man and
materializes norms of courage, toughness, and fearlessness. The examples
he provided were often moments and experiences from his youth. He
vividly narrated a time when he rushed to help when a fire started in a
nearby housing block. He described the scene of billowing smoke, chaos,
and screaming. Of all the men standing at the entrance (including fire-
fighters), it was he that a woman grabbed and begged: "Samer, my child
is upstairs and nobody can get him but you. Please help him." Without
a second thought, Samer pushed his way through and went up to the

fourth floor, snatched the boy and took him downstairs. He then went upstairs again to the third floor, the site of the fire, and brought down the *ambuuba* (a cylinder of butane gas), which could have exploded and destroyed the whole building.[2] When he relayed this story, Samer always noted how many people asserted that he was a real man (*raagil bi saheeh*) and commended his courage and gada'na. Another memorable example occurred when he was twenty and the city bus he was riding in hit a pedestrian. Samer was the only one who dared to go under the bus to pull out the body of the victim. He would also tell the story of an ill-tempered seller of *fuul* and *ta'miyya*, two fava-bean-based Egyptian popular dishes, who, during a fight with one of his customers, started spraying people with boiling oil. One woman screamed, "Isn't there a man around here who can stop this guy?"—an exclamation intended to incite the men nearby to act. Samer overheard her and jumped out of the balcony where he was standing, rushed to the man, and managed to quickly flip down the pot with the hot oil.

His other examples included the fights that were imposed on him or in which he felt compelled to get involved to help someone or correct a wrongdoing. One of his favorite examples occurred when he was nineteen and riding the city bus with two of his friends. They noticed a young boy who was crying, trying to retrieve his watch from a young man, whom I will refer to as Bilia. The boy had received the watch as a gift from his father, and Bilia had somehow managed to convince him to exchange it for a much cheaper plastic watch. When the boy realized that he had been tricked, he started crying and pleading with Bilia to give the watch back. Samer and his friends supported the boy and tried first to persuade and then to pressure Bilia to give the watch back. In a few minutes, Bilia had mobilized several of his own friends (who were scattered on the bus) to help him confront Samer and his two friends. Fearing getting caught in a fight involving pocketknives (*mataawi*),[3] the other passengers moved away from the brawl and the bus became like a *saaha* (a fighting arena). Throughout the fight, though Samer suffered two stabs in his leg and was bleeding heavily, he made sure to protect his face. For him, scars on the leg are rarely seen by others but the face is a "mirror" that everybody looks at. As bodily hexis, facial scars could be interpreted by others not only as signs of defeat but also as signs of criminality and troublemaking.[4]

Samer would describe how scared members of his family were when they saw his injuries but would also talk about the pride he sensed in their reactions and in their telling and retelling of the events to neighbors and relatives. He knew that even when they clearly disagreed with his quick interventions that could cause him bodily harm, they were still proud when others complimented him and recognized his ruguula. Indeed, his relatives always stressed Samer's bravery but criticized his hastiness, complaining that he often did not think before interfering in risky and potentially dangerous situations. Nonetheless, one of his sisters commented proudly that even when he was a young boy, people often referred to Samer as *agda' min raagil* (more capable than a man). Such testimonies, as he himself emphasized, were central to the formation of his masculine trajectory. They endorsed, consolidated, and celebrated his conduct and the stands he took. However, the criteria for people's judgments and reactions are not always clearly defined, fixed, or easily learned. As Samer once told me, "one does not really know if what he is going to do will be viewed by others as the manly thing to do. I just do things without thinking about them and then hear people's reactions to what I've done." It is this interplay between the doing and the judging, between the act and the meaning given to it, between bodily hexis and its interpretation, between recognition and misrecognition that is the focus of this chapter.

It is important to mention here that the examples offered by Samer were supported by his family and friends and there is no reason to doubt their authenticity. Yet, my point here is not to judge their genuineness but to call attention to their significance in informing Samer's feelings about himself and his views of how masculinity is understood in his neighborhood. They bring a past (even if imagined) into dialogue with the present as well as individual experiences into dialogue with collective expectations. They underscore that there is a set of loosely defined social norms (such as courage, strength, and the ability to use violence when appropriate) that informs a masculine trajectory. They show that an important part of this process lies in the hands of others (including men and women, friends and enemies, and neighbors and strangers), who could grant or deny the social recognition central to the making of men. This interplay is often ambiguous and demands negotiation that has to take place in different contexts with various audiences in order to cultivate and garner desirable meanings. The changing role of the body is central to this process.

This chapter critically draws on Bourdieu's work on the body and social divisions to explore how young men groom their bodies and present them to others in diverse contexts as well as the various interpretations people (including potential brides) make of specific bodily presentations and representations. It traces some significant moments in Samer's masculine trajectory to elaborate on the importance of work, engagement in community life, getting married, and becoming a father in the construction of a masculine identification. The discussion aims to give a sense of the shifting (temporally and spatially) nature of masculinity as a socially meaningful project and an ongoing practical achievement that is strongly linked, but cannot be reduced, to the corporality of the body.

Embodied Inequalities

In theorizing the reproduction of social inequalities, Bourdieu viewed the body as the "most indisputable materialization of class taste" and one of the main sites for the inscription and reproduction of class divisions (in the case of France) and gender hierarchies (in the case of Algeria). He argued that the ways we inhabit our bodies reveal "the deepest dispositions of the habitus," which is "a socially constituted system of cognitive and motivating structures" and "durable, transposable *dispositions*" that are structured by socioeconomic conditions and that structure daily practices, perceptions, and tastes.[5] Furthermore, Bourdieu argued that one could "map out a universe of class bodies, which (biological accidents apart) tends to reproduce in its specific logic the universe of the social structure."[6] The foods we eat, the sports we play, the clothes we wear, and the ways we walk and talk are all structured by our location in a certain social space. Taste, "a class culture turned into nature, that is *embodied*, helps to shape the class body."[7] This embodiment naturalizes social inequalities and ensures their reproduction. Bodily hexis, Bourdieu explained, "is political mythology realized, embodied, turned into a permanent disposition, a durable manner of standing, speaking, and thereby of *feeling* and *thinking*."[8] In the case of Algeria, he observed that the opposition between men and women was displayed and reinforced in the various ways they inhabited their bodies in daily life. Thus, "the specifically feminine virtue, *lahia*, modesty, restraint, reserve, orients the whole female body downwards, towards the ground, the inside, the house, whereas male excellence, *nif*, is asserted in movement upwards, outwards, towards other men."[9] Although this opposition that fully separates men and women and assigns them to separate domains misses the key role that women play in the making of proper men, Bourdieu makes an important point about how the daily embodiment of gender and class inequalities situates the habitus below consciousness and ensures its reproduction with little effort and thought.[10]

Scholars have used Bourdieu's notions of habitus and bodily hexis to analyze the embodiment of piety, ethics, order, and beauty in Egypt.[11] Yet, in doing so, they have revealed the limitations of Bourdieu's work, especially his lack of attention to the "manner and process by which a person comes to acquire a habitus" and his inability to illustrate that bodily hexis "is always subject to multiple interpretations."[12] Saba Mahmood presents a particularly compelling critique of Bourdieu's work and argues for the need to recuperate an "Aristotelian notion of habitus" that would better problematize "how specific kinds of bodily practice come to articulate different concepts of the ethical subject, and how bodily form does not simply express the social structure but also endows the self with particular capacities through which the subject comes to enact the world."[13]

There is much value in Mahmood's critique, but my work in Cairo, unlike hers, aims to highlight the diverse discourses and actors that compete to shape the embodiment of subjectivities and places class at the center of that analysis. Mahmood's work on how women cultivate a virtuous self tends to overestimate "the role self-directed action plays in the learning of an embodied disposition."[14] This emphasis may describe the experience of religious activists who reference a set of traditions and authority figures to legitimize particular discourses or practices as pious, but it is less useful when looking at the many actors, discourses, and images that shape embodiment in urban Egypt. For the women affiliated with the mosque movement described by Mahmood, religion may offer a sense of stability and coherence where each one has the chance to "interpret the moral codes, in accord with traditional guidelines, in order to discover how she, as an individual, may best realize the divine plan for her life."[15]

Their ultimate goal and reward is to satisfy "God's will" and secure "God's pleasure."[16] Thus, religion becomes an authoritative discourse that secures solidity and legitimacy to the realization of notions of self, virtue, and piety. For the majority of Cairo's men (and women), religion is only one discourse (albeit an important one) among several that mold their practices and identities. This multiplicity both facilitates and complicates the constitution of bodies and selves. In a pious context, individuals could possibly appeal to the final judge (God) as the ultimate meaning maker, who would see their acts for what they really are and judge their intentions. In contrast, in daily constructions of masculinity, it is men and women, friends and enemies, and neighbors and strangers who judge, recognize, and proclaim someone as a man or not. In an urban context like Cairo, this hailing, recognizing, or denying is negotiated in various spaces and with several audiences. As Samer's trajectory shows, masculine identity is elaborated through the interplay between structures (especially of gender and class) and practices, individual actors and judges of acts, deeds and contexts, bodily hexis and situated observers.

Samer's Trajectory

Samer was born in the popular quarter of Bulaaq Abu 'Illa in downtown Cairo but his family was relocated to al-Zawiya in 1980 as part of President Sadat's project to modernize and beautify Cairo.[17] At the age of ten, Samer moved with his parents and seven siblings from their one-room dwelling to a two-bedroom apartment in a public housing project in al-Zawiya. Before their relocation, at the age of five, he started working in Bulaq, which had many small workshops and businesses. He first worked at a local workshop (*warsha*) for polishing aluminum kitchen utensils, sweeping the floor and running small errands for the workers. At the age of ten, he discovered auto body repair. The job appealed to him as a young boy, he says, because of the hammering and the other sounds the workers generated. He went to school until the fourth grade but quit because, he explained, he saw the benefits of earning money and the disadvantages of the beatings he got at school at the hands of his teachers, who were often frustrated by his inability to complete his schoolwork. He would often return home very tired and would fall asleep before doing his homework. Samer was also beaten by his usta, who was training him to become an auto body repairman. Whenever he sent him out to buy things and he was late or forgot what he was supposed to buy, the usta would beat him. Samer recalls that, at the time, parents were complicit in this type of disciplining. They would bring their children to an usta and say, "Beat the boy and be very strict with him. Do whatever it takes to teach him a good skill or trade." These beatings were coupled with care, affection, and a strong bond with his usta that lasted many years. Samer's work brought him money and distanced him from the disciplinary power of the school and, at that time, he found great satisfaction in his choice.[18] Like the British "lads" studied by Paul Willis,[19] Samer found working and earning money more rewarding than schooling and, in the process, contributed to the reproduction of his status as part of the working class.[20]

This "(forced) choice" shaped in fundamental ways his material, cultural, and social capital and structured his trajectory as a man.[21] At the age of fifteen, Samer became an usta himself. His good and careful work earned him respect and secured him continuous work for nearly twenty-five years. Since he became an usta, he has moved between different workshops inside and outside his neighborhood. Unlike teenagers who had to go to school and thus depend financially on their families, Samer had the ability to earn money, which enhanced his freedom and ability to tour Cairo and enjoy its offerings. This mobility and his job enabled him to interact with the educated and the illiterate, the decent and the criminal, the strong and the weak, and the ordinary citizen and the police officer. These interactions as well as his knowledge of his neighborhood and other areas in Cairo shaped his sense of himself and how others viewed his standing as a man.

The above examples of Samer's understanding of ruguula as mawqif largely stem from the days of his youth, when he was between fifteen and twenty-five years old.[22] This is the period when most young men begin to enjoy a great deal of freedom of mobility. This is especially true for working men, who earn their own money. They spend their free time (usually one day of the week or after work late at night) in coffee shops, streets, and more recently, gyms and Internet cafés.[23] One exception applies to youths who are under pressure to be successful in school. During the school year, families struggle daily to restrict and control the mobility of boys and adolescents to make sure they devote their time and energy to their homework and studies.

For many young men, "the street," as was emphasized by Samer, becomes an important space for male socialization. He argued that even military service, which in his case lasted three years, did not teach him much about ruguula but only about toughness (*khushuuna*), while the street allowed him to interact with many types of people and taught him much about how to conduct himself as a man. As described in Chapter 1, the street has contradictory meanings. Parents try to limit their children's access to the street for fear they will acquire bad habits and ill manners, but they also recognize that learning from life in the street is key to developing the knowledge that men are supposed to accumulate about their neighborhood and the city at large. It also allows them to develop bonds with other young men. On the street, young men can spend time away from their families and the watchful eyes of siblings and neighbors. They may experiment with alcohol, drugs, and smoking as well as flirt with and court young women.

Young men are not limited to their neighborhood but may also go in small groups to walk the streets of downtown Cairo, watch movies, stroll in malls, and check out stores in middle-class neighborhoods, sit in public gardens, and walk around the Nile Corniche.[24] Most young men are permitted to stay out late, a privilege usually denied young women. In fact, part of the assertion of young men's authority and status as men is strongly linked to their ability to control the mobility of younger female relatives, usually sisters. A brother may use violence to punish a sister who stayed out relatively late or who does not ask for explicit permission from her parents before an outing (this topic will be discussed further in Chapter 4). Young men's freedom of mobility contrasts sharply with the limitations imposed on older men, who are expected to spend most of their time working and attending to the needs of their families and to limit themselves to socially and economically meaningful mobilities.[25] Through their outings, young men get to know the city, master its transportation system, explore its economic opportunities, enjoy its entertainment facilities, frequent some of its spaces, and learn how to interact with its diverse population. Phrases like *laff we daar* (literally, "he went around in circles") capture the sense and sensibility cultivated through roaming around and moving about the city. A man who *laff we daar* during his youth becomes *midardah*: educated in city ways, knowledgeable of its life, aware of its tricks and frauds, and polished in his interaction with its diverse population. He acquires practical knowledge that marks his urban identity and makes him feel at home in the city so that no one can outsmart him. A *midardah* man, for example, knows how to prevent taxi drivers from taking advantage of him. Because most cabs lack reliable meters, the fare is negotiated. Asking about the fare at the beginning of the trip is a risky affair because the driver would most likely ask for more than the passenger would want to pay. Not paying him what he asks for at the end of the trip could lead to a loud verbal confrontation. The same is true if the driver is severely underpaid. Thus, a knowledgeable man would be able to figure out a reasonable fare to pay without the need to check with the driver. This man is viewed positively, and this type of knowledge contributes to his standing as a real man. This was clearly reflected in the case of Samer, whose reputation and standing as a real man were directly related to his days as a youth and the knowledge he accumulated of the city and its various social groups, the good and the bad, the close and the distant.

Over the past two decades, however, I have noticed the increasing restrictions on the mobility of young men and their access to various urban spaces. They have been increasingly excluded from the city by new techniques of "spatial governmentality."[26] This type of governmentality focuses on "managing risks rather than enforcing moral norms" and deploys policing practices "to diminish risks through the production of knowledge about potential offenders."[27] The category "young men" in general and "young working-class men" in particular has become associated in the state public discourse with threat, danger, and disorder.[28] This discourse stresses that these men should be controlled, regulated, and excluded from several spaces to protect a particular public (for example, rich Egyptians, tourists, shoppers, and investors). Downtown Cairo, the area that young men usually enjoy visiting, has increasingly become labeled as a risky and dangerous zone that should be strictly policed. Hotels, malls, and banks have come under heavy surveillance. Police cars, watchdogs, blocked streets, security gates, and guards surround these spaces, judging who belongs and who does not. The mere existence of these monitoring devices is enough to discourage young men from even thinking of entering such spaces. These exclusionary practices, I believe, have been a main factor contributing to the strong support the youth displayed for the revolution and its attempts to reclaim downtown Cairo's public spaces such as Midan al-Tahrir.

Moving in the city taught young men about various forms of inequality (including age, gender, and class) as well as the various moral codes and bodily presentations that would enable them to pass in various spaces. Even though young men were able to (temporarily) escape the disciplining eye of the family and neighbors, they were nonetheless always subjected to the power of the state. Through their movement in the neighborhood and Cairo at large, they came face-to-face with the disciplining gaze of the police. Whenever trouble took place in the area, young men were the first suspects. Many men reported having been stopped, searched, and taken to the police station during the days of their youth; some were even beaten or kept in detention for a few days. Samer, who had to go through police harassment and detention several times, told stories about innocent men who were tortured and confessed to crimes they did not commit; he highlighted a couple of cases of detained men who threw themselves from police station windows and died in the attempt to avoid the beatings of policemen. In addition to carrying their ID cards, young men were keenly aware of the importance of their bodily hexis in their interaction with the police and thus often tried to dress and present their bodies in ways that would allow them to pass as good and respectable citizens.

In general, young men pay great attention to their looks and bodily presentations. They invest as much money as they can spare to buy fashionable clothes and are careful to wear neatly ironed outfits with well-coordinated colors for their outings. They are aware they will be under the gaze of others and will be partially judged by their appearances. They may use lotions and masks to cleanse, clarify, and lighten their skin. Hair and its management are particularly important. Teenagers use gel, mousse, spray, and colors to style their hair in fashionable ways. According to one of the barbers I talked to, the service young men most frequently seek is the straightening of their hair, which is seen as key to attractiveness and good looks.[29] "Cool kids" follow popular fashions and ask the barber to trim their beards and moustaches accordingly. National and international popular singers (for example, Amr Diab or Michael Jackson), actors (for example, Leonardo DiCaprio), and Egyptian and foreign soccer players are especially important in al-Zawiya, and one can see their photos decorating local barbershops. One of the popular beard styles, for example, was called a "doglas" after the goatee beard that Michael Douglas wore in one of his movies. Similarly, the "rough beard" became popular after several Egyptian singers and actors appeared with stubble on TV. Some English words such as "spiky," "curly," and "new look" have become com-

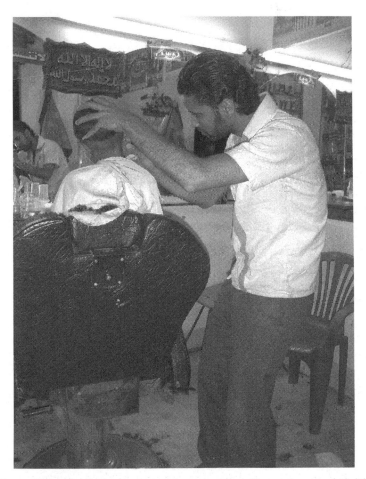

Regular visits to the barbershop are part of the presentation of boys and men in daily life.

mon words used by young men and barbers to refer to specific haircuts and styles. The management of hair is strongly liked to fashion, gender distinction, social conventions, and religious piety. Facial hair in particular may convey several meanings. Untrimmed beards may indicate religiosity, political dissidence, a sense of despair or unhappiness, a state of mourning, or dire economic need.

The circulation of discourses and images that depict desirable bodies, the availability of different products and spaces, and the growing emphasis on consumption are transforming some of the ideas about bodily forms. More and more, young men are associating masculine identities with physical strength and muscles. They increasingly focus on upper body muscles, for example. Muhammad, a 20-year-old college student, told me that he was trying to build up his upper chest and arms to become bigger and look *himish* (tough and strong). As another male interlocutor said, "looking big" (*tuul bi 'ard*, literally "tall and broad") is often enough to deter others from challenging a man and engaging him in a fight. Some young men go to local gyms to lift weights, and some take drugs and supplements to enhance their chest and arm muscles.[30] Some wear tight shirts to show the strength of their upper bodies. Parents remember earlier times when other standards were used to judge the attractive male body. For example, a man in his early sixties remembered how, in the past, a potbelly (*kirsh*) was rare and was considered a sign of wealth in his village in the Egyptian Delta. His 22-year-old son reacted with disgust to such a view and emphasized that contemporary young men dislike belly fat and work hard to avoid it. Some diet, some exercise, while others use vibrating waist belts to get rid of a *kirsh*.

Differences between parents and children in their respective tastes and preferences sometimes lead to tension and conflict, especially if young men ignore their schooling or work or if their experimentation with drugs or alcohol becomes excessive. Tension also erupts between parents and children over the type of clothes the adults feel young men should wear and hairstyles they deem acceptable. For example, parents abhor long hair and certain hairstyles, jewelry such as necklaces, and tight and low-waist jeans. Parents worry about the possible negative interpretations of such bodily presentations, which could be seen as signs of emasculation.

One of the barbers explained to me that, to avoid conflicts with their parents, some young men come to him to fix their hair in certain styles just before they leave to visit other areas where such styles are considered "cool" and try to avoid their families for as long as possible. Other young men color their hair using temporary dye to avoid the wrath of their fathers, which could take the form of verbal, financial, and physical punishment. A 17-year-old man, whom I have known since he was three, loved his hair and spent hours caring for it. Frustrated with his son's obsession with his hair and neglect of his schoolwork, his father took a pair of scissors one night and cut the boy's hair when he was sleeping. The young man was heartbroken for a while but his barber soon managed to trim his hair in another fashionable way. Young men thus must negotiate competing ideals in the management and presentation of their bodies.

Making and Spending Money

Young men's relative freedom of mobility and spending are usually accepted by parents as part of growing up and becoming a man. They are seen as an important part of their spatial and social knowledge of the city. It is expected, however, that a young man will come out of this phase by his mid-twenties and grow into a responsible, serious, and productive individual who abides by social norms and fulfills his family's demands. Soon after they finish their military service (usually three years for young men without a high school diploma),[31] their families begin to pressure them to earn and maintain well-paid jobs and to save as much as possible. Economic productivity and financial success become central parts of a man's masculine trajectory. This centrality has been further enhanced over the past twenty years by the growing emphasis on consumption, the withdrawal of the state from offering basic services, and the increasing responsibility of families for the education and health care of their members. If a young man shows interest in a prospective wife, the family (especially the mother and the sisters) evaluate her and, if they deem her acceptable, encourage him to work harder to make enough money to be able to propose to her. Finding a spouse becomes central to a masculine trajectory and a man's status in the eyes of others. Men's heterosexuality and desire to be married is taken for granted.[32] People think that the only thing that could conceivably prevent this expectation is the financial ability to marry. Over the years, a popular man like Samer became familiar with several women and even brought some of them home to meet his mother and sisters, a step showing his seriousness about them as potential wives. His female relatives raved about the beauty of one of them in particular who had light skin, long dark hair, and green eyes, and who was madly in love with Samer. He refused to marry her, however, because of the educational differences between them. She had much more education (a college degree) and he worried that would create problems after marriage and undermine his standing as a man.

In general, most young men find a fiancée between the ages of twenty-five and thirty and seek to marry by their late twenties or early thirties. Their priorities are often clear: they want to save money and start a family. Over the past two decades, getting married has become more and more challenging. Both media and scholarly work have recently focused on a "marriage crisis" in Egypt, which is reflected in a growing number of men and women who are not able to marry or who marry at a much later age compared to the past generation.[33] It is important to note that the current "marriage crisis" is often depicted by both policy circles and media as a woman's problem. As shown in several recent TV series (such as 'Ayiza Atgawiz, or I Want to Get Married), the supposed crisis is presented through women's (often desperate) attempts to find husbands so that they may conform to social norms and fulfill the expectations of their families and society at large. Rarely are men brought into the discussion, and we do not have a sense of the type of pressure that men who are viewed as old and unmarried have to negotiate in their daily life.[34] The assumption continues to be that women are single out of necessity (no one is proposing to them) while men are single out of choice (they could always manage to marry no matter how old they become). However, many men are single out of economic necessity and have to face continuous social criticisms and pressure to marry as soon as possible. The standing of a man may be undermined if he fails to earn and save enough, get engaged, rent or buy an apartment, and purchase the furniture and appliances requested by the families of most brides before the consummation of the marriage. This challenge is illustrated by Samer's trajectory.

The Wasteful Man

There is no doubt that Samer earned a good income by al-Zawiya's standards. However, for a long time he was not able to save enough to make progress toward getting married. The problem was that, as his family describes it, Samer was *hinayyin* and *illi fi geebu mish lih* (too generous, literally "the money in his pocket is not his"). His excessive generosity was seen as his main failing. He did not pay attention to his money but carelessly spent it. In this context and as argued by other scholars,[35] we see a tension between some aspects of the construction of manhood outside the home, where men are required to be generous, and family expectations that demand prudence with their money and savings for the future. Things became tense when Samer's family discovered that he had managed to get involved with a "bad crowd" (including women and drugs) and wasted his money on them. Despite his family's urgings, Samer would not change his lifestyle. Things became even more stressful in the summer of 1997, when he became unemployed. His family blamed him for losing his job because he stayed up very late, leaving him too tired to be productive during the day. His then fiancée and her mother criticized him for not finding a job immediately. There was nothing worse for a man, they argued, than not having a job and an income when he had so many financial obligations, such as payments for savings associations. Under such strong pressure, he accepted one of the first jobs he found, even though it was in a workshop far from his neighborhood. He argued that the location and the number of hours were not as good as he would have liked but that it was a better alternative than staying without a job and being subjected to incessant criticism. Despite the hardships of his travel and work, he regained part of his authority at home and seemed much happier than when he was unemployed.

No matter how hard Samer worked, though, he could not save enough to fulfill the expectations of the people around him. It was not just that Samer started saving later than most men his age: the increasing desire for consumption in general also heightened the demand for more and fancier items and the shortage in housing made finding an affordable apartment very difficult. Over time, Samer came to understand what his family had been seeing (and saying) all along and realized that he would not be able to save much if he stayed connected to the bad crowd that drained him of money and kept him up all night and tired all day. In addition, he needed to earn more than was possible by his work in Cairo. Samer's solution was to remove himself from that setting by traveling to another country, where he could find a higher-paying job. He managed to find an opportunity in Libya and spent several years working there sporadically—first for three years, after that for two years, and most recently for fifteen months. Luckily, these trips allowed him to save enough money to buy an apartment in another neighborhood. Despite the relatively small size of the apartment and its distance from al-Zawiya, his family was thrilled to see him spend his money so wisely. He grew more conscious of how his money was spent but often could not manage it himself. His younger sister, Afaf, became an important source of support by managing his money, finding workers, paying monthly installments, and looking after his apartment when he was abroad. Samer continued to depend on her while he was in Cairo because, as he emphasized, she was good at saving him money. For example, when they were adding the final touches to his apartment, he asked Afaf to oversee its furnishing because he worried that he would spend too much money on tips and would be tempted to hire people to do some errands that his sister could enlist relatives and neighbors to do for free. With the support of his family, Samer was now well positioned to materialize another set of norms that define a proper man: marriage and fatherhood.

Unmarried at Forty

Despite his hard work and family's assistance, in the summer of 2010, Samer was forty and still unmarried. He had his apartment and his share of the furniture, including for the bedroom, as well as the stove, the refrigerator, the TV set, and the fans. As is customary, the bride would be expected to bring the furniture for the living room, carpets, curtains, kitchen cabinets, appliances, utensils, and china. Yet Samer had no bride, and his mother was particularly distraught. Her worries made her sick and unable to sleep; she could not believe that he was "getting so old" without being married and living in his own home. "When will he be able to have children and raise them?" she wondered. In addition to her eagerness to see him happily married, she was growing older and her health did not make it always easy for her to look after her son's needs. Even though Samer had his own apartment, he continued to live with his family. Men and women are not expected to move out of their homes before they marry. Although Samer cooked his own food and made his own tea while working in Libya, in al-Zawiya his female relatives are expected to carry out these tasks. Thus, his mother, a woman in her late sixties, especially resented that she still had to get up in the morning to make his tea and ensure he was not late for work.

Samer's mother lamented the money that he earned and wasted over the years, and she bemoaned his failed engagements to two lovely women who would have made excellent wives. These women came from good families and were devoted to Samer, but he had broken up with both of them after disagreements with their families. The first engagement he broke off because he wanted his fiancée to stop working and the second because he refused to give in to her continuous demands and ultimatums,[36] the most recent of which was her insistence that he should borrow money to expedite their marriage plans. He was also engaged to a third young woman, but his family did not approve of her. His siblings and friends agreed that the woman, despite her beauty, would not make a good wife for Samer. She was not suitable, they argued, not only because she was divorced but also because she lacked modest behavior and would not make a trustworthy wife. They flagged her provocative dancing and revealing outfits at weddings as well as her tendency to tease, flirt, and joke with male neighbors as transgressions that Samer would not tolerate in the future and that could lead to serious marital problems. Given Samer's insistence on the young woman, they finally gave in and reluctantly agreed to the engagement but were delighted when the couple eventually broke up over an argument about her talking flirtatiously to a male neighbor.

Samer himself found it ironic that he was the most popular of his brothers with women, yet they all married much younger than he did. His older brother married at the age of twenty-three and his other three brothers married in their early thirties. During his twenties and thirties, his married friends used to envy him because he did not have to worry about a wife and children. They would tell him how lucky he was for not having a wife who would "nag" him about money and his whereabouts. They envied the nice clothes he continued to buy and the freedom of mobility he enjoyed. By the age of forty, however, Samer felt that the pressure and need to get married and start a family outweighed the conveniences of his single life. People around continuously reminded him of his unmarried status. This was especially acute in summer 2010, when his nephew married at the age of twenty-six. Many of the wedding attendees asked why Samer was not married yet and prayed to God to grant him a good wife. He also saw his friends with their teenage children and worried that he may not have enough time to father and raise his own offspring. He appreciated the bond his peers have fostered with their children and felt that he would like to experience something this precious before he gets too old.

At the same time, Samer realized that he was not able to earn as much income as before. His work was physically very demanding. It included working for many hours under hard conditions (such as enduring terrible noise and the hot summer weather). Due to inadequate safety measures, he ended up with several bad cuts and eye injuries. His hands, nails, and arms reflected many years of work and the injuries and burns he suffered. Most of the time, Samer hardly ate during the day and merely smoked and drank sweet tea. Some days, he joined his fellow workers and shared some ready-made food that was sold around such workshops but, most often, he waited until midnight for his main meal. His work surroundings, eating habits, and long hours have been causing him some health problems, especially with his digestive system.[37]

Although he used to tolerate his work conditions and rarely complained, at the age of forty he could not imagine working in auto body repair for much longer. Other ustas at his age usually have their own workshops and hire young workers to do the demanding physical labor while they themselves become supervisors and managers. Samer tried in the past to establish his own workshop but, as he explained, people around him were impatient with his inability to quickly make money and could not understand that a new warsha needed more time to succeed and acquire the reputation that would attract regular customers. He had to end that project and he increasingly found himself with limited options, though he had been considering cab driving (not an easy occupation in a city like Cairo) as a future alternative. He regretted that he did not pursue his education and partially blamed his parents, who did not make him stay in school. He also recalled with a sense of sorrow the pride he felt when he used to spend his money on his friends, who stayed in school. "Look at where they are now and where I am!" he told me a couple of times. He was referring to the fact that they either have well-paying jobs in good companies or have two jobs that supplement their families' income and that their children are becoming teenagers.

Under the Gaze

While I was in al-Zawiya in the summer of 2010, Samer, after returning from his last trip to Libya, decided that he wanted to get married as quickly as possible. His neighbors and siblings were actively trying to find him a wife and introduced him to several young women. After refusing to propose to most of them either because one was too dark, another was too short, or a third did not have nice facial features, he eventually agreed to propose to a woman who was nine years his junior.[38] Despite the difference in their ages and educational backgrounds (she had a college degree), his family was confident that she would agree to the marriage proposal given that, in her early thirties, she was thought unlikely to find a better match. Samer groomed himself and dressed very nicely before going to visit the young woman and her family. They had a promising first meeting and she preliminarily agreed to the marriage; however, she soon changed her mind. Samer's sisters speculate (and Samer eventually concurred with them) that the reason for her eventual refusal was that he made the mistake of visiting her the second time in his work clothes without having shaved and looking his best. His younger sister pointed out that the white hair dotting his beard and the stained clothes that he must have been wearing were enough to make any young woman rethink his marriage proposal.

I have not had the chance to ask the woman herself about her rejection of Samer's proposal, but I think the reason given by his sisters is plausible. Even though his body was fit and strong, it was clear that his hair was thinning and his hands and body reflected the difficult conditions of his manual labor. From the beginning of the search, his sisters were very aware of the importance of his appearances in appealing to a potential wife. One of them severely scolded him when he spent a day on the beach under the burning sun. She said that it was imprudent of him to make a mess out of himself (*ibahdil nafsu*) during a time when they were trying to find him a wife. Samer is naturally dark and spending more time under the sun, the sister worried, would make him even darker.[39] She was fully aware that Samer would be evaluated and judged by potential wives and knew that was a time when he should be particularly meticulous about his appearance to make a good impression on the woman to whom he would propose and her family.

I have heard of several other cases where young women rejected suitors because of their appearance, especially their clothes, hairstyle, and shoes. One young woman rejected a potential groom who was viewed as a good catch by her family because his shoes had buckles. The buckles, according to the young woman and some of her friends, revealed that the shoes were old and unfashionable. Shoes, another young woman explained to me, reveal a lot about a man: his taste, knowledge of fashion, and how much he cares about himself. When one of my close informants was in her

Styling their hair and wearing coordinated colors is especially important for these young men when attending social occasions such as weddings.

late twenties and her family was desperate for her to get married, she rejected a suitor who came to visit her family in dusty shoes. People assured her that he worked at a bank and earned a substantial monthly salary, but his dusty shoes coupled with his tardiness in arriving at her family's home indicated that he took the city bus instead of a cab. This choice implied that he was either miserly or could not afford the taxi fare, neither a good quality in a future husband. Keeping one's shoes clean is a very challenging task given the dusty streets of Cairo, especially in low-income areas like al-Zawiya. In addition to cleaning and polishing them before leaving home, young men and women keep an eye on their shoes while traveling between different areas and wipe them off whenever there is a need. Thus, clean shoes are subtle indicators of a man's financial standing as well as the amount of care he invests in his body and its presentation.

Since it is well known that a man should look his best when he visits a potential bride to make sure that he meets her approval, I was surprised by Samer's conduct, especially because he usually tended to his appearance carefully. At work, he dressed in simple and old clothes, but in his neighborhood and when he was going to travel to and from work, he usually wore very nice clothes. On his day off, he would visit the barbershop to shave his beard, apply masks and lotions to treat his skin, and trim and fix his hair. He would make sure his clothes were ironed, either at home or at a local shop, and would only wear matching colors. On more than one occasion, Samer also strongly asserted that men should take care of their appearances and declared that the woman he was interested in would never see him any less than fully groomed. It was thus strange that he defied these norms during his second visit to his potential bride. Samer explained to me that he had wanted to ensure the young woman would know what he would look like when returning from work. He did not want any surprises that could strain their relationship after marriage. His siblings, however, believed that it was yet another indication of his impulsiveness and hastiness. They thought that he was so determined to get married in two months that he carelessly tried to expedite the process. Thus, he did not think about his looks and their implications before appearing at the woman's doorstep.

Above all, I think this mishap reflected Samer's liminal state and his attempts to materialize competing norms that defined his standing as a man.[40] As a bachelor attempting to attract a spouse, he should have looked his best; yet, as a 40-year-old man, Samer should be less concerned with his looks than younger men usually are. As stated previously, most men at Samer's age already had families and tend to be focused on their children and their household needs. On several occasions, married men complained that their wives become suspicious when they pay attention to their looks and attire. They are faced with questions, such as Why are you dressed up? Who are you going to see? Are you having an affair? Why don't you spend the money on the children and their education? In a way, Samer was betwixt and between two different social states. His privileging of the norms linked to productivity (closely related to his sociobiological age) over attractiveness and physical appeal (closely related to his social status as a potential groom) jeopardized his initial marriage proposal. Samer recalled with regret the good old days when a *sanaay'i* (a skilled worker, or artisan) would go to a wedding or a social visit wearing his work clothes and people would warmly welcome and praise him for being a *kaseeb* (a man who earns good money). These days, Samer states, one has to shower, shave, and wear nice clothes before going out. To be appealing as a potential groom and earn social approval, one has to have the looks as well as the ability to earn good money. A man has to show a sense of style, good taste, and diligent attention to his looks and bodily presentation. This change has been shaped by global flows of information, images, and products and the increasing emphasis on consumption and its role in daily life in general and the management of the body in particular. It captures the fact that even though manual skilled labor continues to be highly regarded and is viewed as the most reliable source of income, there is also a growing appreciation of cultural capital (in the form of schooling, a college degree, knowledge of English, and computer training) as part of the promise of upward social mobility. We see this appreciation clearly reflected in the efforts of parents to train their children in a profession (*san'a*) and to make sure they get as much formal education as possible.

Despite the value they place on a potential groom's looks, some young women I have known have consciously accepted the proposal of a man who lacked one of the features they thought was important (such as height, attractiveness, youthfulness, or thick hair) because the suitor offered an exceptionally good living arrangement. In this case, they would follow the proverb that *er-raagil ma i'aybuush illa gaybu* (literally, "nothing shames a man except for his pocket"), meaning that the only flaw in a man is the inability to provide. In the case of Samer, although viewed as a potentially adequate provider, he did not obviously excel in this capacity and, by not grooming himself, his bodily hexis did not communicate the type of attractive qualities that would appeal to a potential bride.

More important, I think that Samer's lapse of judgment when visiting his prospective fiancée had also made visible the disparity in cultural capital between him and the young woman. While originally his family and his presentation of himself aimed to downplay the educational differences between the two sides, his appearance in her living room in his work clothes made the differences noticeable and thinkable. It visibly punctuated his identity as a manual worker who was not highly educated and who did not carry the promise of social mobility. Embodied signs of manual labor such as rough hands, dark skin, and stained clothes, which signal productivity and the ability to earn money, in this context signaled instead Samer's failure to develop his own business, which would have allowed him to stop depending on his own physical labor and enjoy the financial benefits and symbolic capital associated with hiring, training, and supervising younger men to do manual work. Thus, his bodily presentation made his limited economic and cultural capital more visible and the woman found few advantages in his marriage proposal.

Although Samer told me that he did not mind the rejection because he was not in love with the woman and he could find another bride, I nevertheless sensed it was still a difficult moment for him. For one thing, he thought of himself as settling for much less than he wanted by proposing to this woman, who, according to him, was not beautiful and did not have any *unusa* or femininity (neither her voice nor her gestures indicated any feminine qualities, as he explained). In addition, as Samer's sister also commented, the bride was not a good or entertaining speaker. He agreed to propose to her, he explained several times, simply because he felt under pressure to quickly marry and to start a family with a woman who had a good reputation and could be trusted, two qualities that strongly distinguished the woman locally. Yet she turned him down even when he already possessed an apartment and the required furniture, a distinct advantage in a groom as it means that the couple would not have had to wait many years before finalizing the marriage. Perhaps more importantly, her rejection left Samer in need of a wife who could contribute to the materialization of his abilities as a provider, a husband, a sexual partner, and a potential father.

Samer, however, was not discouraged. He continued to search for a suitable bride. Early in the fall of 2010, I learned over the phone that Samer had met a woman whom he quickly married. The bride, Sabah, was, as his sisters described, decent (*bint halaal*), outgoing, and had good communication skills. However, she was not exactly what Samer had in mind because she was in her late thirties, much darker than he (and his mother) had desired, and worked as a nurse in a distant hospital (Samer did not want a working wife). Nonetheless, his family was ecstatic and relieved and Samer himself was bursting with happiness when I called to congratulate him.

When I saw him and his wife in the summers of 2011 and 2012, they both were very happy. They spoke warmly and affectionately about each other. Sabah explained how they met through the husband of one of her friends and how they liked each other from the first meeting. She liked how he talked and dressed, but particularly emphasized an outing that demonstrated Samer's *ruguula* and confirmed her love for him. Soon after their engagement, Samer took her out to celebrate a Muslim holiday in a public garden. When he saw how crowded the place was, he held so tightly to her and shouted to the others to make way for them to avoid any physical contact between her and other men. That *mawqif* impressed Sabah deeply and inspired her love and devotion for Samer. He also was happy with his wife's energy and social skills. She was supportive, quickly responded to his wishes, and carefully looked after his health (including making sure he ate better and smoked less). She also maintained good relationships with Samer's family and cultivated friendships with his sisters and sisters-in-law. They both wanted to make each other as happy as possible. Supported by his wife, Samer has begun taking steps toward executing his plans of becoming a taxi driver: he bought a rundown car that he was trying to fix to use to practice driving.

His marriage, however, signals only the end of one chapter and the start of a new one in Samer's masculine trajectory. Immediately after their marriage, his family, friends, and relatives as well as his wife's family, friends, and relatives started inquiring about his wife's pregnancy. Becoming a father would be another significant facet of his trajectory as a man. Pregnancy would not only demonstrate his virility and affirm his standing as a heterosexual man, it would also socially define him as a father, a central component of the masculine trajectories of men of his age group. Both Samer and Sabah are acutely aware of the urgency of pregnancy for a couple of their age (especially Sabah, who was approaching forty). They both have been consulting doctors and Sabah is going through some medical treatment. As of March 2013, the couple and their families are waiting and hoping.

Stands and Trajectories

Samer's trajectory shows that manhood needs to be continuously reasserted and reestablished over time and in various contexts and for several audiences. It is in the mawaaqif, the stances one takes in specific situations, that a man becomes noticeable and recognized by others as such. As aptly put by a 32-year-old worker, "there are attitudes (mawaaqif) that show the quality of a man and reveal if he is a fraud or of high quality, but you can't measure a man by only one attitude." These points were clearly articulated during the Egyptian revolution. Among his family members, Samer was one of the strongest supporters of the revolution. He never wavered in his support, even when people around him were moved by Mubarak's speech on February 1, 2011, and wanted to give him another chance. When I asked Samer why that was the case, he replied, "from what I saw." In addition to his many negative encounters with the police and government officials in Egypt, he was enraged by the condition of Egyptian workers in Libya. He described how the smallest African country had representatives available to assist its citizens in Libya while he never found that type of support from the Egyptian embassy.[41] But above all, the rebels materialized the notion of *er-ruguula mawqif*, which Samer emphasized. Their determination, decency, and bravery resonated very well with his own views of what constitute ruguula. Their stands were contrasted to the pro-Mubarak supporters, who were seen by Samer and his neighbors as cowards, thugs, and corrupt.

Masculine trajectories shift over time and men are expected to modify their conduct and the management of their bodies accordingly. Unlike the pious selfhood that Mahmood describes as cultivated by the women in the Egyptian mosque movement, Samer's sense of himself as a man is not informed by "authoritative sources" and "foundational texts" that would provide the point of reference for his attempt at materializing various facets of masculinity.[42] It is not canonical sources but the eyes, ears, and tongues of others that are important in judging, legitimizing, and recognizing him as a man. The sources that authorize and legitimize Samer's conduct as a man are diffused in many spaces, over several media, and among diverse audiences both inside and outside his neighborhood. The same act may be viewed as violating the law by the police, as confirming bravery by neighbors, or as revealing hastiness and irresponsibility by family members. As Gregory Starrett contends, bodily hexis is open to multiple interpretations.[43] A scar on the face, a stain on a pair of pants, dust on one's shoes, or an unshaven beard have different meanings in different contexts and to different people. However, the number of interpretations is not unlimited but, rather, is structured by specific social inequalities.

Rather than simple transitions from one stage of life to another, masculinity is about inhabiting particular norms in certain interactions and at specific times. As the notion of mawqif shows, being a real man is always related to a certain context and conduct. The mawaaqif one takes and how others interpret them are central to the social coherence of a masculine trajectory. It is the ability to respond to the shifting social expectations, new possibilities, and emerging challenges as well as to embody the proper norms in the appropriate context that is key to the making of a real man. This process is supported, challenged, and legitimized by various actors. Samer's family and neighbors played an important role in circulating narratives that celebrated his achievements but also exerted pressured to make sure he conformed to the social norms that define a real man. Not only men, but women also play an important role in the making of a proper man. This role, especially of sisters and wives, will be the focus of the next chapter.

3

Women and the Making of Proper Men

> We learn about men only outside the company of their imme-
> diate families, outside the circle of paternal love, outside the
> intimacy which would lead to self-reflection.
>
> Robert Fernea, "A Limited Construction of Masculinity"

IN ONE OF THE RARE ACCOUNTS of male circumcision in the Middle East, Abdu Khal, a Saudi novelist, vividly described the circumcision of a young boy in a Saudi village during the 1950s. The boy, Yahia, had lost his father and became the man of the family at an early age. To mark his shift to manhood, he had to undergo circumcision. As a central part of this rite, the boy stands in front of attendees while the circumciser cuts part of the foreskin, taking the pain of cutting without flinching or showing any fear. When Yahia stood in front of the circumciser, surrounded by his relatives and neighbors and the festivities that marked this important point in his life, he was determined not to shame his mother and kin. After the first cut, he was enthralled by the compliments of others around him. Praises by his uncles such as "Khadija's [his mother's name] son has enabled us to hold our heads high" and "A man from the loins of a man" motivated him to ask the circumciser to cut more to affirm his bravery and strength.[1] It was his mother who rushed to snatch him urging him: "Don't kill yourself, my son."

As far as I know, this type of circumcision is not currently practiced in any Middle Eastern country and male circumcision no longer signifies "the arrival of manhood" in most of the region.[2] This story, however, captured my attention not because of the nature of the rite of passage but because of the centrality of women to a rite that aimed to make a man out of Yahia. It was the mother who instructed the son before the ritual: "Be careful not to flinch. Don't let people gloat over us. Don't let them say you're a sissie [sic]. Don't blink and so shame us and yourself."[3] It was the mother who ululated to show joy and pride in her son's conduct. It was the mother who rushed to save him when she felt he was overdoing it and could do serious harm to himself. It was the mother who nursed his wounds, cared for him for three months, and celebrated his recovery.

Such a story as well as my research in al-Zawiya left me wondering about the lack of serious scholarly discussion of the role of women in the making of proper men. This is particularly puzzling in light of the shift over the past two decades toward theorizing gender as performative. This conceptualization entailed a shift from seeing gender as *being* to viewing it as *becoming* and from viewing it as what one *is* to viewing it as what one *does*. Rather than viewing them as simple performance, i.e., the enactment of a foundational truth by a fully formed subject, various scholars have argued that gendered subjectivities are "the product of a set of regulatory practices that construct the categories of woman and man and open them to resignification."[4] This focus on the performative nature of gender has led to a more dynamic analysis of gendered constructions. A growing number of studies have shown the importance of context in analyzing how femininities and masculinities are made and remade. Yet, most studies continue to assume that "masculine self-identification relies on male-centered cultural practices and forms of sociality" and to "proceed as if women are not a relevant part of the analysis, and therefore to analyze masculinity by looking only at men and relations among men."[5] Despite the move "towards an understanding of how selves are formed in and through relations with others,"[6] these "others" are largely regarded as men. Women are mainly viewed as objects that should be sexually and socially controlled or as a "negative pole,"[7] an oppositional category that is used to project biological, psychological, and social differences that define manhood.

This trend has been especially true in the Middle East, where there was assumed to be a clear dichotomy between men (equated with the public domain) and women (equated with the private domain). Despite feminists and anthropologists moving beyond simplistic assumptions about the divide between public and private and despite the wealth of studies that show the power women exercise both in public and private,[8] little attention has been directed to the role of women in shaping masculine subjectivities and the making of men.

A notable exception is Suad Joseph, who advanced the notion of "connectivity" to capture how "the social production of relational selves with diffuse boundaries . . . [requires] continuous interaction with significant others for a sense of completion" and elaborates on how "one's sense of self is intimately linked with the self of another such that the security, identity, integrity, dignity, and self-worth of one is tied to the actions of others."[9] Unlike most studies, which tend to ignore sibling connectivity, Joseph looks at the brother-sister relationship as key to understanding the sociocultural and psychological dynamics that contribute to the reproduction of Arab patriarchy. Through their intimate relationship, brothers and sisters learn the meaning of gender distinctions and how to equate love with domination (in the case of men) and subordination (in the case of women). Thus, the power-love dynamic is critical to a brother's "empowerment and masculinization" and to a sister's "domestication and feminization."[10]

There is much value in Joseph's provocative and astute analysis. However, a few issues are worth rethinking, in particular the role of female relatives in the shaping of the masculine trajectories of their brothers, sons, and husbands. First, most of Joseph's analysis is focused on the older brother, who enjoys a certain status that is not necessarily shared by the other brothers. Second, in Joseph's examples, the brother is always viewed positively by the sister as the ideal man, and she aspires to find a husband like him. In contrast, in al-Zawiya, there were many examples where the brother represented the undesirable type of man, who failed to materialize appropriate norms of masculinity and exemplified the type of man that should be avoided as a marriage partner. Third, by drawing on a Weberian notion of power as "the capacity to direct the behavior of others, even against their will,"[11] power for Joseph becomes oppositional and monopolized by the brother, who is depicted vividly as shaping the conduct and feminine identification of his sister. Joseph's frequent emphasis on "the subordination of the sister to the brother" ends up underestimating the role sisters play in the production of their brothers as men.[12] Although Joseph's work gives us a lucid sense of how the brother controls his sister's movement, choice of clothing, and actions, it does not capture how the brother, as a patriarch, is also "an extension of others in the household, just as they themselves are extensions of him" nor account for the full extent of the role of sisters in shaping the conduct of their brothers and their cultivation as proper men.[13]

As the discussion below shows, a Foucauldian approach, which looks at power "as a way in which certain actions may structure the field of other possible actions" and recognizes that power is dispersed throughout the social body, allows us to capture the significant power women exercise in shaping masculine trajectories.[14] Furthermore, the power-love dynamics described by Joseph shift over the span of a man's life. Not only do men protect, they are also protected; not only do they shape, they are also shaped; not only do they provide, they are also provided for. As will become clear soon, women keenly work to protect the economic and social vulnerabilities of their male relatives, in the process profoundly contributing to their standing as men. Alternatively, a woman who chooses to expose these vulnerabilities could undermine the view of others of the masculine identification of her husband or brother.

As the preceding two chapters have illustrated, a masculine trajectory is a collective endeavor shaped by many actors, diverse discourses, and several institutions. This chapter argues that women contribute to this project in al-Zawiya by conforming to the social norms that define their responsibilities as dutiful daughters, obedient wives, and respectful sisters. When necessary, women step in to both materially and emotionally support their male relatives' attempts to become proper men. They also instruct their sons, brothers, husbands, and male neighbors about the proper way of being a man. These women defend their family members' reputations and standing as men in various spaces and contexts, monitor their ways of dressing and acting, and strongly critique their actions when they deviate from the socially defined ways of enacting manhood. These interventions and instructions are performative and forcefully contribute to the creation of what they name (i.e., the proper man). They are part of the "technologies of the self" that are key to the production and embodiment of masculinity. These technologies refer to techniques and practices that "permit individuals to effect by their own means or *with the help of others* a certain number of operations on their bodies and souls, thoughts, conduct, and way of being, so as to transform themselves in order to attain a certain state of happiness, purity, wisdom, perfection, or immortality."[15] Such technologies range from taking care of one's body and its presentation in daily life to conforming to social norms that relate masculinity to economic productivity, assertiveness, courage, and good manners. These technologies are focused on individual subjects and their acts, but they also encompass the contextual and relational complexities that shape masculine trajectories and link, yet separate, men and women.

This chapter approaches these issues by first looking at a young man, Zaki, a worker in his early thirties. I have followed his masculine trajectory since he was a teenager. Over the past two decades, I have observed major transitions in his life, including military service, movement between several workshops in and around his neighborhood, and his engagement to a young woman in his neighborhood. In considering some aspects of Zaki's life, I would like to highlight the important role that his

Contrary to common stereotypes about gender segregation, men and women interact daily in different spaces in Cairo, including Tahrir Square during and after the January 25 Revolution.

mother and sisters played in cultivating him as a man. I do not here claim that his conduct outside the house, his interaction with his peers, and his ability to enact specific notions of masculinity in various public spaces are not important to the construction of his identity as a man. These are indeed important and I have discussed some of them throughout the book. The point of this chapter, however, is to show that our understanding of masculinity remains inadequate if we do not pay close attention to how women verify, support, and question the male relatives' attempts to materialize gendered social norms. After discussing Zaki's case, I will compare him to one of his older married brothers and draw on other examples to illustrate how the role of women in the formation of masculinity shifts over a man's lifetime. It is important to keep in mind that women do not constitute a homogenous group but are diversified agents who can relate to the making of men in multiple ways. The following discussion juxtaposes the brother-sister relationship with the husband-wife relationship and accentuates their changing significance to how one's standing as a man is evaluated and judged by others. It is precisely because there is a recognition of the important roles women play in the crafting of men that the husband-wife relationship becomes so key to the definition of a man, especially during the first few years of marriage.

Zaki, His Mother, and Sisters

When Zaki got engaged at the age of thirty, his family was delighted. This engagement, they thought, would force him to become more serious and financially responsible. From the moment he announced his interest in a beautiful young neighbor named Fatma, his mother, brothers, and sisters worked diligently to realize his plans to marry her. Zaki first needed their support in approaching Fatma's family. This entailed not only visiting and presenting some initial gifts but also the presence of his family as witnesses to the initial plans made between the two sides, an important event that signified Zaki's seriousness about the proposal and ensured that his relatives would work with him to fulfill the agreement. The two families had to agree on who would buy what items, the time it would take to buy different pieces of furniture, when Zaki would find an apartment, and when the couple would marry.

Immediately after his engagement, Zaki began to face increased pressure from his mother and siblings to save as much money as possible. His younger sister, who earns a relatively high income for her work at a textile factory in a middle-class area, tried to help him start his own shoe-making workshop in the neighborhood. She lent him some of the money needed to buy machines and one of his older sisters kept track of his accounts. After two years of unsuccessful attempts to sustain the business and much debt, largely because he was not well connected to the market and could not respond efficiently to fluctuating demand, Zaki had to bow to the pressure of his family (who were joined in their demands by his fiancée) to rent the warsha out and go back to working for a weekly salary in another workshop. They all agreed that he needed a more stable and steady flow of income that could feed into savings associations so that he could later purchase items needed for the marriage.

At the same time, Zaki's mother and sisters started complaining bitterly about his conduct. In particular, they were disappointed that Zaki was not "acting like a man" in front of his in-laws. The refrain "*mish yi'mel raagil*" (he was not making himself a man) was often repeated to refer to Zaki's diffidence and unwillingness to take stands that would make him a man. For example, his family felt that he gave in too quickly to Fatma's preferences, such as her request that he visit her on his day off each Friday. His mother and sisters thought weekly visits were too frequent and urged Zaki to "man up" (*i'mel raagil*, literally, "make a man of yourself") by showing self-control and assertiveness in front of Fatma. Teasingly, his younger sister would imitate Zaki's gestures when he was talking to his fiancée over the phone: he spoke softly and lowered his chin down to his chest, gestures that indicated weakness and submission. Zaki's relatives, including cousins and in-laws, criticized the fact that he continuously gave Fatma's family the wrong impression by overstating his earnings, accepted their new and unrealistic demands, and did not defend his choices, which were limited by his financial abilities. For example, Fatma's family insisted that Zaki should buy a fully automatic washing machine instead of a conventional one and that he should acquire an apartment with three rooms instead of two. He accepted these demands even though he knew that he would not have the means to meet their expectations in a timely manner, which would delay the marriage and further displease Fatma's family. His sisters often compared him to other men, such as his older brothers, the fiancé of Fatma's younger sister, and the husband of her older sister, all of whom conducted themselves like proper men and asserted their views (and encouraged Zaki to do the same) in front of their in-laws.

Using such men as authoritative points of reference and models to be emulated, Zaki's family deployed several tactics and strategies to encourage him to man up. For example, his mother prevented him from using the phone for long daily chats with Fatma. She also chased him out of the house when he wanted to spend too much time in front of the window waving and gazing at Fatma. When he did not obey, the mother and sisters sometimes refused to do the daily chores he expected from them, such as heating his dinner when he returned home late at night. They verbally "nagged" him all the time about his conduct and the improper things he was doing, instructing him about the proper way of conducting himself as a man. *Khalleek raagil* ("Be a man") was an expression often used when praising or critiquing his ways. His female relatives feared that he would be viewed as *khawal, hafa', kheekha,* or *'ayyil.* As argued in Chapter 1, these words are usually used to indicate one's lack of social competency or inability to embody the norms that define a real man. They signal a person who is not "good at being a man—a stance that stresses the *performative excellence,* the ability to foreground manhood by means of deeds that strikingly speak for themselves."[16] Furthermore, Zaki's sisters were outraged because they felt he was eroding not only respect for himself but also the dignity of his brothers (*bisaghar nafsu w bisaghar ikhwatu*).

Yet, along with these criticisms, Zaki's mother and sisters always stepped in to support him morally and financially. They exempted him from contributing to the household expenses. They supported him when his in-laws complained about him or pressured him to expedite the wedding date. For instance, his older sister visited Fatma's family on a couple of occasions to "reproach them in a nice way" (*hazzatuhum bi-elzook*), as she said, for their impractical demands, which were complicating Zaki's plans, and to urge them to be flexible when it came to the deadlines that they and Zaki had agreed on. She also kept a close watch on his financial situation, documenting his wages, his spending, and his contributions to rotating savings associations, which she helped organize with (largely female) friends and neighbors to make sure Zaki would be able to get the sums of money he needed. When Zaki failed to meet his first yearly deadline, specified by Fatma's family to show that he made good progress on buying key furniture and household appliances, his family stepped in. His mother sold a golden necklace and bought him a new refrigerator. His older sister joined a savings association and borrowed money from friends to help Zaki purchase furniture for one of the rooms. One of his older brothers bought him the automatic washing machine that, according to Fatma's family, was an essential part of a new home.

Zaki's inability to meet the first major deadline by himself and the fact that he needed his family's support early in the process prompted his older sister to suggest including his fiancée in the discussions of his financial troubles. She reasoned that if Fatma really loved Zaki, she would join his family in encouraging him to work harder and to save more but would protect him by not telling her immediate male relatives about his financial affairs. Fatma was very upset to learn of Zaki's difficulties but shared the news only with her mother, and they both decided to keep it hidden from Fatma's male relatives. In particular, they did not want to undermine Zaki's standing in front of Fatma's father for fear that he might break up the engagement. Fatma and her mother joined Zaki's family in keeping track of his earnings and savings. All the women on his side and his fiancée's side worked together to maintain the impression of his success as a provider and to elevate his standing, especially in front of Fatma's male relatives. I have seen this pattern in other contexts when the man was not able to provide adequately because of sickness, unemployment, lack of skills, or pure negligence.[17] Sisters, wives, and mothers often stepped in to help uphold the norm that a brother, a husband, or a son was still capable of providing. They borrowed money, participated in savings associations, sold their jewelry, or worked near or around the house to help secure the needed money.

During this period, money talk became a fundamental part of Zaki's life. He comments with surprise at how suddenly and visibly money became of great importance in defining his status as a man and how everyone around him started discussing his income and evaluating his success and failure based on the amount of money he allocated every month to buying furniture or to savings associations. He comments sadly, "One could be gada' and a real man but his need for money might force him to accept certain things or overlook others that he wouldn't otherwise have accepted. If he can't satisfy the needs of his family, then a man has to be flexible with other matters." Paradoxically, he felt that he had to make compromises that potentially undermined his view of himself as a man in order to satisfy the requests of others that were essential to socially producing him as a man. This compromising and flexibility is reflected in how his relationships with the women around him have shifted over time. Two examples are sufficient to convey a sense of some of these changes. First, Zaki's relationship with his sisters changed deeply. As a young man, Zaki asserted his masculinity in part by keeping track of his sisters' whereabouts and by making sure that they conformed to the social norms that defined the conduct of proper women. As I said in Chapter 2, the divide between freedom of mobility for young men and restriction on young women's mobility is one of the most visible manifestations of gender inequalities.[18] I recall a period when Zaki monitored his sisters' movements and dress code, occasionally using violence to discipline the younger sister. In particular, once, when she was sixteen and he was eighteen, he beat her severely because she went out with some of her friends and stayed out late without clear permission. He was commended by his neighbors for his action and even the sister saw his beating as a sign of care, fully agreeing that she brought this physical punishment on herself. He was seen as a real man, protecting the reputation of his sister and family.

As a grown man, however, Zaki is expected not to use violence against others, especially against his sisters, who have become a major financial and moral support for him. Even verbally insulting them during a quarrel could be taken seriously and could lead to negative repercussions for him. The sisters may stop talking to him for days, refuse to do his laundry or prepare his dinner, and withdraw their moral and material assistance. The older he gets, the more Zaki is expected to become selective and limited in his use of violence. At the same time, a different relationship based on mutual support and interdependency is growing between him and his sisters, which makes the use of violence unwise and unwarranted.

The second illustrative example of a change in Zaki's relationships with women was his surveillance of Fatma and her movements soon after their engagement. He showed great interest in monitoring and regulating when she was supposed to leave her family's apartment and where she was going. All involved in the engagement viewed this initial interest as a sign of his *ruguula* and love for Fatma. However, when he started "smothering her" (*yukhinuu'ha*) with his regulations, she shared her frustrations with his mother and sisters, and they criticized and ridiculed him. The sisters would say "*Huwa 'amil 'aleeha raagil 'ala aeeh?*" (He is making himself a man in front of her for what?), questioning why he was trying to exercise manly rights over her when he had not done enough to warrant that right.[19] Since he was not living up to the norms that equate masculinity with economic success and providing for others, it was not appropriate for him to assume the other rights of control and regulation. Similarly, his sisters assumed his inability to show steady economic progress was the reason for Fatma's family refusal to let her go out with Zaki or visit his family as frequently as expected. Therefore, enactment of norms that emphasize providing and those that emphasize control and domination become increasingly intertwined over a man's life span.

Husbands and Wives: Love and Domination?

The concerns that Zaki's family have been expressing over his relationship with his fiancée and her family, especially his willingness to give into her demands and show too much affection and dedication to her, are rooted in an anxiety about his relationship with his future wife. In addition to a husband's role as the provider for his wife, the relationship between them is one of the most important elements that could enhance or undermine his standing as a man, especially during the early years of marriage. A husband's ability to assert his domination and the wife's acceptance of (or at least appearing to accept) this domination significantly reflect on a man's standing. He should show that he is able to shape his wife and her conduct while clearly resisting her attempts to influence his ways of doing and being. Since sisters and mothers are fully aware of the strong role women play in the production of men, they are especially sensitive to the relationship between married relatives and their spouses and usually seek to limit the role of a new wife in affecting the conduct of her husband as much as possible. An examination of one of Zaki's older brothers, Muhsen, will illustrate some aspects of this relationship. Muhsen is a particularly good example as he was frequently used as a point of reference when criticizing Zaki's conduct. Unlike his brother, Muhsen was considered by his family to be a real man. Besides being a good provider financially, he had been exemplary in his ability to assert himself in front of his wife and in-laws.

In the summer of 2010, Muhsen, at the age of forty-four, was a worker in a printing company in another part of Cairo. He had been married to Manal for twelve years, and they had three children. Muhsen worked six days a week; he usually left home around seven in the morning and returned around eight in the evening. However, when he worked overtime, which he did frequently, he arrived back home closer to ten in the evening. His wife worked as a clerk in a company in a middle-class neighborhood; she worked five days a week and also left home around seven but returned at four in the afternoon. In addition to her job, Manal was the one who did all the household work and provided all the child care.

Most of the time, Muhsen was well regarded socially for his conduct as a man. He was credited for being generous but reasonable, assertive but not antagonistic, and kind but still able to stand up for himself. Examples about his standing as a real man drew on his premarital days when he was still engaged and always expressed his views in front of his tough father-in-law. Unlike Zaki, who accepted occasional mistreatment by his future father-in-law, Muhsen never tolerated any lack of respect. For example, Zaki had to put up with Fatma's father's refusal to let them go out together. Depending on the financial abilities of the man, such outings might be a walk in the neighborhood or a visit to a relative, a stroll near the Nile, a meal at a restaurant, or a movie in downtown Cairo. Unlike his brother, Muhsen would not accept restrictions imposed by his in-laws. I was told several times by Muhsen and his family of one occasion when he angrily departed from his fiancée's home because he had wanted to take her out and her father had refused. Muhsen stayed away for several days until the father-in-law himself called and told him to take Manal out the next day. Unlike Zaki, who often accepted new demands even when he knew he would not be able to fulfill them, Muhsen knew when to stand his ground. Even though he worked in Kuwait for several years and earned a decent living, he always made a point not to exaggerate the gifts he sent to his fiancée and wisely managed his money so that he could secure an adequate home in the future.[20]

Upon marrying, Muhsen wanted his wife to quit her job. He made it very clear that his income was enough and he did not need his wife's salary. This was important for him to assert because women's work after marriage is not highly regarded and could be viewed as a sign of the inability of the husband to adequately provide for his family. After much negotiation, he accepted the argument of Manal's family and several of his friends that it would be imprudent to force the wife to leave her job and lose her benefits, especially her future pension. His father-in-law as well as Muhsen's friends assured him that he would retain the right to ask his wife to quit if at any time he felt she neglected him or their home. Due to this agreement and because, as he said several times, he does not want his wife to get used to his assistance, Muhsen made a point of not helping with any household chores. When he saw her looking exhausted or when she uttered the slightest complaint about all the work she had to do, he would simply state that she could just stop working if she was too tired or if she could not balance her duties as a wife, a mother, and an employee.[21]

When Muhsen was in Kuwait, his mother and sisters were key in reinforcing his standing as a man in their neighborhood by saving his money, helping with securing his apartment, buying the furniture needed, and maintaining good relations with his in-laws. Manal and her family soon joined them in repeating stories that celebrated his abilities, financial success, and wise management of his resources. Through these actions and narratives, they collectively produced him as a good and successful man. After his return and marriage, his sisters and mother proudly pointed out that because of Muhsen's standing and firmness,[22] his wife meticulously kept the couple's big apartment spick-and-span, carefully looked after the children and their education, always made sure a hot meal was waiting for her husband when he returned back home in the evening, and quickly responded to all his needs (such as ironing his clothes, matching them in colors, and making sure they were ready for him to wear whenever he needed them).[23] Manal's family has been a strong source of support and significantly contributed to her ability to satisfy the needs of her husband and children and combine work inside and outside the house.[24] Her mother and unmarried sister in particular have been instrumental in helping her take care of the children and fulfilling some of her household obligations. For example, the mother looked after the younger child, who did not go to school, and prepared for Manal some of the time-consuming dishes (such as stuffed vegetables) while the sister helped with an assortment of chores (such as ironing and cleaning the apartment for major events). At the same time, the couple has been careful to invite Muhsen's family for special meals during Ramadan and other appropriate occasions. Manal would make a point of serving an array of foods that showed her skills as a cook and a housewife. She also tried to visit Muhsen's family as often as possible, exchanged gifts and foods with them, and attended important social occasions (such as engagement parties, birth celebrations, and funerals) related to his extended family. From his success as a provider and assertiveness in front of his in-laws to his ability to father children, control his wife, and make his preferences respected, all of these achievements were interpreted as signs of his status as a real man, who was consistently able to enact the proper norms in the right context.

The focus on the relationship between Manal and Muhsen is part of a broader pattern that places the wife–husband relationship at the center of a masculine trajectory, especially during the early years of marriage. The broader view on this matter was well summarized by a 40-year-old man: "The wife is the one who can make the husband feel his ruguula. If she respects her husband and his family, obeys his wishes, especially in front of others, takes care of their home, looks after the children, and does not complain about him to others, then he would feel he is a real, good man. Other people would judge him as such as well. Alternatively, a woman who seems to be out of control, leaves the house whenever she wants, fights with the neighbors, publicly disobeys her husband's instructions, and neglects her home and children could undermine her husband's standing as a man in front of his extended family, neighbors, and friends."

In contrast to the ideal exemplified in Muhsen's marriage, when parents and relatives perceive a clear destabilization of the hierarchy that privileges men over women, they are troubled and will work to reestablish the domination of the husband over the wife. After marriage, relatives, neighbors, and friends keep a close eye on the relationship between the husband and wife and deploy several strategies such as joking and teasing, direct criticism, verbal instructions, and, in few cases, physical discipline, to ensure that the hierarchy between the two sides is maintained. They closely monitor the interaction between the couple and pay special attention to bodily gestures (such as the way she looks at him) and language exchanges (such as the wording and intonations of her reactions) to confirm that she shows deference and obedience. The case of Muhammad, a plumber in his late thirties, illustrates some of these points. Muhammad got married when he was in his early thirties to a woman he deeply loved. His work in Saudi Arabia allowed him to offer her a nice big apartment and she was considered very lucky by many of Muhammad's neighbors and family members. He was severely criticized, however, by both male and female acquaintances because he went out of his way to help his wife, who did not work outside the home. He made a habit of buying all of their daily supplies (including vegetables, which is usually done by women) and allowed her to stay with her family in another neighborhood for extended periods of time. When she became pregnant, he started helping her with daily chores, such as mopping the stairs, cleaning the bathroom, and washing the windows. In a (male-female) mixed group discussion, he explained to us that he worried about her falling and hurting herself while pregnant. His male friends did not approve of his explanation and conduct. One of them asked, "Why marry if you're going to do all this stuff?" Another one went on to criticize Muhammad's wife because she often made hissing sounds from their apartment's balcony to call her husband home, even while he was in the middle of a conversation with his friends. While Muhammad saw her behavior as a sign of love, his friends dismissed his reasoning and saw his wife's action as a sign of disrespect and an indication of her dominance. After Muhammad's departure, one of his friends explained to me that Muhammad is not able to control his wife (*yushkumha*), which undermines his standing as a man. The women present also strongly criticized his ways, especially doing chores like mopping the stairs, that could be publicly seen by others. The women understood that there might be times when the husband should help his wife (by looking after the children if the wife is too busy, ironing his clothes if she is sick, or fixing his breakfast if she has to be away), but they emphasized the need for such help to be discreet and kept away from the eyes of others. Visibly defying social norms usually invites criticisms from others, who interpret the conduct of the husband as an indication of the domination of the wife and evidence of a shift in the hierarchies that structure the husband-wife relationship.

Over the course of marriage, we see more interdependence cultivated between spouses, most of whom mutually support each other. Husbands may offer help at home and wives may use their earnings (few work outside but some do part-time work such as selling clothes, spices, juices, or cooked food) to help support their families. At the same time, the definition of manhood expands to encompass other matters, such as fathering and educating children, marrying one's daughters and sons, and maintaining good relationships with others. Moreover, most women learn to uphold the appearance of men's domination while expanding their ability to exercise power in various aspects of daily life. Umm Ali, a woman in her late fifties and the mother of four children, brilliantly mastered the art of making her husband seem like the driving force in their life while in reality she oversaw the important decisions about almost everything related to their family.[25] Since I met her in 1993, when she was in her early forties and her children were still young and in school, I have been impressed by how efficiently she managed her household and cared for her children. She was savvy about managing the family's limited budget, securing its daily needs while saving as much as possible, and keeping track of her children's schooling and social relationships. Over time, I watched her make almost all the decisions related to her children's education, marriage, and the new home that the family eventually built in another part of Cairo.[26] Abu Ali, who had two jobs and worked very hard to provide for his family, was rarely present and often went along with whatever his wife decided. Yet Umm Ali always made it seem as if he were the one who made all the decisions about their life and would always claim to the neighbors that she was going to check with him on even the most mundane decisions. She often used his authority in strategic ways when she wanted to avoid undesirable obligations. When she did not want to do something or hesitated about it, she would tell a neighbor, a friend, or a relative that her husband would not approve of it. She was always eager to compliment and praise him in front of others for his hard work and often put herself down to underscore his important role in her life. She would describe how he taught her everything she knows and repeatedly emphasized that, without his knowledge and support, she would have continued to be the peasant girl she was when she moved from her village to Cairo after their marriage. Such acts and verbal statements helped support the standing of Abu Ali as a man and ultimately garnered for him the kind of public recognition and legitimacy central to a masculine trajectory.

In other cases, when a wife visibly defied the expected conduct by ignoring her children and apartment and disobeying her husband's requests, social consequences were expected. The husband may be encouraged by family members and friends to reassert his standing and make sure his wife abides by his wishes, even through the use of physical violence. Divorce may result if the wife does not amend her ways, especially early in the marriage. The case of Abdu highlights this possibility. Abdu married a woman he very much loved. She was beautiful and strong but had a bad temper and quickly managed to antagonize her husband's family and all the neighbors, whom she frequently insulted and fought with. No matter how much Abdu reasoned with his wife, she did not change her ways. Eventually, he had to find housing in another neighborhood and leave al-Zawiya to avoid, as he said, the embarrassment caused by his wife's conduct. After the birth of their first child, he returned from work one day to find that his wife had fought with his mother, who was visiting them to help with the baby, and slapped her on the face. This was such a grave offense that it could not be ignored. He felt that overlooking her act would have totally undermined his standing as a man in front of others, especially his family. Though he still deeply loved his wife, he felt that the only appropriate response to her offense against his mother was divorce. Even though divorce is not encouraged and is usually viewed negatively, in this case, people reacted positively to Abdu's decision and commended his assertive stand.[27]

Other cases proved to be much more complicated than Abdu's and divorce was not a practical possibility, leaving a husband with no tangible options. This was clearly the case for Safwat, a man in his late forties, who has been working in Kuwait for the past ten years. He usually spends two years or so abroad before returning for two or three months to see his wife and five children. When he returns, he is loaded with gifts for his family, neighbors, and friends. Soon after he arrives, troubles usually start between him and his wife, Hana', a strong and skilled woman but "not a good wife," as described by Safwat and his relatives. They complained that Hana' does not pay enough attention to the couple's small apartment, which is usually filthy, untidy, and infested with insects. She does not care enough for her children either, who run around in soiled clothes and with uncombed hair and dirty faces. She is also socially awkward and managed over time to strain her relationships with Safwat's family and friends. On top of all this, she is a jealous woman who suspects that her husband is having or will have an affair with any woman he encounters. In particular, she became very unhappy when he returned to al-Zawiya in the summer of 2011 and saw that he had lost a lot of weight,[28] had fixed his teeth, and had dyed his hair, which made him look several years younger than his real age. Observing these changes, Hana' became convinced that he must be planning to take another wife. They fought constantly and he left their apartment for a couple of weeks until she, under pressure from her family, apologized to Safwat and begged him to return home. Soon after he returned, however, they started fighting again and Safwat found himself with few options.

Safwat's case is remarkable because it defies many of the stereotypical expectations about the Arab man, who supposedly enjoys unlimited power in managing his family (especially in terms of his presumed right to divorce and remarry).[29] Although Safwat is a good man, has a great sense of humor, and is liked by many, he became helpless when dealing with his wife's conduct. He tried reasoning with her and asked their relatives (both male and female) to mediate and talk with Hana', but this failed to alter her behavior. He tried violence and occasionally beat her, but that did not prove to be effective either. He considered divorce, but feared what would happen to his young children. He considered taking another wife, but that would be expensive and would compromise his commitment to the well-being of his children. Safwat found the best solution was to continue to work abroad away from his wife. This option allows him to fulfill his obligations as a provider (he sends his wife a monthly allowance) while staying away from continuous and direct interaction with Hana' and having to work hard to reassert his standing as a man in front of her and others.

The Power to Make

My discussion reveals the multifaceted ways women contribute to the shaping of a masculine trajectory and the making of men. These ways have not been sufficiently addressed by the literature and there is a need not only to look at oppositions and separations but also interactions and connections between men and women as key to the constitution of gendered subjectivities. One study that is worth mentioning here is Salwa Ismail's analysis of gender politics in Bulaq al-Dakrur, a low-income neighborhood in Cairo. Focusing on R. W. Connell's concept of "marginalized masculinities," Ismail argued that the changing role of women in the household and their expanding role as mediators between their families and government officials as well as the violence exerted by state agents and the humiliation young men face almost daily had created "injured masculinity."[30] In trying to reconfigure gender relations to reassert male domination necessary for "hegemonic masculinity" (represented by the ruling elite), young men in Bulaq al-Dakrur developed a masculinity that was "scarred, bearing the wounds inflicted through its articulation with class and state power."[31] Young men in Bulaq al-Dakrur sought the "recovery/restitution" of their masculinity through the control of women and their movement outside the home.

Two points are worth highlighting regarding Ismail's intriguing analysis. First, I find the notion of "injured masculinity" unproductive because it implies another type of intact, uninjured, and complete notion of masculinity against which other enactments are measured and evaluated. As argued by scholars in other contexts, the assumption that there existed a time when men enjoyed "a straightforward confirmation of a masculine identity" is problematic and difficult to substantiate.[32] If we understand masculinity as a process of becoming, as enacted in various contexts and different circumstances, it would be tricky to think of injury and recovery. At the same time, it is not clear how hegemonic

masculinity is specified (is it only state-sponsored and -supported masculinity?) and how it is communicated to young men in Bulaq al-Dakrur.

Second, women play multiple roles in the creation of men. Through
abiding by social norms that determine the behavior of a proper woman,
offering material and emotional support, and instructing, monitoring,
and modifying the conduct of their male relatives, women can greatly
enhance or undermine the standing of a man in social life. Like Ismail's
descriptions, men in al-Zawiya do present negative depictions of women
by accusing them of being lazy, morally corrupt, and prone to moral
transgression. Yet it is important to explore how these narratives are situated and to think of the category "women" as diverse, including sisters,
mothers, wives, mothers-in-law, cousins, and more. Similar to what
Ismail notes, some men in al-Zawiya complain that their wives waste
their income either because they are "lazy" and "incompetent" or because
they want to drain the husband of money so he does not spend it on
others, minimizing the risk of his taking another wife.[33] Simultaneously,
while men in al-Zawiya often criticized women as a collective abstract
group, most of them presented a different narrative when talking about
their own female relatives. They usually celebrated the skills, knowledge,
and resourcefulness that their mothers, sisters, and wives displayed when
dealing with merchants, teachers, drivers, and government officials.
These skills are assets and foundations of support for men and the family
at large. In fact, rather than threatening and undermining their standing
as men, such interventions often enhanced and supported the attempts
of sons, brothers, and husbands to materialize norms that define masculine identifications.

Looking at some moments in Zaki's life and thinking about the trajectories of some of his neighbors enables us to see that not only other men
but also women are judges of normality who monitor how men conform
to norms that define a proper man, evaluate shortcomings, and exert pressure to modify conduct. Their daily instructions, criticisms, and financial
and moral support are all important parts of the technologies that help
to cultivate a masculine self that is recognized and legitimized by others.
Here, we do not find a unidirectional flow of power (male powerful/female
powerless, male makes/female made) but a complex web of signification
and multiple flows of power that structure how masculinity (and, for that

matter, femininity) are embodied, reproduced, and transformed in various contexts and over time.

These strategies include and go beyond "the bargaining with patriarchy" argument.[34] The acts, interventions, and instructions I have discussed above are not simply "interpersonal strategies that maximize their [women's] security through the manipulation of the affections of their sons and husbands" and that aim at "maximizing their own life chances."[35] It is true that enhancing the standing of male relatives as men also enhances the standing of the family in the neighborhood; having a real man for a son, a brother, a husband, or a father reflects well on the respect, distinction, and good reputation of the whole family. But it would be inaccurate to think of women as mainly motivated by narrow personal interest and the desire to maximize their future gains. In fact, most women are realistic about their expectations of their male relatives, especially the brothers, who often struggle to support their wives and children. Fundamentally, women's support, instructions, and corrections are structured by social norms that define proper men and by a strong desire to see their male relatives become men who are respected and cherished by themselves and others. Women are not isolated and segregated but are entangled in the broader cultural and social universe that defines the proper man and they work diligently to materialize that understanding in the trajectories of their male relatives. Thus, my discussion of the contribution of women to the making of men should not be understood as an argument that a counter or alternative type of masculinity is being produced. Rather, women, especially mothers and sisters, work to help ensure that male relatives master or perfect existing norms that define the proper man. In fact, their interventions are often geared toward reestablishing the hierarchical relationships that privilege men over women and that reinforce the dominance of husbands over wives. The importance of maintaining and reinforcing such hierarchical relationships is key to understanding socially sanctioned uses of violence, especially in the domain of the family, the topic of the next chapter.

4

Gendered Violence
Local and National Articulations

> Violence is part of a system of domination, but is at the same time a measure of its imperfection.
>
> R. W. Connell, *Masculinities*

IN THE SUMMER OF 2010, a murder case captured the attention of many people in al-Zawiya. For days men and women repeatedly recounted the events of such a rare crime, each concentrating on different facets of the events and the characters involved. The story started when Kirsha, a young man of twenty-five, began acting like a baltagi. Kirsha became notorious in the area for the many fights he got into and, most recently, for his attempt to extract *'itaawaat* (protection money) from owners of local shops and businesses. This had already begun to create a sense of resentment among the residents of the area, but these feelings sharply increased when Kirsha was accused of raping a married woman, a grave offense in al-Zawiya. He allegedly went to her apartment at 4 am and found her taking a shower. He raped her and left her naked in the living room until her husband, who works all night, came back late in the morning. She told him what had happened and they went to the police station to report the assault. The police, according to the neighbors, quickly apprehended Kirsha, who was well known to them because of his previous offenses. The medical examination of the woman and Kirsha showed that she was either "raped," according to her, or had sex, according to him. Here, the neighbors differ in their narratives. Some believe that the woman was indeed raped while others doubt that she was forced into the sexual act, claiming instead that she was having an affair with Kirsha. She got angry, they claim, when he visited her apartment with two of his friends, thereby publicizing their scandalizing affair.

Regardless of these differences, consensus holds that Kirsha's family, especially his mother, did not want him to be convicted of an "honor crime" (*gariimat sharaf*).[1] They quickly contacted the woman and managed to offer her a modest compensation to drop the charges. She agreed and soon Kirsha was out of prison. Shortly after his release, rumors have it that he and the woman started seeing each other regularly and he could be seen going up to her apartment with food and presents.[2] Things got very tense when one of the neighbors made an insinuating comment either criticizing the woman for having an affair with Kirsha or proposing that he too could have an affair with her. The woman was infuriated and told Kirsha about the encounter. He was furious and gave the man, called Atif, a good beating. *'Aganu* (a verb, which literally means kneading him like dough) is how people described the thrashing and humiliation that Atif received at the hands of Kirsha.

Atif, a married man in his late thirties and the father of three children, was known in the area as a nice but rowdy man. Usually, he was kind, shy, devout, and well-mannered. However, when he was *mibarshim* (i.e., took *birsham*, drugs taken orally by some men),[3] he became violent, rude, and out of control. Gossip had it that his beating at the hands of Kirsha greatly offended Atif and his family, especially his mother. The neighbors said that the whole family incited Atif to get back at Kirsha. A fight between Kirsha and Atif ensued, but soon their families (male and female) joined the fight, as is usually expected. One of Kirsha's brothers, who was respected in the area and who had been critical of his brother's conduct, heard about the fight while sitting at a local coffee shop and joined in (some say he was fighting along with his brother while others say he was trying to put an end to the fight). During the commotion, Atif stabbed Kirsha's brother, who died of his wounds a few hours later on the doorsteps of a hospital in downtown Cairo.[4] The police arrested both Atif and

Kirsha, and the former's family and their close relatives had to flee their apartments and move to unknown locations.

There was a lot of speculation about how this case would end. A sense of uncertainty and ambiguity arose as the case unfolded within the two parallel methods used for resolving similar conflicts: the official legal system and the informal social norms that regulate the use and counter-use of force. There was a need to deal first with the state apparatus, the police, and eventually the court system. Both families would have to hire lawyers, recruit witnesses, and attend court proceedings. They would also make and circulate narratives to persuade neighbors and the legal authorities that their side was right and the other was wrong. Some claim that one of the policemen did a big favor for Atif by cutting his (Atif's) abdomen to make it look like he was defending himself when he killed Kirsha's brother.[5] Others emphasize that Atif cut himself after the fight to enhance a self-defense argument.[6] At the same time, his family has spread a narrative emphasizing that Atif was protecting the honor of his family. According to the neighbors and a weekly newspaper,[7] Atif's family claimed that Kirsha was about to sexually assault Atif's young daughter (the neighbors say it was his sister) and that her father was trying to protect her honor (*sharafha*) when he accidentally killed Kirsha's brother. Using violence to protect female relatives, especially when they are threatened sexually, is socially expected, accepted, and legitimized. Neighbors tend not to believe in this story but think it is a good account to offer to the police, who could easily buy it because of Kirsha's violent record.

In addition to the complexity of working within the formal legal system, social expectations and norms could complicate the ending of this incident. Some neighbors argue that no matter what the court rules, Kirsha would have to avenge the death of his brother. The victim's family (following the traditions of their native Upper Egypt) refused to accept condolences after his burial, a clear indication that they wanted revenge. Several neighbors think that Kirsha would not kill Atif, who is viewed by some as *saaye'* (worthless, or good-for-nothing). Instead, Kirsha would target, as he had promised, Atif's best brother to "burn their [the family's] hearts" (*'alashaan yihriq qalbuhum*). Others think that Kirsha would not dare take revenge because this would be a premeditated murder and so could land him in prison for a very long time. Some men I spoke to think that he may badly hurt one of Atif's brothers, something that Kirsha is skilled at doing, but that he would avoid any fatal blows. Others believe that instead of a violent retaliation, the victim's family may eventually accept a compensation that would help to support Kirsha's brother's three young children.[8]

Even though such extreme events rarely happen in al-Zawiya, I find this case significant because it shows the complex meanings that people attach to the use of physical force and its relationship to masculinity. In particular, the responses to this incident relate to broader views of the legitimacy of violence and its appropriate uses. As is argued by other scholars, there is a strong relationship between violence and the construction of masculinity in different parts of the world.[9] Although gender distinctions are largely supported and legitimized by social conventions, cultural meanings, legal codes, and religious discourses, force is occasionally used to support inequalities among men and between men and women. While violence is not a privilege in itself, it is "part of the practice by which particular men or groups of men claim respect, intimidate rivals, or try to gain material advantages."[10] Similarly, in al-Zawiya, men are expected to use violence both at home and outside to assert their standing as men. In this chapter, however, I would like to go beyond the literature on violence and masculinity, most of which tends to focus on its gendered nature and distribution, by looking closely at the type and amount of violence deployed, how it is viewed socially, when it is sanctioned, and when it is stigmatized, scorned, and rejected.

The use of force is not arbitrary. Rather, I argue that a man displays his social skill and reinforces his social standing by selectively using, or avoiding, violence. Notions such as *gada'na*, *baltaga* (thuggery), and *ghabaawa* (social incompetence), as will become clear later in the chapter, are social concepts that differentiate between several uses of violence and how they relate to social inequalities. My discussion shows that there is a strong connection between the legitimate use of violence and upholding cherished social norms as well as reinforcing the hierarchies that structure relationships between men and women, old and young, and parent and child. It illustrates that violence is a social practice: an exercise of power that is productive (note that I do not say "positive") and performative. The deployment of violence produces the subjects (such as real men—gid'aan—and baltagiyya) that it claims to simply represent and reinforces the inequalities that make its practice possible in the first place. After looking at the politics of using various forms of physical force both in the domain of the family and outside it, I explore how the categories people use to classify, regulate, and evaluate proper versus improper uses of violence framed the attempts of men and women in al-Zawiya to make sense of the protests and changing events that have been profoundly shaping Egypt's political and social landscapes. The discussion pays special attention to the interplay, tensions, and contradictions between localized categories and national discourses and debates over the legitimate uses of force.

Daily Dramas

If you had the chance to walk the streets of Cairo, most likely you would have seen two or more people (usually men) yelling or even attempting to reach out to grab each other. Such occurrences might have given you the false impression that force was central to how people interact with each other and how they run their affairs. I myself made the mistake of initially feeling uneasy and apprehensive when I heard a driver and passengers exchange some harsh words, noted men at the bus station insult each other, or saw men on the side of the street reach out to get hold of each other to start a fistfight. Over time, however, I learned what these gestures and verbal exchanges indicated and relaxed when witnessing such scenes, which normally ended quickly and without the use of actual violence.[11] The loud voices usually attracted the attention of others—drivers, passengers, or passers-by—who immediately interfered to restrain the parties and put an end to their disagreement. In fact, I have learned that rather than actual violence, it is often the threat of its use that is loudly and visibly asserted. Mothers, for example, would threaten their children many times before they actually beat them.[12] Husbands frequently use the threat of beating (especially during the first few years of marriage) but rarely inflict violence on their wives. Young men may challenge each other verbally but rarely resort to the tangible use of violence. Older men are assumed to have the ability to use violence against family members but a major part of their distinction and standing is the result of their ability to avoid its use.

Like the "social dramas" described by Victor Turner, fights in al-Zawiya have a beginning, a middle, and an end. Social dramas usually ensue when a "public breach has occurred in the normal working of society, ranging from some grave transgression of the code of manners to an act of violence, a beating, even homicide."[13] A breach "may take the form of unhappy chance: a quarrel round the beer pots, an unwise or overheard word, an unpremeditated quarrel."[14] This breach constitutes a crisis that is addressed swiftly to prevent its escalation into a broader and deeper conflict. Redressive mechanisms (for example, arbitration, formal or informal legal action, rituals, or policing) are deployed by social agents such as the elders, officials, lawmakers, religious figures, or community leaders, who work to end the conflict and mend relationships.[15] The result is "either reintegration or recognition of schism."[16]

Like social dramas, fights in al-Zawiya have their own ritualized insults, bodily language, and ways of settlement. A fight usually starts with shouts. If it is between women, soon one hears verbal insults exchanged. In some cases, women and children may use the lids of cooking pots to make loud sounds that accompany their own insults or distort the other party's slurs. If conflict is between men, they shout threats and often grab each other's clothes to indicate a willingness to physically attack each other.[17] Being loudest is important to assert rights, show courage, and declare the need for others to either watch and hear the exchange or intervene to help.[18] While neighbors look through windows and doors to observe and monitor what happens, relatives, friends, and close neighbors quickly appear (failing to do so could strain relationships), in some cases to help one party against the other or, more often to put an end to the conflict.[19] They use social and religious phrases and formulas, such as *ma'alish* (It's okay, or Don't worry about it), *haqqak 'alayya* (I owe you an apology, or Let me apologize to you), *waheed illah* (Witness the oneness of God), *sali 'ala in-Nabi* (Say a prayer to bless the Prophet), or curse Satan, to soothe the disputing parties, remind them of the bonds and values that connect them to each other, and urge them to end the dispute. Although both parties usually resist being the first to end or abandon the quarrel, they can most often be persuaded to stop. In fact, rejecting mediation and persisting in fighting is socially discouraged and could strain the relationships between the mediators and the individuals involved in the conflict. Those who *ma bikabruish had* (literally, "they do not make anyone big," indicating that they do not defer to any person, including senior and distinguished mediators) are labeled quarrelsome and most people are not willing to intercede on their behalf. Most of the quarrels I have witnessed in al-Zawiya, however, quickly fizzled out and normal social relationships were often restored before long.

My emphasis on peaceful resolutions to most breaches and the infrequent use of physical force does not mean that violence is absent. As indicated in the case of Atif and Kirsha, it is sometimes deployed, even with tragic endings. Violence is used both inside and outside the home. Mothers may beat their children as part of teaching them the correct way of behaving;[20] husbands may strike their wives to show their frustration and reinforce their dominance; teachers may use physical punishment to maintain order in the classroom; the usta may beat his young apprentices as part of their training in a trade; policemen may use force to extract a confession from a suspected criminal; and young men may use violence against others to assert courage and dominance.[21] As the case of Kirsha and Atif shows, violent encounters between two men could also expand to include family members and could escalate to cause serious bodily harm or even death. Thus, it is important to consider how the violence deployed by men is part of a broader setting where some type of violence is (at least occasionally) used to discipline individuals, shape their conduct, and restrict their choices and movements. In particular, the brutality of the state, which most young men are subjected to, should be central to any adequate understanding of the relationship between masculinity and violence.

Within the Family

Although there are multiple social, religious, and legal discourses that support and legitimize gender inequalities, physical force is sometimes used to discipline female and younger family members.[22] As opposed to most national surveys and current literature, which tend to lump all acts under the label "domestic violence," people in al-Zawiya attach different meanings to violence depending on how and when it is deployed. It is seen as legitimate under some conditions but not under others. If it is measured and deployed for a socially acceptable reason, the use of violence is sanctioned. When used to uphold social norms and cultivate proper men and women, violence is positively viewed. For example, when Zaki, the young man discussed in Chapter 3, hit his sister because she stayed out late, his family members and neighbors viewed his act positively. He was seen as a real man who was protecting his family's reputation by making sure his sister behaved properly. Even the sister saw his beating as a sign of love and care.[23] Similarly, an uncle who hit his teenage nephew was praised for looking after the interest of the "boy" and turning him into a young "man." Tariq, who was sixteen at the time, did not want to go to work or school and was not interested in learning a craft but wanted to spend most of his time roaming around with his friends. For a while, he took an interest in working as a money collector on mini-buses that connected al-Zawiya to nearby areas. His family, however, thought the job was very risky,[24] paid very little, and did not promise him a good future. His parents and uncles found him alternative jobs, but he quickly quit them. Eventually, one of his uncles took him to work in his own workshop but soon became frustrated when the young man dawdled on his errands or came back after a long wait with the wrong things. His paternal uncles and aunts argue that since Tariq is the only child, his mother was not firm and tended to spoil him while his father tended to overreact and treated him harshly. The mother tried to protect Tariq from his father's rough treatment by turning to his paternal uncles, whose attention and occasional use of measured force were thought to help make him more serious and a bit tougher (*yikhshan shwayya*).

The use of violence becomes especially important in situations where the man is expected to clearly show his ability to dominate younger female family members, especially the wife. The pattern in al-Zawiya parallels what has been stated about the United States, where "males are more likely to be violent when they see their female partners as insufficiently submissive and not servicing their emotional and sexual desires."[25] The most frequently cited acceptable reasons for beating a wife in al-Zawiya include her failure to take care of the apartment, her inability to prepare a meal on time, her neglect of the children, and her dismissal of her husband's instructions.[26] Both men and women tend to agree that men work hard outside the house and have to endure many nuisances (such as the ineffective transportation system, harassment by the police, and long hours of work under difficult conditions), so the least they should expect when they get back home is a clean place, a home-cooked meal, and children whose needs have been addressed by the mother. But above all, the husband should not accept disobedience in front of others. Failure to use violence when one of these norms is breached could have negative consequences for a man's standing and reputation. For example, people severely criticized a man named Fahmi who did not slap his wife on the face in front of others when she would not obey his instructions to stop insulting the neighbors or go inside their apartment. His neighbors described him as *mish raagil* (not a man) and saw his wife as in control and dominating. Similarly, Fahmi was criticized by his mother and neighbors because he could not control his wife, who went out whenever she wanted, neglected the apartment, and frequently forced her husband to buy ready-made food for their children. Fahmi's mother was furious when she visited her son's apartment and found the place filthy, noticing that even the couple's bed was smelly and stained with the children's urine. The mother had to take matters in her own hands and slapped Fahmi's wife on the face when she responded impolitely to her mother-in-law's concerns about her conduct and the condition of the apartment. Fahmi's father also interfered and threatened to kick his daughter-in-law out of the apartment if she did not mend her ways. Fahmi was considered by some of his neighbors and friends as *ghalbaan* (a poor soul) and his wife as strong and controlling.

For it to be acceptable, however, violence should be measured and infrequent. A slap on the face is the most common type of physical disciplining of family members and is often a symbolic gesture that asserts the power of the man in front of others. Although more severe forms of corporal punishment are sometimes deployed by husbands, fathers, and brothers, these forms are usually discouraged and negatively viewed. A man who indiscriminately uses force is linked to *ghabaawa*, which usually refers to stupidity but in this context refers specifically to "social incompetence" or the inability to materialize the appropriate social norm in the right setting. For example, a man who hit his mother was considered *ghabi* (a man who displays ghabaawa) and *mish raagil*. A mother should be respected and cherished, and using violence against her is a very serious violation.[27] A little child should also be protected from severe physical disciplining. A grandmother was so upset by the beating her son-in-law inflicted on his young son that she threatened to call the police. She argued that the child was not his alone and that she and her family made sacrifices to raise the child when the father was abroad working. While she often emphasized that a little bit of beating should be used to discipline children and teach them good manners, she criticized the severity of the beating that her grandson suffered and worried that excessive violence could harm him both physically and psychologically. Similarly, a husband who unjustifiably and frequently beats his wife is considered *muftari* (unjust and brutal) and is looked down upon. On some occasions, family members interfered to limit the excessive violence inflicted on their married female relatives, and brothers and fathers ended up having fistfights with the offending husbands. In general, and no matter what the cause of the use of force, neighbors and relatives quickly stepped in to end the beating of a wife, a sister, or a son. This interference is expected and welcomed by most people, and failure to interfere in family brawls could strain relationships between neighbors. In this sense, violence within the domain of the family is not a private matter but a public and communal concern that should be quickly contained.

As is often the case with gender dynamics, where masculine trajectories involve the use of violence, a "misrecognition" grants men the productive aspects of its use while women are blamed for the use and misuse of force both at home and outside.[28] Women are often viewed as provoking men to use physical force by failing to do what is expected of them. They are assigned the burden of containing the violence of men inside the home by following social norms and catering to the needs of male relatives. If a wife respects herself (*btihtirim nafsaha*) and does all her duties, many argue, the husband would not have a reason to beat her. Similarly, women are also often blamed when their male relatives commit violent acts in public. Such instances are either because mothers did not raise them properly or because they incite them to use violence against neighbors or family members. This was the case with Atif's mother, who was frequently held responsible for spurring his violent encounter with

Kirsha. In addition to the fact that she always supported him morally and materially (implying that she supported his drug addiction), neighbors claim, she often bragged about his violent actions when he was under the influence of drugs and sometimes threatened the neighbors that she would prompt him to respond violently if they did not do what she wanted. For example, some say that Atif's mother got upset because one of her neighbors began a business selling *gallabiyyaat* (women's long gowns) that rivaled Atif's mother's monopolizing enterprise. She went to the neighbor and told her "we do not need Atif [implying that she is willing to sacrifice him], I'll ask him to take *birshama* [a pill] and kill your husband." Neighbors also claim that she was the one who gave Atif the knife and urged him to use it if Kirsha ever attacked him again. The mother was held responsible for inciting the terrible violence that led to the death of a young man and the imprisonment of her own son.

When I asked about the fathers, I learned that Atif's father has been working in Saudi Arabia for the past two decades and Kirsha's father has been jobless for years and spends most of his time roaming around the area without much influence on his family. The sons, as argued by several men and women, do not feel they owe their fathers any respect and do not listen to anything they may have to say. The phrase *tarbiyyet niswaan* (raised by women) was used to explain the excessive violence and lack of restraint on Kirsha's and Atif's behaviors. The phrase strongly implies that someone failed to become a man (*mish raagil*) because he lacks some of the main characteristics (such as a sense of responsibility and courage) that define a proper man. It signifies that the boy was spoiled by the mother, who may encourage him to be violent toward others and not think about the consequences of his actions, as in the case of Atif. Contrarily, the phrase may indicate that the mother—like Hiba, discussed in Chapter 1—may be too strict with the boy. A mother may hit him too much, prevent him from going outside to play with other children, and turn him into a sissy who is not able to stand up for himself. The paradox here, as I have argued in the previous chapters (especially Chapter 3), is that women are active in the making of men in several significant ways. Yet, socially, the fathers are credited for the positive conduct of their sons while mothers are usually blamed when sons fail to conform to social norms that define proper masculine conduct. Such misrecognition ensures the reproduction of inequalities that configure relationships not only between men and women but also between young and older men. It allows men to continue to be strongly associated with positive meanings and socially cherished values while women endure the burden of being associated with socially unacceptable and stigmatized meanings.[29]

This tendency was painfully expressed during protests in Cairo in December 2011 when the horrific images of soldiers beating and stomping on the bare chest of an unconscious young Egyptian woman (widely dubbed in Western media as "the girl in the blue bra") were circulated in the media. People were outraged by the images but still many (including some of my close female interlocutors in al-Zawiya) condemned the woman, arguing that she herself brought on the beating because she infuriated the soldiers by using vulgar gestures and offensive language. Many questioned her moral standing and why she was in the street in the first place. She was even criticized for not wearing more clothes under her outer garment as a precaution against potential exposure. Through these accounts, the soldiers were viewed as victims of the woman's aggression and incitement and, rather than focusing on the physical violence and violation the woman was subjected to, the attention quickly shifted to affirming the virtue of the soldier who covered the chest of the woman after she was repeatedly trampled by the other soldiers. This soldier's conduct was highlighted, especially by military leaders, to counter claims that the soldiers violated the woman's rights and bodily integrity.

Structured Uses

As in many other patriarchal societies,[30] the physical squabbles of boys and young men outside the home are part of life in al-Zawiya. As discussed in Chapter 1, boys are taught the importance of defending themselves and fighting back. Most families do not want their children to be the aggressors, but parents usually encourage their sons to stand up for themselves and respond appropriately when they find themselves in a fight. Parents often punish boys who initiate fights with others but also scold and may physically discipline a boy who does not fight back when attacked first by his peer(s). For young men in particular, engaging in some form of physical scuffles is often viewed as part of growing up, and using violence in the right context could be the source of distinction and prestige. Fighting to protect and control female relatives, back one's friends, restore respect to older people, or support the weak against the strong are viewed positively and could contribute to boosting one's standing as a man.

As described in Chapter 2, Samer vividly remembers and proudly describes some of the fights that others began with him as a young man. He rose to the occasion once to help a young boy who was being bullied by an older youth, another time to support a young man and his fiancée who were being harassed by a group of thugs, and another time to assist a humble worker who was unjustly attacked by a well-connected, influential owner of a sweet factory and some of his employees who supported him. To Samer, these memories were important moments when others recognized him as a man because he was not the instigator of the conflicts but managed to either counter some form of unjust deployment of force or bravely confront others (even when they outnumbered him) who were violating norms that *sha'bi*, people like Samer, from popular or low-income neighborhoods, value. Bullying a young boy on the city bus, harassing a woman on the street, or insulting an older man in the market are offenses that defy the sensibilities of men like Samer, who are expected and feel obliged to intervene to correct such conduct.[31] Although at the age of forty he is not expected to use violence in his dealings with others, Samer unequivocally states that he would retaliate violently if a man deliberately stares (*yibuss*) at a woman walking with him in the street. "Why would he gaze at her? Does not she have a man walking with her?" He interprets the stare as a direct attack on the woman and a clear challenge to him. In such a situation, his use of violence could be viewed positively by others and could be taken as a sign of his standing as a real man.

Men can and do choose not to use force.[32] The phrase *maluush fil-khinaaq* refers to a man who is not interested in fighting and who deliberately avoids physical confrontation. It could indicate a cowardly man or a humble individual (*ghalbaan*) with no one to support him, but most often it refers to educated, respectable, and well-mannered people (*nas muhtarama*) who voluntarily shun violence and avoid using it (even though they are able to) in daily life. There are also several mechanisms to contain violence, including the moral obligation to intervene to separate parties engaged in an altercation. In the same way that socially appropriate uses of violence can enhance one's standing, it is considered foolish for a man to get into a fight that he cannot win. For instance, Shireen described her husband's uncle who embarrasses himself and his kin by getting into fights, even when everybody knows that he is not able to fight back. She described his *'abeeta* (silly or foolish) way of fighting and the many times he ended up being severely beaten. She laughed hard when recalling the few times her husband (who does not like to fight) had the bad luck of being around and felt obliged to join his uncle's brawls. They ended up either with torn clothes or covered with sand from rolling on the ground. The uncle, Shireen emphasized, was bringing humiliation (*bahdala*) not only to himself but also to his kin, who were growing impatient with his ways.

In general, as he gets older, a man is expected to minimize his use of force both inside and outside the home. Older men are expected to avoid the possibility of being humiliated by others, especially younger men and the police.[33] After a certain age (usually the early thirties), using violence outside the home becomes a sign of immaturity and irresponsibility. As Muhammad, a 46-year-old married man and father of four children stated, "Now, I have to be more rational (*'aqlaani*) and think of my kids and responsibilities. It is not like the old days when I ran to offer my free services (*agaamil*) whenever there was a fight." At his current age, he is expected to end fights, not initiate or participate in them. Thus, unless a major violation demands his attention, he would not use physical violence against other men. Though the possibility of using violence at home never ceases, an older man is expected to use it as little as possible. For older men, being wise, thoughtful, pious, and diplomatic becomes a better option than using force.

A man can diminish his standing, however, by avoiding the use of force when there is a clear need for it. A man who runs away when confronted is stigmatized and his ruguula is questioned. Umm Saaleh, for example, criticized her neighbor Abu Waleed because he did not respond firmly and violently when another neighbor insulted him in the street by declaring that Abu Waleed was "not a respectable man." She emphasized that her husband would have responded very strongly to such a statement and would certainly have beaten any man who would offend him in this manner. In a way, Abu Waleed confirmed the man's allegations that he was not a proper man by not reacting to him. She contrasted Abu Waleed's passive response to her own firm reaction to one of her neighbors, who tried to intrude on the space near their house, when she asserted her family's rights by loudly and firmly declaring that she was fathered by a real man and would never allow the neighbor to execute his plan. Even the neighbor's wife and son took Umm Saaleh's side when they saw how strong she was and pressured him to stop his plans to prevent escalation. If a confrontation unfolds, both men and women are expected to respond and assert their ability to stand up for themselves.

Gada'na Versus Baltaga

Knowing when to use or avoid violence, the right context for its use or avoidance, and amount of violence to use is an important skill that is not mastered by all men. This knowledge and the purpose of the violence are exactly what differentiate the positive concept gada', the decent man, from the negative concept baltagi, the thug. Kirsha in the case mentioned above was universally viewed as a baltagi. His actions were *qillet adab* (lacking in good manners) and *sayyaa'a* (hassling and irresponsible), not acts of ruguula or gada'na.[34] Almost all of the residents, including his own family members, reacted negatively to Kirsha's conduct because he tried to profit at the expense of others. He hoped to boost his reputation and increase his material and symbolic capital by forcing people to give money to him and show respect that was not deserved. Most of the neighbors were happy to see him imprisoned and wished that Kirsha had died instead of his brother. They condemned the acts of both Kirsha and Atif because the two men sought personal gain rather than serving the social good and because their violent behaviors were excessive and unmeasured.[35] People gave Kirsha credit, however, for his ability to engage in many fights without fatally injuring anyone, whereas they reprimanded Atif for his inability to injure without killing. In general, leaving an opponent with a scar to remember and that would flag him to the police as a troublemaker is a difficult skill that not many men master.[36] As this fight demonstrated, Atif was *ghasheem* (inexperienced), as described by a

40-year-old man. A more experienced man would have caused Kirsha's brother some harm without fatally stabbing him. It is this experience that men draw on to support their belief that Kirsha would in the future cause Atif's most respected brother some major harm but without killing him and exposing himself to a long incarceration.

Yet, the terrible conduct of Kirsha was contrasted with the positive concept of gada'na. The term *gada'* refers to a person who excels in materializing social norms that define "the moral universe of Egyptian popular classes,"[37] including intelligence, valor, toughness, reliability, and decency. As in other popular (*sha'bi*) quarters in Cairo, in al-Zawiya the adjective *gada'na* refers to a mix of gallantry and "nobility, audacity, responsibility, generosity, vigor, and manliness."[38] A gada' is a person who "does not accept injustice or tyranny and usually stands for the weak against the strong."[39] The label gada' was applied to several residents: A man who quickly offered a loan to a needy friend, another who rushed to carry his next door neighbor's 5-year-old son when he fell and broke his arm, the worker who stepped in to help a boy who was bullied by an older youth on a city bus, and a 12-year-old brother who rushed to help his 10-year-old brother in a fight with several children in the street. In al-Zawiya, parents desire their sons (and daughters) to be gid'aan, to be supportive and assertive but without oppressing others (*min gheer ma yiftiru 'ala hadd*). As stated in Chapter 1, not all men are gid'aan and not all gid'aan are men. A woman or a boy who materializes key aspects of gada'na could acquire this symbolic label. Action, not gender, determines who deserves this label and who does not.

A key part of gada'na is to not resort to violence except in the proper contexts, including defending oneself, aiding friends and relatives, and protecting vulnerable individuals and family members (especially females). In contrast to a gada', a baltagi is someone (usually a man) who uses violence to impose his own will (as in the case of Kirsha) on others and to further his personal interests.[40] This concept has a long history that goes back as far as the Ottomans, when it was used to refer to a group of men who were usually armed with knives and axes and charged with protecting and serving the sultan and his family.[41] It was redefined, however, by the Egyptian government in recent times to refer to and control what it termed "social terrorism."[42] The deployment of this concept became part of the broader neoliberal policies of the state and its attempt to discipline young men and subject them to new regimes of productivity and surveillance. Whereas government representatives and journalists in the late 1980s and early 1990s used the phrase mainly to refer to Islamist leaders, since the mid-1990s, "social baltaga" primarily has referred to the violence that has erupted between government agents and young men in popular quarters.[43] Law 6 on thuggery was passed in 1998 to regulate behavior deemed "antisocial and threatening" and proposed stiff penalties for acts thought to intimidate others.[44] This law was coupled with the emergency law (employed in Egypt since 1967) to grant security forces extensive powers to stop, search, question, and detain individuals suspected of threatening order and security.[45] Central to this process has been the control of various spaces (such as streets, mosques, and local markets) and their uses, especially by young men. At the same time, baltagiyya were "appropriated as useful tools of the police,"[46] who trained and paid thugs to counter protests, scare opposition groups, intimidate voters during election times, and generate a sense of chaos that justified the need for heavy policing of various spaces and groups.

Unlike this legal framework, which has tended to lump young men together as potential baltagiyya, the understanding of baltaga in al-Zawiya focuses mainly on the improper uses of violence in daily life. Contrary to the gada' who aims to help and protect others, a baltagi is a person who uses force to bully others, take over their property, extract money from them, or coerce them to comply with his wishes. He does not work to further the public good or serve the community but is focused on his own well-being, and his loyalties are easily bought. In addition to his conduct, both his weapon (mainly the *singa*,[47] a long knife usually carried visibly to intimidate others) and his appearance (the way he dresses and, more important, the visible bodily scars of previous injuries that reveal his willingness to use violence) identify him as a baltagi.[48] Through their own observations and the testimonies of relatives and neighbors, people are usually able to recognize who is socially defined as a baltagi in their community and try to avoid, control, or defeat him.

This distinction between baltagi and gada' became particularly relevant during the recent Egyptian revolution and strongly framed the shifting feelings of my close interlocutors toward the changing events in

Cairo, especially in Midan al-Tahrir, or Liberation Square, the epicenter of the protests in Egypt since January 25, 2011. As the next section shows, the conduct of the protestors, while initially viewed suspiciously and negatively, became over time legitimized and equated with notions of gada'na. Simultaneously, the conduct of Mubarak and his supporters was gradually delegitimized and equated with baltaga. These shifting uses show the importance of looking at the overlaps, tensions, and contradictions between local meanings and national discourses and projects and how they transform feelings, views, and stands.

Gid'aan in the Midan

Knowing about their frequently negative encounters with the government and its agents (especially the police), the economic hardships that structured their daily lives, their political marginalization, and the history of protest movements in their neighborhood, I expected people in al-Zawiya to immediately and fully embrace the calls for social and economic justice. During the first few days, however, the families I talked to over the phone were uncertain about what was happening, how long the demonstrations would last, and who the protestors even were.[49] The residents, especially day workers and families with no savings, felt unsafe and worried about their livelihoods. They blamed the protestors for disrupting their access to work, threatening their safety, and destabilizing the country. Because of the government censorship, many watched TV channels that were limited to supporting the official position.[50] They thought poorly of the activists and used the lines offered by government propaganda, describing the protestors as troublemakers who were paid a daily allowance in Euros by outsiders and who were served free meals from Kentucky Fried Chicken.[51] These feelings were especially strong in the immediate aftermath of an emotional speech by Mubarak on February 1, in which he warned against potential chaos and disorder generated by the demonstrations, promised that he would neither run again for the presidency nor pass his position to his son, and declared that he had served Egypt for most of his life and would like to die and be buried on the soil of Egypt. This speech moved many people in al-Zawiya, who fully supported the president and his plans for change. They felt that he was offering major concessions and that the protestors would be unreasonable if they refused to give him a chance to finish his term in September 2011. Their feelings and views, however, changed rapidly and drastically after the attacks on the demonstrators in Liberation Square on February 2.

During the eighteen days that led to the demise of Mubarak's rule, Midan al-Tahrir was transformed into an epicenter of a moral geography that connected Egyptians in various locations into the same political and ethical project. The Midan's spatial centrality and its historical significance enabled millions of Egyptians to come together as citizens who shared pressing grievances and demands.[52] Despite initial clashes with the police, the demonstrators continued to grow in numbers. The police withdrew on January 28, when they were replaced by members of the army who declared that they would not shoot at the protestors. On February 2, however, so-called pro-Mubarak supporters attacked the Midan. Many of us watched with horror as men riding horses and camels attacked the square, wielding stones, whips, clubs, knives, sticks, and fire bombs against the peaceful protestors.[53] These attackers were immediately seen by many Egyptians (including people in al-Zawiya) as baltagiyya, thugs commissioned by government officials to frighten the demonstrators.[54] The aggressors were met by strong resistance from the peaceful protestors, who managed to chase them away and erected barriers and fences to protect the square and regulate access to its vicinities.[55]

My interlocutors' narratives and media coverage clearly mark these attacks and the successful defense of Tahrir Square as among the most important moments in the recent revolution. The attacks brought to the foreground a set of associations between the past and the present, the local and the national, and the proper and improper uses of violence that shaped in vital ways the views many Egyptians held of the protestors and the pro-Mubarak supporters. Whereas the rebels (el-suwwaar) had proven themselves to be gid'aan, brave and decent men and women willing to sacrifice their lives for the dignity and good of the whole nation, Mubarak's government and its supporters were seen as baltagiyya, thugs who protected their own interests.

Notions of gada'na and ruguula as mawqif became clearly articulated both in al-Zawiya and Midan al-Tahrir. In particular, that the inhabitants of the two sites worked in similar ways to aid, protect, support, and contain violence generated both emotional and political connections that linked them to the same moral and political project. The mobilization of people in al-Zawiya against the potential threat of baltagiyya was particularly significant. Over the years I have heard of a few baltagiyya in al-Zawiya, but baltaga was never felt as a collective and direct threat until January 28. On that day, the police station in al-Zawiya (like other police stations in other parts of Egypt) was burned, the police withdrew from the streets, and rumors spread widely, warning of looming attacks of baltagiyya from a nearby community.[56] All of my interlocutors (especially women and children) vividly described the terror that struck the area and the fear that engulfed them for days. Local mosques urged men to sacrifice themselves to protect their homes and families, and men rose to the occasion and worked together to defend and aid their community. This period both reflected and reinforced a strong sense of camaraderie and solidarity. In the summers of 2011 and 2012, people remembered with pride the way the men stood together, the unity they displayed, and the type of real ruguula they materialized.

Going through the fears, the worries, and the task of protecting their neighborhood, it was not difficult for many people in al-Zawiya to increasingly identify with the protestors who were also subjected to the violence of baltagiyya, especially on February 2. Just as al-Zawiya's residents attempted to defend and care for their neighborhood, those in the square also protected it, cleaned it, and offered emotional, medical, and material support to its occupants. Through such parallel actions and emotional connections, the protestors were redefined as gid'aan and national heroes:[57] well-educated, reliable, and trustworthy young people who were willing to sacrifice financial success and easy living to advocate freedom and social justice.[58] Like other gid'aan in al-Zawiya, el-suwwaar were working to challenge and transform the inequalities that privileged el-nizam (the system) over el-sha'b (the people) and that enriched Mubarak and his family at the expense of ordinary Egyptians (el-ghalaba).

The protestors' stands (mawaaqif) reflected the type of ruguula which, as discussed in Chapter 2, is highly regarded in al-Zawiya. A sharp ethical contrast was created between these cherished heroes, who avoided using violence as much as possible but who were brave enough to defend themselves and protect Tahrir Square, and the baltagiyya who unjustly used violence against peaceful protestors for the sole purpose of defending the interests of few corrupt politicians. Just as people condemn a husband who uses excessive violence against his wife, or a father who severely beats his young son, or a man (like Kirsha) who uses force to impose his will on others, they criticized, condemned, and resented the acts of baltagiyya against unarmed demonstrators. Whereas the occupants of Tahrir represented the nation's aspirations for a brighter future, the acts of baltaga became closely linked to the state and its arbitrary use of violence, habit of breaking its promises, and tendency to use illegitimate means to serve the interests of a small minority at the expense of the whole nation. As one of my female interlocutors in al-Zawiya, who was originally moved by Mubarak's speech, told me, "The president was making all these promises and asking people to trust him and the next thing we hear about is the attacks on al-Tahrir. How did he expect us to believe him after that?" She critically reflected on her earlier emotional reaction and strong support for Mubarak after his speech and explained to me that almost all her relatives and neighbors felt as she did because they are 'atoufeen, kindhearted and forgiving. They truly believed the president's promises and wanted to give him another chance. By the summer of 2011, however, she instead praised the protestors for not accepting Mubarak's "empty promises" and for insisting on their demands. She detailed with dread the terrible consequences that could have resulted had Mubarak stayed in office.

At the same time, the events in Tahrir Square and in al-Zawiya clearly confirmed what many had known and believed for a long time about the illegitimate use of force by state agents. Samer argued that, like baltagiyya, the police used force to obtain illegitimate payments (such as bribes) and to enable the government to extract exorbitant taxes from ordinary citizens. In fact, he concluded, not only had the previous government used baltagiyya to intimidate its political opponents, but its officials themselves were also baltagiyya because they used the techniques of baltaga. The stunning magnitude of the use of these techniques by the previous government and its financial corruption, widely reported in the media since the beginning of the revolution, currently constitute a major source of rage for Samer and his neighbors. Thus, the figure of baltagi, utilized by Mubarak's government to control youth and their spatial mobilities, became central to the discourse that condemned the government's actions, undermined its legitimacy, and framed the anti-regime feelings of many Egyptians.

Shifting Meanings

Over the past two years, the threat of baltagiyya has become a major public concern in Egypt as well as a significant discursive tool in the struggle over legitimacy and visibility. When I visited al-Zawiya in the summers of 2011 and 2012, all of my interlocutors were concerned about baltagiyya and the threat they posed to public order. Stories circulated about the kidnapping of people for ransom, the theft of cars, the snatching of handbags and jewelry from women in broad daylight, the shooting of police officers, and the beating (even killing) of ordinary citizens. Such events are typically narrated as taking place in other neighborhoods, but they nonetheless had a strong emotional impact on residents of al-Zawiya.[59] Whereas such criminal acts were easily classified by people as instances of baltaga, over the past two years, the concept has become more ambiguous, contested, and politicized.

The media report daily accusations and counter accusations of baltaga and different groups use this term to discredit their opponents. The Supreme Council of the Armed Forces, which ruled Egypt from February 2011 until August 2012, has used the term *baltaga* in various contexts to assert its legitimacy and delegitimize the actions of "others," a broad and shifting category that included but went beyond the protestors. The council reactivated the thuggery law, which gave it vast authority in detaining and severely punishing a wide range of individuals. Many were critical of the ways the Supreme Council used the term. Activists in particular had disapproved of the tendency of the council to use it to malign those who defied its orders and to "discredit Tahrir Square protestors and turn their image from *Thouwar* (revolutionaries) to *Baltagiyya*."[60] Many have viewed such accusations as an indication of continuities between the current and the previous regimes, claiming that acts of baltaga were deliberately commissioned by the supporters of a counterrevolution to undermine the accomplishments of the January 25 Revolution. In short, baltagiyya "have become anonymous, the masked actors on behalf of what the government, the military, media and public now call generically the 'hidden hands,'"[61] who seek to spread fear, chaos, and instability in the whole country.[62]

The multiple and contradictory uses of this term in several contexts and for various purposes had made it more complicated for the public to judge whether those accused of baltaga by politicians and media actually had done anything illegitimate. My interlocutors in al-Zawiya tended to listen to miscellaneous opinions and then used their own knowledge to evaluate such accusations. They closely observed the type of act committed, its location, the accused groups and their history, the accusers and their relationship to the previous and current regimes, and the TV images, including the clothing of the accused and the accuser. For example, while we were watching news of the clashes next to the Ministry of Defense in Abbasiyya on July 23, 2011, between protestors (who presented themselves as activists who had marched all the way from Tahrir Square but were viewed by the Supreme Council as baltagiyya) and what the council described as "concerned residents" of Abbasiyya (but depicted by protestors as baltagiyya), the viewers commented on the facial features of those interviewed, the way they were dressed, and their ways of talking as well as the methods used to vandalize cars, stores, and apartments. They dismissed the claims of some of those interviewed because they did not look "respectable," concluding that those who attacked the beautiful apartments, nice cars, and fancy-looking businesses must be baltagiyya who deliberately incited violence and discord. Yet the political leanings of men and women are increasingly exerting influence on ways of interpretations. The term *baltagiyya* continues to refer to those who illegitimately deploy violence but local uses are increasingly linked to national accusations and discourses.[63] Thus those among my interlocutors who have Islamist leanings tended to follow the line of Islamist leaders who accused those who remained in Tahrir toward the end of July of being baltagiyya. Others, who sympathized with the army and saw it as the source of legitimacy during this transitional period, tended to accept the classifications offered by the Supreme Council. Such overlaps, tensions, and contradictions between localized notions and broader national events and discourses are important for capturing the shifting feelings of people in various parts of Egypt and how they position themselves vis-à-vis the changing events in the country. Not only did existing categories frame people's interpretations of the use of violence by thugs against the protestors in Tahrir Square, but national discourses and debates are also exerting influence over how these local categories and views are defined and redefined.

Power and Violence

As is clear from the discussion above, the definition of a real man and the type of respect that he garners is strongly linked to the knowledge of when to use violence and when to avoid it. Being the aggressor and starting fights are considered acts of baltaga. If several men attack a single man, the behavior is strongly criticized. A man who frequently engages in fights is looked down upon and is avoided socially. Violence therefore must be seen as "a social act that is always related to some form of instrumental rationality" and "a form of 'cultural performance' . . . with special rules, etiquettes, and codes that may be—and have to be—decoded."[64]

The occasional use of violence (both inside and outside the family) is expected and sanctioned when it clearly upholds specific social norms and hierarchies. When it is employed to support established inequalities between men and women or old and young, it is accepted and viewed positively. An older sibling beating his younger sister or nephew or a man slapping his wife when she does not obey him in front of others is praised and his identity is affirmed as a caring brother or a real man. Force here is used to reestablish and support social hierarchies that privilege male over female and the older over the younger. However, when violence flows in the reverse direction, such as a wife beating a husband, a son striking a mother or father, or a younger person attacking an older one, the act becomes highly stigmatized.[65] Similarly, when violence is frequent, excessive, or used to enhance one's own interests at the expense of others, it is negatively viewed and denounced. When it is deployed to protect and aid others (especially children, female companions, and vulnerable men), then it is considered an act of gada'na and is socially accepted and valued. This ability of others to monitor, classify, judge, and attach meanings to various violent acts as well as the fact that they are expected (in fact obliged) to interfere to stop the use of force is key to the regulation and management of violence both at home and outside.

The regulated use of violence also shapes people's views of the future and how they reimagine the relationship between the government and the citizens. The changing views of the police exemplify some aspects of this relationship.[66] Originally content with the humiliation inflicted on the police, which helped curb the arbitrary violence they exercised and limited their role in public life, many people soon realized the significance of having the police as a force that maintains public order and security. The increased rate of real and imagined crimes in Cairo and other parts of Egypt has generated feelings of uneasiness about the current climate of safety and security. There are calls for restructuring the police force to make sure its primary responsibility is redefined as assisting the public instead of protecting the regime. The hope is to shift its role from one that parallels the conduct of baltagiyya, who intimidate, coerce, and brutalize, to one that materializes the ethos of gid'aan, who aid, care, and protect.

Tragically, violence can end in significant bodily harm or death, as in the case of Kirsha's brother, who has been mourned by his family and neighbors and is remembered as a good man. More recently, in early February 2012, violence erupted after a soccer game in the city of Port Said and over seventy boys and young men were killed and more than a thousand injured. Many people drew parallels between the violence inflicted on the protestors on January 28 and February 2 of 2011 and the events of Port Said, causing another round of strong protests that rocked Cairo for days. All sides argued that baltagiyya were to be blamed, but the question became who commissioned or incited them. Many Egyptians believed that the violence was either instigated by loyalists to the old system or deliberately orchestrated (or at least facilitated) by security forces to discipline the supporters of al-Ahly, the oldest and most popular soccer team in Egypt, who played an important role in the Egyptian revolution and have continued to confront the police over the past year.[67] Most Egyptians, including people in al-Zawiya, mourned the young men and considered them to be martyrs. Enraged street protestors chanted *"Raagil fi hayaatu, shaheed fi mamaatu"* (A man in his life, a martyr in his death).

This phrase captured a strong link that people in al-Zawiya often make between the deeds of a young man and the nature of his death. This link was particularly important when people tried to make sense out of the unexpected death of young men caused by sickness and accidents. It is to this subject that we turn in the next chapter.

5

Sickness, Death, and a Good Ending

Patriarchy is the single most life-threatening social disease as-
saulting the male body and spirit in our nation.

bell hooks, *The Will to Change*

There is a growing consensus that death and dying is one of the
last taboos of modern industrial societies.

Alexandra Howson, *The Body in Society*

ON JUNE 6, 2010, a 28-year-old Egyptian man from Alexandria was
pronounced dead. According to his family and eyewitnesses, Khaled Said
was beaten to death by the police for posting a video showing police officers dealing drugs. According to the police, the young man choked while
trying to swallow a packet of marijuana, implicating him as a drug addict
and dealer. Soon, however, the photos that circulated on the Internet cast
deep doubts over the police's story. Here is how Wael Ghonim, a Google
marketing executive and an Egyptian activist, describes the first time he
saw one of the images:

> It was a horrifying photo showing the distorted face of a man in his twenties.
> There was a big pool of blood behind his head, which rested on a chunk of
> marble. His face was extremely disfigured and bloodied; his lower lip had
> been ripped in half, and his jaw was seemingly dislocated. His front teeth
> appeared to be missing, and it looked as if they had been beaten right out
> of his mouth. The image was so gruesome that I wondered if he had been
> wounded in war.[1]

Ghonim was so moved by the image of Said's tortured body that he felt
he could not "stand passively in the face of such grave injustices."[2] Seeking
justice for the victim and aiming to end police cruelty, Ghonim estab-

lished the now famous Facebook page "Kullena Khaled Said" (We Are All Khaled Said). This name aimed to communicate Ghonim's feelings that the same type of violence could be inflicted on him and all young middle-class Egyptians. Very quickly "Kullena Khaled Said" became a major site for the organization, publicization, and mobilization of millions of Egyptians, and it played a leading role in calling for the January 25, 2011, protests. Khaled Said's death and battered body became national symbols of the brutality of the police, the oppression Egyptians had to endure, and the type of justice young people aspired to see. He became a martyr (*shahid*), highly celebrated by most Egyptians, including people in al-Zawiya. The meanings invested in his homicide and the killing of hundreds of other young Egyptians since the beginning of the protests strongly resonated with some of the key meanings and ideals that people in al-Zawiya drew on to make sense of the tragic and unexpected deaths of young men.

This chapter looks at the life, sickness, and death of two men (the first died at the age of sixty-four and the second at thirty-eight) to interrogate the deep intersection between class and gender in the making of bodies and selves. In particular, I argue that patriarchal structures, market forces, and medical systems intersect to regulate and discipline the male body to produce an economically productive and politically obedient subject.[3] In the process, the materiality of the body is both elaborated and negated, highlighted and downplayed, produced and consumed. These contradictory tendencies shape in forceful ways the materiality of the male body and how it is defined and redefined during life and after death.

The chapter begins by looking at current scholarly discussions of the relationship between masculinity and health, underscoring the need to look carefully and thoughtfully at the intersection between gender, class, and age in shaping bodies and health. Then, I look at some moments in the masculine trajectory of Abu Hosni, a man I knew for eighteen years, and explore how specific structural forces shaped his health, sickness, and death at the age of sixty-four. The discussion reflects on how the decline of his health redefined his standing as a man and his relationship with his wife and children. I then compare his death to that of a young man I call Karim,[4] whose death was sudden but universally viewed by his family, relatives, and neighbors as *moota kwaisa* and *moota tisharaf* (a good and honorable death). My discussion accounts for some of the cultural meanings, social ideals, and religious discourses that his family and friends drew on to make sense of his death and frame it within the highly cherished notion of "good ending" (*husn el-khaatimah*). In addition to the intersection between gender and class, this part of the chapter draws attention to how religion is also a significant force that shapes life and death. It also points to the important link between the collective production of a proper man and the collective construction of a good death. Relating my analysis of good ending to the killing of young men in the recent Egyptian revolution, I argue that this notion is not a negation of life, a sign of fatalism and irrationality, a call for people to value only the afterlife and ignore the current life, or an indication of a "culture of death" (which many Westerners are increasingly associating with Islam). Instead, I argue that the notion of "good ending" establishes a strong relationship between this life and the afterlife, one's religious devotion and engagement with the community, and one's deeds and intentions.

Gender, Illness, and Health

Until recently, most scholarly (and policy) attention was directed toward women's health issues. As argued by several scholars, "sociologists, medical researchers and other health professionals have all contributed to cultural portrayals of men as healthy and women as the 'sicker' gender . . . , to strongly held beliefs that men's bodies are structurally more efficient than and superior to women's bodies . . . , and to the 'invisibility' of men's poor health status."[5] Over the past two decades, however, feminists have forcefully questioned the tendency to make the male body the norm against which women's bodies and health are measured.[6] At the same time, a growing number of studies have shown the many health challenges men are facing in different parts of the world.[7] "Masculine roles" may have often secured economic and political advantages for men over women, but several scholars have argued that these same roles were also harmful to men's physical and emotional well-being.[8] To conform to "traditional masculinity," men are expected to take physical risks, suppress their emotions, and deny their pain and physical discomfort.

Various studies have documented a significant gap between men and women in morbidity, mortality, and health-seeking practices. Ironically, however, just as women's bodies and health used to be measured against the male body, currently men are being evaluated using women's health-seeking practices as the norm.[9] Both in scholarly work and policy circles, there is a strong assumption that men are "in fact responsible for their ill health and that, if they actually asked for help, acted differently and got involved in health prevention, the gap between men's and women's health would be overcome."[10] Simultaneously, most studies on men's health depend primarily on only a few specific methods such as surveys and focus groups and tend to neglect historical, critical, and in-depth analysis needed to understand the complex factors that shape health and illness. Such methodological choices reveal the strong link between scholarly work and narrow policy programs and "the pursuit of 'quick fixes' to what are complex problems."[11] But more important, "pathologizing" masculinity and assuming that it is the cause of men's health problems risks depoliticizing, individualizing, and medicalizing vital structural issues.[12]

To avoid this danger, the intersection between gender and other structures, especially class, must be seriously considered as central to any understanding of the masculine trajectories I analyze in this book in general and in this chapter in particular. The political, urban, and environmental context is also imperative to keep in the foreground when we consider issues of men's health and health-seeking practices. In a city like Cairo, pollution, contaminated food and water, and the pressure of urban life as well as lack of safety measures, adequate health insurance, reasonable compensation systems, and accountability of health professionals are among the key factors that increase the possibilities of injury for men and limit the possibility of finding time to seek medical attention or to nurse injuries and illness.[13] While it is true that men are encouraged to engage in hazardous behaviors, deny their pain, and suppress their emotions, it would be simplistic to assume that social norms that define masculinity could solely (or mainly) explain men's daily enactments, illness, and health. A man who falls when trying to jump on or off the bus, for example, should not be assumed to be simply enacting norms that link masculinity with daring and risky actions. Rather, we should explore his unfortunate accident within the broader context where there is limited cheap public transportation, where Cairo's congested streets make arriving at work on time a real challenge, where overcrowded buses are not able to accommodate more passengers who desperately need to reach specific places, and where the overworked and underpaid bus driver tries to navigate competing demands (including terrible traffic, anxious passengers, and bureaucratic requirements). These structural factors intersect in forceful ways to shape the life, health, and death of men in al-Zawiya. The next section further illustrates these points by looking at some moments in the masculine trajectory of Abu Hosni, a man I met in 1993, when I first started my research in al-Zawiya. Looking at this remarkable man's health and how it deteriorated reveals some of the forces that shape men's life and death.

Days of Health, Days of Sickness

When I first met Abu Hosni, he was in his mid-forties with a stocky body, a full head of neatly trimmed black hair, and a serious face. As soon as I talked to him, Abu Hosni grasped the meaning of my anthropological work and he asked his wife to show me how things were done without pretenses and told her to take me to visit other people, local markets, mosques, shops, and much more.[14] He would frequently ask about the progress of my research and would delight in spending many hours talking about various topics related to his neighborhood, home village, and Egypt at large.

Over time, I got to know Abu Hosni not only as a disciplinarian father, a strict husband, and an assertive man, but also as an outstanding interlocutor. A knowledgeable and articulate man who was born and raised in a small village near Cairo and moved to the city as a young man seeking work, he had a broad perspective on life in Egypt. As a driver for an Egyptian ministry, Abu Hosni interacted with engineers, high-ranking officials, and foreign visitors. His job also opened new opportunities for him to know Cairo's streets, neighborhoods, and spaces. These experiences stimulated a strong aspiration for social mobility and granted him undisputed authority when discussing many themes that ranged from politics, economics, and religious extremism to gender distinctions, notions of modernity, and urban problems. When I look at my notes from 1993 to 2000, I see how forthcoming, expressive, and eager Abu Hosni was in sharing his ideas with me. I only needed to ask him one question about any topic and he would spend the next three or four hours moving from one issue to another, expressing compelling views on various subjects and a deep knowledge of life in Cairo in general and his neighborhood in particular.

As a husband, Abu Hosni was strict with his wife, expecting her to comply with his requests, attend to their apartment, and look after the children. He discouraged her visits to neighbors and family members. His children also feared him because he monitored their activities and sometimes resorted to violence to impose his will on them. I remember him once severely beating his older son, who was in his early twenties at the time, because he refused to agree to Abu Hosni's plan for him to propose to his cousin (Abu Hosni's brother's daughter). Hosni was in love with another woman and was trying to enlist his mother's support in front of his father. After several verbal disagreements, Abu Hosni was so outraged by his son's insistence that he attacked him and had already bloodied his face when the neighbors managed to pull them apart. But most of the time, Abu Hosni was deeply invested in the education of his children and expressed tremendous pride in his two younger sons, who were able to earn college degrees.

When I visited them in 1997, Abu Hosni and his wife talked about the beginning of his recent serious illness.[15] One day a few months earlier, he had not been feeling well at work so he returned home earlier than expected. Unfortunately, his wife, who often served as a buffer between Hosni and his father, was out on a group trip to the beach, so he instructed his older son to stay home until he returned from the doctor's office.[16] When the father returned, he discovered that Hosni had defied his explicit instructions, a habit that had long caused confrontation in their relationship. Abu Hosni became enraged and almost fainted.[17] He had to be taken to the doctor again, who informed him that his blood pressure had skyrocketed and that he had nearly had a stroke. He recommended that Abu Hosni rest at home for a few days to recover, but the dedicated worker and father would not hear of it. His wife commented on his unwillingness to quit smoking, which the doctor strongly recommended, or to take any time off from work. They were married for twenty-seven years, she teasingly said, yet he never took her to the beach or on a casual outing. He responded by stressing that he would rather work overtime and earn more money to support and educate his children than waste his time on vacations or outings.

As well as refusing to take time off, Abu Hosni stubbornly refused to change his diet. To help him comply with the doctor's instructions, his wife tried to serve him foods to control his blood pressure and diabetes. Like most people in al-Zawiya, Abu Hosni strongly preferred fatty, salty, and sugary foods. This parallels what Bourdieu described in his discussion of the French working class, who also had a strong "preference" for fatty and salty foods, which are cheaper and more filling than other types. Bourdieu viewed such preferences as representing "the taste of necessity" because they are structured by the limited economic and cultural resources available to the working class.[18] Although they are defined by one's class positionality, they are usually accepted as mere preferences and voluntary choices. Because they are deeply internalized and embodied by social agents, they become very difficult to question or transform. Thus, when Umm Hosni encouraged her husband to eat the things the doctor recommended, Abu Hosni strongly resisted the idea, suggesting that she was trying to control him and expose his physical vulnerabilities to others. He rejected her attempts to offer him alternative foods and found the low-fat, low-sodium dishes she prepared tasteless. When his wife tried to limit his access to unhealthy foods, he insulted her and yelled that she had not paid for the food and had no right to deprive him of his favorite dishes. Even when he tried, it was very difficult for him to change his tastes and adjust to new ways of eating. At the same time, his long work hours made it difficult to control and regulate his blood sugar so he had to rely heavily on medication. Both the nature of Abu Hosni's work and his tastes, a "forced choice," to use Bourdieu's phrase, structured by his class positionality as well as his understanding of his status as a man complicated the attempts of his family to help him alter his practices and contributed to the worsening of his sickness.

Each time I saw him after that, Abu Hosni's health had further declined, but nothing prepared me for his condition in the summer of 2005. When his wife opened the door to welcome me after one year of absence,

I was shocked to see a frail man who could not stand on his own for more than a few seconds and who soon started crying, something that I had never seen him do before and never expected to see. Controlling one's emotions is an important part of the construction of masculinity in al-Zawiya. The display of certain emotions such as rage and anger are expected and accepted of men, but other emotions, especially sadness and sorrow, are expected to be kept under control. The tears of men are precious and are reserved for extraordinary events, and those instances of crying are recalled as evidence that signifies the magnitude of the loss and depth of feelings experienced at those moments. As I mentioned in Chapter 1, young boys are explicitly taught about the need to control their emotional reactions and limit their crying. Abu Hosni in particular was a very proud man who never showed any signs of "weakness," so seeing him cry was more than I could endure.[19] I also broke into tears and both of us sobbed as his wife informed me that Abu Hosni had a stroke, which left him unable to walk properly and limited his ability to speak. She explained that because of the stroke, he had to retire at the age of fifty-eight, earlier than expected, which broke his heart.

Over the next five years, despite his stopping smoking and his wife and sons taking him to good doctors, making sure he had all the required tests and X-rays, and bringing him needed medicine, Abu Hosni's health worsened rapidly. His wife thought a major part of his condition was "psychological" because he felt "sorry" for himself. He was heartbroken because he lost the job that was a source of great power for him, and because he was not allowed to drive anymore, he could not go to many of the places he loved (especially his home village). Concurrently, his physical mobility became limited and he required assistance in order to visit nearby friends and relatives, frequent local mosques to pray and socialize with others, or simply sit in front of an adjacent shop to observe passersby.

Unfortunately, soon after that, Abu Hosni fell in the bathroom that his family had shared with another family for more than thirty years.[20] He broke his femur and, because of his diabetes, the doctors decided not to operate on him (other doctors later said this was a grave mistake). He was put in cast for almost four months. When I saw him in the summer of 2008, he had lost a lot of weight, had no teeth, and had gone totally bald.

Now tiny and feeble, he could not even stand to greet me. He seemed to be in constant pain and screamed whenever his wife turned him from one side to the other or helped him sit up. When the doctors removed the cast, which had to be reapplied twice because of a medical error, they found that his healing leg was 6 cm shorter than the other leg. This, combined with his stroke, left him unable to move at all without help. Even sitting up in bed demanded the assistance of his wife or children and, by the time I saw him in the summer of 2010, Abu Hosni was not able to have an intelligible conversation and had become entirely immobile. His wife explained, "He is like a child" (zai el-'ayyil), one who had lost control over his bodily functions,[21] cried most of the time, and did not want her to leave his side even for few minutes. She told me, "He clings to everything" (bi-yishbbat fi kul haaga), a phrase that is usually used to describe children and their inability to control their passions and needs. His sons came regularly to help bathe him, shave his beard, and carry him up and down the stairs when needed (such as for visits to the doctor's office) while his wife fed him and took care of all his daily needs. This immobility became detrimental to his health and social relationships, which became limited to his immediate family.

When he became sick, Abu Hosni became the object of the medical gaze: his body was examined, x-rayed, monitored, and medicalized. His family invested money, time, and energy in taking good care of him. Rather than healing him, his interaction with the medical system seemed to have contributed to the decline of his health. His wife blamed much of this on the mistakes the doctors made such as when they did not operate on his femur and then the mistake of casting his leg in a way that made it shrink. Such lack of accountability on the part of the doctors has led to major health risks and permanent damage to other people in al-Zawiya and similar low-income neighborhoods. Mild examples include extracting a healthy tooth instead of a decaying one, giving the wrong medicine, and casting the wrong limb. In extreme cases, as well reported in Egyptian media, doctors left instruments (such as small scissors) or pieces of cloth or cotton in the body of a patient during surgery, stitched the cut incorrectly, or removed the wrong organ. Yet there are no accessible and effective mechanisms for people either to hold medical professionals liable or to get adequate compensation for their injuries. To be fair, it is important to note here that many doctors work under very difficult conditions, especially in the crowded, understaffed, and underfunded government hospitals and clinics. I visited a few public hospitals and was struck by the terrible conditions under which (mainly poor working-class) patients received treatment. Yet glaring mistakes also happen in private practice, where people pay a lot of money to make sure they and their families get adequate health care. Under these circumstances, families are often left to shoulder the burden of caring for their loved ones. Over the period of my fieldwork, I have been impressed by the amount of medical knowledge many people, especially women, accumulate and how they become key mediators between doctors and their sick relatives.

Changing Relationships

Over time, I saw Abu Hosni's relationships with his wife and children change dramatically. He went from being a strong, assertive, and demanding husband and father to becoming totally dependent on his family. Umm Hosni recalled how, in earlier years, she often dreaded his return home and described how her legs would wobble when she heard his footsteps coming up the stairs before she was done making his meal or tidying up the apartment. He would often yell at her and sometimes hit her when she did not abide by his wishes. With his sickness, she became much more mobile than he and became his main caregiver. But most important, Umm Hosni, who was previously silenced by her husband, eventually became his tongue. Because the stroke left his spoken words intangible, she became a "translator" for him. She also spoke for him, describing his condition, the medications he was taking, and his reactions to the visits of his children and grandchildren. She herself saw the irony in how things had changed and reminded me of the times when she would not be able to say anything. Whenever I visited and he was at home, Abu Hosni would sit talking to me for hours without giving Umm Hosni the chance to participate in our conversations. He would make fun of any comments she tried to interject and would often quiet her by asking for more tea or coffee. She half-jokingly told me that after his sickness, she was making up for the years she was silenced by talking on his behalf and hers and freely expressing her own feelings and views.

Similarly, Abu Hosni's relationship with his sons changed greatly after his sickness. In addition to his inability to impose his wishes on his children, he became dependent on them and their support. I was interested to note how, over time, the third oldest son, Yassir, who held a college degree and worked for a big pharmaceutical company, became the most influential person in the family. Unlike his two older brothers, neither of whom had a college degree, and unlike his younger brother, who had a college degree but lacked the social skills that could facilitate his interaction with others, Yassir had both the cultural capital and social competencies that enabled him to become an effective interlocutor with the Egyptian bureaucracy and the medical institution. Because of his education and thoughtful ways of interacting with others, he managed to marry a nice and educated woman, acquire a beautiful and spacious apartment in another area, on the outskirts of Cairo, buy a fine car, and start a small workshop in al-Zawiya to supplement his income. Both his material and cultural capital have added to his standing in his family, and his mother does not stop talking about his success and numerous achievements. With this success, Yassir acquired symbolic capital that was reflected in his relationship with both parents, especially his father. For example, the father and son developed a warm joking relationship that did not exist with the other sons. Simultaneously, his car enabled Yassir to take his father to medical appointments and his work in the pharmaceutical industry gave him medical knowledge that his father respected. Over time, Yassir became the only one who could exert any pressure on his father and persuade him to abide by the instructions of the doctors and refrain from bad habits such as smoking.

Sickness thus rearranged relationships that connected Abu Hosni to his family and the community. He shifted from being a feared and assertive man to being a child who had to be fed, cleaned, dressed, and moved around. Originally enjoying freedom of mobility enabled by his driving skills and gender, he became totally immobile and limited to his home. No longer able to visit others, including people in his home village, he also was rarely visited by others. Most of his friends, his wife told me, either had died or were unable to move around. The decline in his health altered the materiality of his body, its ability to produce, move, and communicate and transformed his social stance as a man. When I saw him last in the summer of 2010, I was not sure I would see him again. Sure enough, when I called in early 2011 to check on him and his family, his wife told me that Abu Hosni had died two weeks before my call. She tried to make me feel better about his death by saying that he finally rested in peace (*irtah*) because he had been in great pain. With all the suffering that he had to endure during the last couple of years of his life, his death was largely seen as an honor granted to him by God (*rabina karamuh*) to end his suffering.

Death without Aging

Unlike the gradual sickness and death of Abu Hosni, the death of Karim was sudden. Whereas Abu Hosni saw his four sons married and fathers of happy and healthy children, Karim left two little children, without even having the chance to see one of them. Unlike the death of Abu Hosni, which was quickly accepted as an ending to his pain and suffering, Karim's death was unexpected and generated rich narratives that connected his life, death, and status in the afterlife. The rest of this chapter looks at these accounts and how they depicted his death and related it to his deeds, relationships, and conduct as a good man.

Although I do not have the statistics to support this claim, my sense is that more young men than young women die in al-Zawiya.[22] Partially the outcome of their work, partially related to their freedom of mobility, and partially the product of the norms that equate manhood with risk-taking, more young men end up suffering fatal accidents than young women.[23] Such instances include the electrocution of a young electrician who left his wife pregnant with their first child, the drowning of a 20-year-old soldier who took a dip in the Nile to cool down on his way home, the college student who was hit by a train when trying to cross the railroad tracks, and the stabbing of a man who tried to break up a fight. There were also other stories about young men who got sick or who just suddenly died while waiting for a cup of tea or chatting with their friends or relatives. As has been well documented by many anthropologists, death is not just a biological event but also a social fact that is culturally and religiously elaborated and interpreted within specific structures and systems of meaning.[24] Perhaps because these deaths are unexpected and tragic, because young men are equated with strength and endurance, and because male death generates significant socioeconomic rearrangements of households, sources of income, and relationships between families, deaths of young men usually evoke a series of vivid accounts that seek to contextualize and relate them to religious discourses, cultural meanings, and social ideals. Unlike the deaths of older men like Abu Hosni, which are mourned but quickly accepted as part of the natural order of things and God's will, rich narratives forcefully relate the life of the young deceased to the nature of his death and expected status in the afterlife.

These narratives are contextualized by religious discourses that view the increasing number of such deaths as *aaya sughra*, a minor sign that the Day of Judgment is approaching. Different sheikhs draw on the death of individuals in their prime of life to emphasize the fragility of human life, the universality and inevitability of death, the need to prepare for it from an early age, and the necessity of redefining widespread but not properly Islamic views of death, mourning, grieving, burial traditions, and paying condolences. Through these accounts, they work on people's feelings and cultivate a sense of morality that should govern the daily life of young men and women. They emphasize the notion of a "good ending" (*husn el-khaatimah*) as something to aspire to and work toward. They offer advice on how to attain that ending and elaborate greatly on the rewards awaiting those with good endings both in the grave and the afterlife. They also warn of a "bad ending" (*sua' el-khaatimah*) and vividly describe the torture and horror associated with it. Through defining the meaning of good and bad endings, a plurality of religious authorities tries to regulate and shape the most minute and mundane aspects of daily life as well as the emotional dispositions linked to life and death.

Family members, relatives, and friends draw on such religious discourses as well as social ideals to construct narratives that clearly link the life of the departed with his good ending. In this context, the life the deceased had led in addition to the timing and nature of his death, the place of burial, and testimonies by people who attend the washing, praying, carrying, and burying are all important in authenticating a good death. Just as the meaning of a proper man is defined by both the conduct of the person and the recognition of others, a good ending is also largely defined by the deeds of the man and the judgments, testimonies, and words of his family, friends, and community members. I will further explore these themes by focusing on Karim's death, the discourses that were circulated around his life and death, and the bodily signs that were seen as indicators of the good nature of his death. As was emphasized by his relatives, even total strangers marveled at the auspicious timing of his death and the distinguished site of his burial. Because she was wearing black, a sign of mourning, at a young age, people were often curious and asked Karim's wife directly about the reason for her mourning. As his wife said, she hardly opens her mouth and tells people, be it in the post office, the mosque, the school, or on the bus, about her husband's death, when they tell her: "What a lucky man! We wish we could have that kind of death." What made his death good? How does his death and its narrations help us understand the relationship between the materiality of the body and masculine trajectories? How does his death and status in the afterlife relate to his standing as a man in this life?

Before I address these questions, it is important to note that the notion of "good death" also exists in other societies. In some places, it could mean death "when a person has completed the life cycle, in old age," a quick and painless death, or one that gives the person the chance to prepare for his death (as was the case in Medieval Europe).[25] In other places, such as Japan, death in old age (especially when one is sleeping) and dying without causing difficulty for others is considered good, natural, or peaceful.[26] Among British Hindus, death "should be entered voluntarily and peacefully; in a sense it should be 'willed,'" and passing away while chanting the name of the God Ram is considered a good death.[27] These meanings shift over time. For example, historians have shown that "'good death' in contemporary America, that is, to die in one's sleep without suffering or awareness of dying, was precisely the 'accused death' of the Middle Ages because it did not allow one to contemplate and prepare for death."[28] Thus, any meaning of death is contextualized by specific social, religious, and economic discourses that are important to keep in mind.

The following sections offer a thick description of Karim's death and explore the deeds and signs that people pointed to as signaling his good ending. My discussion draws on conversations with Karim before his death and with his wife, mother, father, siblings, and in-laws before and after his death. These conversations took place both in al-Zawiya and Upper Egypt. I frame my discussion of his life and death with my broader ethnographic knowledge of masculinity, health, death, and embodiment.

From Village to City

Karim was born to a family that lived in a little village overlooking the Nile in Upper Egypt. He was one of eight children, five boys and three girls. Compared to his other brothers, he received very little education. All the other four male siblings managed to receive degrees from al-Azhar University and three of them are currently teachers in or around their village. But Karim, it seems, was not interested in going to school. Most likely because he was picked on by his teacher, who beat him severely on several occasions, Karim left school after only three years to work with his father farming their land.[29] At the age of fifteen or so, he traveled from Upper Egypt to Cairo to work with a relative who owned a construction business. Karim learned the art of and then became a master of plastering. He worked in Cairo for over ten years and his life changed dramatically when, in 1994, his family found a man willing (for a substantial amount of money) to help him travel to Saudi Arabia. Karim's remittances helped his family build a big house and contributed to the improvement of their living conditions. His parents always (before and after his death) spoke of their appreciation for his hard work and willingness to share his income with them and his siblings. In 1997, he proposed to my friend Hiba, who lived with her family in al-Zawiya. They were married in just a couple of weeks, an anomaly at the time. Most young men and women had (and still have) to wait for several years after their engagement before managing to get married and starting their life together. In the case of Karim, his work in Saudi Arabia allowed him to build an apartment in Upper Egypt and save enough money to pay for the furniture and the wedding expenses. Hiba also had her share of what was required for marriage. Like most young women in al-Zawiya, Hiba and her family started accumulating her trousseau when she was very young. She worked for three years in a sewing factory to save enough money to cover the expenses of the living-room furniture, kitchen appliances, carpets, and curtains she was expected to bring to her future home.

Hiba and Karim tried to conceive a child during the first few months of their marriage but did not succeed. After three years of marriage and two returns home on the part of Karim, Hiba became pregnant. Karim went back to Saudi Arabia before the birth of his first child, a boy they named Ahmed, whose boyhood was the focus of Chapter 1. When Karim was in Saudi Arabia, Hiba usually stayed with her family in Cairo, but they would pass most of the months Karim spent in Egypt in their apartment in his village in Upper Egypt. On his last trip to Egypt, Hiba became pregnant again. Karim was in Saudi Arabia when his second baby was born. He heard of the birth of his daughter over the phone but never saw her. Five months after her birth, Karim fell ill and died suddenly in a hospital in Saudi Arabia. It is important to note that unlike the tendency in the West to attach a specific cause for each death, a step that aims to distance death from the self,[30] the cause of death is not the main concern for people in al-Zawiya. In fact, many people are hesitant about allowing autopsies of loved ones so that they can avoid the desecration of the body. Unless clear circumstances indicate foul play and an autopsy is required by law, most families tend to privilege the integrity of the body and dignity of the dead over the certainty of knowing the cause of death. Thus, neither Hiba nor Karim's family had specific ideas about the cause of his death but I had the chance to look at his death certificate, which was issued by the Saudi authorities and stated that he could not breathe and that his heart had stopped working.

Choices of Necessity

According to his family, soon after he started working abroad Karim developed an allergy that compromised his respiratory system. His family now believes that it was his work that caused the allergy. One of his brothers, Saed, who could last only a short time doing that type of work, described the year he spent with Karim in Saudi Arabia in 1995. While praising the endurance of his brother, Saed's description indirectly blamed Karim for sacrificing his body and health for the sake of money.[31] Saed spoke of the horrible wells and storage tanks—very dark and hot— that they had to clean and plaster. "You could only spend a few minutes down there" he said, "and then you had to get out to squeeze the sweat out of your shirt, change to a dry one, and get a breath of air before diving back inside." On top of all of this, the tanks were infested with insects and contained chemicals that made the smell incredibly difficult to stomach. While this was just one example of the things he did, everybody knew that Karim worked as hard as he could and that he lived under difficult conditions to be able to save as much money as possible and support his family at home. In addition, operating under the full control of Saudi sponsors and clients who occasionally denied them payments or refused to pay them in a timely manner, and lacking any legal support or representation, workers like Karim live in crowded places and budget their spending to save as much as possible. The pressure, demands, and expectations Karim faced are common and part of the life of most Egyptian working-class men at home and abroad.

For working-class men like Karim, the "body is a means to an end."[32] Its main use is in labor, which is needed to provide for one's family and children. As discussed earlier, those who cannot travel abroad may work at several jobs to earn enough money for their families. Many work for long hours and under unsafe and harsh conditions. So key is the relationship between well-being and labor that people tend to measure good health by the ability to go out to work. For example, when a sick man recovers from an illness, family members verify that by saying that "he went to work" (*nizil el-shughul*). Similarly, when checking on the full recovery of a man, people ask "Did he go to work?" (*Huwwa nizil el-shughul?*). Simultaneously, a masculine identification in a working-class context is strongly tied to the control that a man exerts over his body and its needs. Enduring pain, controlling one's feelings (especially of sadness), overlooking minor health problems, and working hard even when one is sick are expected from men. As argued by Kamran Ali in his study of family planning, men often believed that they "did not themselves need medical advice. It was only the weak, or more, precisely the women and children, who needed to be helped and protected."[33] This view resonated with those I heard in al-Zawiya about a cohort of young men, but by the age of fifty, most men, like Abu Hosni, suffer from serious health problems such as high blood pressure, diabetes, and heart problems, and become the subject of the medical gaze and the center of attention of their families.

A worker uses an open fire to glue the heel of a shoe in a local workshop. A lack of safety measures often leaves workers with burns and injuries that could affect their health and livelihood.

Like Abu Hosni, Karim visited several doctors in Egypt and most of them said he should not be in contact with dust, cement, sand, and all the other basic materials that were central to his work. But that did not stop him. His decision was not solely the product of his masculine identification but of his class positionality as well. In other cases, some men managed to shift their jobs depending on their skills. For example, Mohi stopped his work in plastering at the age of twenty-seven when he was diagnosed with diabetes. He worked as a taxi driver for twenty years. When at the age of forty-seven he lost the sight of one of his eyes because of diabetes complications, his extended family and wife helped him to start a modest fruit stand in the neighborhood. Even if Mohi does not make any money, his family reasoned that the stand will keep him occupied and distract him from his sickness. In the case of Karim, without the cultural capital his brothers had accumulated and without any other skills that could help him quickly and efficiently make the money his family needed, he had little choice but to resume the work that was harming his health. Despite several episodes of allergic attacks and reactions to medicines (including to a wrong medicine given by a doctor), which caused him to stop breathing and nearly killed him, Karim continued (with the help of various medicines) to work in Saudi Arabia. Seeing how much he was suffering, his wife and his parents urged him not to travel again, but he refused and promised that he would stop working abroad after saving enough to start a small business in Cairo.

During his last two trips, his youngest brother, Nadim, who holds a bachelor's degree in religious studies but had wanted to learn his brother's trade in order to save money, accompanied him to Saudi Arabia. Nadim was therefore present when Karim died. As a result of these last trips, Karim saved money to start building a house for his nuclear family in Cairo (a condition his wife's family insisted on before they agreed to his marriage proposal) but he still wanted to save money to open a small business (a bakery). He was hoping to establish himself in Cairo not only to satisfy Hiba and her family but also to reinforce his status as a provider and to signal his social mobility. With the help of his wife, Karim managed to purchase a piece of land on the outskirts of Cairo and started (but never finished) building their future home.

Signs of Good Endings

Karim's hard work, the reason for his travel, the place of his death, the site of his burial, and the testimonies about his life and death became significant parts of the accounts that circulated about his untimely death and its good nature. To start with, people (including his brother Nadim) who were with Karim vividly described his last day of life to his family. A couple of other men from their village happened to be with Karim in Saudi Arabia when he got sick. These men became witnesses whose testimonies underlay Karim's family's narratives about his death. These accounts emphasized his physical appearance before and after death and how they, from the very beginning, signaled his good ending. The case of Karim reveals the significance of the materiality of the body both in life and death. The body, which enabled him to labor, provide, go to the mosque, pray, perform the hajj, father children, and interact with others became also the medium that enabled others to attach specific meanings to his death and relate it to his conduct. Just as appearances play a role in defining a good man, a potential husband, or a decent citizen, as argued in the preceding chapters, the materiality of the body and its appearance also play a role in the construction of a good ending. In both cases, the eye of others is important in evaluating, recognizing, and attaching meanings to bodily hexis.

Early the evening he died, Karim took a bath and wore a new white *gallabia* (long loose dress), both indicators of cleanliness and purity (*tahara*). The description of those who were with him focuses on the beauty of his face, which was white and round, both desirable qualities in life and death. One man jokingly teased Karim, saying "By God, you look more handsome than my own wife." However, Karim refused to join the group of men for dinner and later that night told his brother that he felt unwell. Karim urged Nadim to look after their parents and his wife and children, indicating that he knew his death was imminent. Both his appearance and this knowledge of his looming death were significant because they showed his deep faith and closeness to God. According to witnesses and the interpretations of his family, his closeness to God made his face glow because he was provided with insights that enabled him to foresee his own death. Nadim teased him and tried to change the subject, but around midnight Karim asked his brother to take him to the hospital. Nadim was asked to leave Karim there and go back home. When Nadim went back to see his brother in the morning, he was told that Karim had died at 4 am.

This was a major tragedy for Karim's family. Nadim called one of his brothers, a teacher in a nearby village, and the news soon spread. Karim's brothers called relatives in other parts of Egypt and mourners came from many villages and cities. Hiba immediately traveled with her family from Cairo to Karim's village in Upper Egypt. Their sadness and sorrow was tremendous. While their grief and elaborate mourning are beyond the scope of this chapter,[34] I would like to concentrate on how some of the events surrounding Karim's death soon became the source of rich narratives that effectively highlighted the *karamat* (honors) that God granted him and reflected his good ending. In particular, testimonies about his death crossed national borders and circulated in several places, especially his village in Upper Egypt and al-Zawiya, and were quickly incorporated in the accounts that depicted his good death.

The timing of Karim's death and location of his burial in Saudi Arabia became especially significant. His wife, parents, and other relatives point out that he died just a few days after performing the hajj and only a couple of months after performing the *ummra*, an abbreviated form of the pilgrimage ceremonies that, if conducted during Ramadan (as was the case with Karim), becomes equivalent to a regular hajj. This accomplishment is important because, for many Muslims, performing the pilgrimage serves as a rebirth and cleanses the individual of all his or her sins, so everybody thought that Karim died sinless. He also died Thursday morning and was buried late Thursday evening, an auspicious time for most Muslims. A young boy who died that day was also buried in the same grave with Karim (his mother and wife said literally that he took him in his arms).[35] Both of these facts, as explained by his wife and mother, meant that Karim would be saved from the torture of the grave.[36]

The people who attended Karim's washing (*ghusul*) emphasized that his face was very beautiful, glowing with a special light (*nour*) and a big smile. Such signs in his appearance indicated that he was eager to be buried. This eagerness is usually read as a reflection of a believer's positive attitude toward death and signals a sense of security about meeting God. It suggests that the believer did all he could to satisfy God and had no fears of facing him. If one has a good ending, and to relieve any sense of anxiety, the angels immediately give dead believers a glimpse of the wonderful things that await them in the grave and afterlife. This knowledge is reflected in signs such as a smiling face, an easy ride to the cemetery, and a quick burial. Some of those who attended Karim's funeral swore to the family that they could see light shining out of the grave and could smell the strong aroma of henna and perfume emanating from the grave while they were burying him. These signs implied that his grave was going to be a paradise and not a hell.

Another positive indication of his good death was his speedy burial. His paperwork was handled by the Saudi bureaucracy on the same day, a miracle says his young niece, because it usually takes days, even weeks, before such papers are completed and the burial is authorized.[37] Several traditions of the Prophet emphasize the need to bury the corpse as quickly as possible. One of these traditions, often heard in mosques and repeated by people in other contexts, states: "Bury the dead very quickly. If the deceased was good, then you are doing him a favor. If the person was bad, then you are ridding the community of an evil." Other traditions state that the dead person sees what fortune awaits and manages to either hurry up or slow down the procession based on what he or she sees, so a prompt burial is a good indicator of the deceased's prospects. Before the burial, the departed is in a state of liminality:[38] neither here nor there, neither part of the living nor part of the dead. While the deceased is not able to react to the living, he or she is still thought to be able to hear and feel them. The deceased is washed, managed, and carried by others, yet is able to direct their acts according to his or her wishes. I have heard several stories about a corpse refusing to move until a loved one arrived to witness the burial, or until disagreements between family members were worked out, or until the wishes of the deceased about the burial place or process were respected. A speedy burial, like Karim's, indicates that the deceased knows that good things await in the grave and afterlife.[39]

In addition, thousands of people prayed over Karim's body, another significant sign because the more prayers there are, the more *sai'at*, or bad deeds, are removed from one's history.[40] Several sayings of the Prophet, which were repeated by Karim's family as well as in lessons by preachers on satellite TV channels, emphasize that if a certain number of people (the numbers vary, but forty and one hundred were mentioned by different sheikhs) pray over the corpse, the person will be admitted to paradise.[41] Similarly, testimonies by neighbors and community members (about his or her good manners, willingness to help, readiness to support, and generous giving) are believed to help credit the dead with extra good deeds and eventually contribute to securing a place in heaven. These connections between the living and the dead, as will be addressed below, were significant and continue to shape both sides over time.

Unlike labor migrants who die abroad and who have to be taken back home, Karim was buried in al-Baqia' in al-Medina al-Mounwara in Saudi Arabia, one of the holiest Muslim sites. It is the burial place of the Prophet and many of his companions. Nadim made a point to assure his family that Karim was buried very close to where the Prophet's wet nurse was buried. This place of burial is itself the source of great distinction and religious value. The location acquires even more significance when we know that Karim died a few days after a highly publicized accident of a ferry headed from Saudi Arabia to Egypt carrying thousands of labor migrants and their families.[42] Many parents and relatives, as Karim's wife and mother said, did not even have a body to bury, which for them is a double tragedy. Even though Karim's family did not have a body to bury in Egypt either, they did have the testimonies of Nadim and other men present at Karim's burial. These statements became especially valuable in verifying the proper management of the body, the renowned burial location, and the bodily signs that reflected that his was a good death.

Good Death and the End of the Body

These signs of his good ending were closely related to Karim's deeds during his life. His good qualities as a man, husband, father, son, and neighbor were repeatedly articulated: He respected and cared for his parents. He provided for his children and loved his wife. He never denied his siblings anything. He was kind to his sisters-in-law. He was nice to his neighbors and helped them with their chores. He visited sick relatives and friends.[43] His piety and devotion to God were also emphasized: He prayed on regular basis. He fasted. He performed the hajj several times. He volunteered his labor to renovate the village's mosque. He provided the money needed to buy the loudspeakers for the mosque. Such deeds and memories are important to making and remaking his biographical narrative in order to highlight how his good work was linked to his good death and expected status in the afterlife. He was celebrated not only as a *proper man* but also as a *good Muslim man* who provided, protected, cared, supported, and worshiped. While these two categories often overlap, they are not the same. There are men who are socially viewed as real men but who are not devout or religiously pious, and there are men who are pious but who are seen as lacking some important characteristics (such as courage, providing, or generosity) that define them as gid'aan. In Karim's case, he was seen as both. He consolidated a legitimate masculine trajectory in this life and pursued a pious path that would secure him a good death and a place in paradise in the afterlife. This ideal combination demonstrates that religion is another structural factor that intersects with gender and class in shaping a man's life and death.

Although a person is fundamentally responsible for his own deeds and status after death, it is important to note that his relationship to his family and the community defines part of his status in the grave and afterlife. This relationship does not end with his death. Rather, his status and God's evaluation of his deeds continue to be shaped by his family's and friends' prayers, testimonies, tears, and charitable acts (such as assistance to the poor and donations to build a mosque). In addition to offering the deceased forgiveness for any mistakes committed during his life, family members pay his debts to make sure he rests in peace. In other cases, one can even perform the hajj on behalf of a deceased relative who did not have the time to do so before dying. Moreover, the accounts reiterated by the deceased's family and neighbors are performative in that they (at least partially) create what they describe.

In repeating testimonies about his death, emphasizing his good deeds and his religious devotion, Karim's family and friends were in fact making his death "good" and were contributing to how God would judge him. This performative aspect was emphasized by several sheikhs, who argued on audiotapes, TV programs, and in local mosques that the Prophet emphasized that positive testimonies by neighbors and community members play an important role in God's eventual judgment of the dead. Just as one's status as a real or proper man is collectively produced, his good ending is also collectively defined and shaped. Here we do not see death as the end of an autonomous, independent self that is attached to a clearly defined body, as is the case in most Western societies.[44] Rather the dead, especially if he was a good man, continues to be connected to the living. This connection is cultivated and maintained by family members. Hiba, for example, makes a point of encouraging her children to remember their father and to regularly pray that God blesses Karim's soul and grants him access to paradise. She also makes sure to deposit a few coins on behalf of her deceased husband each time she passes by a mosque with a box for donations either to renovate the mosque or to help the needy. This relationship is not one-dimensional (i.e., it is not only the living who can pray, offer testimonies, contribute to charity, fast, cry, and perform the hajj on behalf of the deceased); the deceased also maintains a presence in the life of his loved ones. This is done not only through the stories people retell about him and his deeds, the mourning practices of family members, and one's children who carry his name and help remember him. But there are also other social mediums that keep the dead connected to his family and community members. Through dreams, for example, the deceased could communicate good and bad news, offer advice, make requests, name babies, predict important events, and comfort loved ones. Karim's older sister told us of a dream in which she saw him dressed in a light-colored robe with a glowing face telling her about a feast he was going to have for his family. When she woke up, she felt as happy as if he were still living. Through such means and through the efforts of relatives and friends, the dead and the living continue to be connected and inform each other's practices and standings.

Culture of Death?

The notion of good ending became clearly articulated during the recent Egyptian revolution. Even though the protests were largely peaceful, hundreds of men and women lost their lives and many more were injured. News stories confirm that no less than thirteen men and one woman from al-Zawiya (most of them between the ages of eighteen and thirty) were killed during the first few days of the protests.[45] According to national media, the police or baltagiyya killed these innocent victims as they were trying to aid or defend their families and neighbors. They were seen as martyrs and their good endings were clearly stressed in descriptions of the moments preceding their deaths.[46] Adil Saleh, for example, was described as a 23-year-old man who was the only provider for his widowed mother and sisters. On January 28, he went out to perform the evening prayer and was gunned down as he left the mosque. Both the endeavor and the space of his death show his piety and signal his good ending. A 29-year-old man, described as an orphan, who heard that his younger brother was shot in the leg quickly ran to take him to the hospital, but four bullets ended his life. This man died while materializing the norms that equate manhood with caring and protecting. A 51-year-old bus driver, who was the only provider for his wife and daughters, was killed while helping a peddler collect orange boxes that spilled in the street. That these two men died doing good deeds indicated their good ending. Another man, age twenty-five, who was to be married in a few weeks, was hit by a bullet as he was helping transport the injured and protecting women and children from baltagiyya. He represented the ethos of gada'na discussed in Chapter 4 and died while doing good deeds, which is expected to be greatly rewarded by God. That all the victims died while trying to be good men by helping others, protecting their families, providing for their children, securing their neighborhood, or performing their religious duties are all indicators of their qualities as good men and positive status as martyrs. When the protestors chanted in the streets, especially after the death of over seventy young men in the city of Port Said, "Raagil fi hayaatu, shaheed fi mamaatu," they were highlighting this exact relationship between being a good man and deserving a good death.

The death of both Abu Hosni and Karim were strongly linked to their class and gendered positionalities. Yet, there were marked differences in the social, religious, and cultural meanings invested in each death. Abu Hosni raised his children until they became grown men, got sick for an extended period, became immobile, and slowly died. His death was mourned but largely viewed as part of the natural order of things and as ending to his suffering. Karim, however, died suddenly and left a young family behind. He was deeply mourned and his death vividly discussed, elaborated, and narrated to highlight and constitute it as good and honorable. This prevalent and public presence of death in daily life and the notion of good death in Egypt may contradict some Western sensibilities. Death in Western societies has moved away from being a social event, when family members, friends, and neighbors participated in taking care of the dying and managing the corpse, to it becoming hidden and relegated to specific and isolated spaces such as hospital rooms and hospices.[47] Death is often viewed as a crisis, an end to the self, a violation of the norms that emphasize youthfulness, productivity, and "collective happiness."[48] Scholars have shown how a complex set of economic and social factors have led to intensifying the fear of death in Western societies, which in turn has led to the growing "bureaucratization of death" and "the loneliness . . . of the dying."[49] As argued by Philippe Ariès, "Death, so omnipresent in the past that it was familiar, would be effaced, would disappear. It would become shameful and forbidden."[50] It "is no longer seen as natural or beautiful or socially significant. On the contrary, it became dirty and medicalized. The dying person is expected to die 'out of sight' in a hospital."[51]

In such a context, one may be tempted to understand the Egyptian notion of good ending as a negation of life, a sign of fatalism and irrationality, a call for people to value only the afterlife and ignore the current one. As argued by Charles Hirschkind, for "many in the West today, Muslim discourses on death are taken as evidence of a diseased culture, one frequently epitomized in the figure of the suicide bomber."[52] Yet this simplistic and hasty conclusion does not capture how the notion of good death establishes a strong relationship between this life and the afterlife, between one's religious devotion and engagement with the community, and between one's deeds and intentions. Such a view also misses the continuous contestation, argumentation, and struggle over the definition and appropriation of religious and social discourses and how they are negotiated in defining a good ending. Instead of viewing the preceding discussion as a dichotomy between "a culture of death" and "a culture of life," it would be best to see the differences as the "product of distinct sensibilities for the place and meaning of death and its structuring significance for human life."[53]

Rather than a sign of fatalism, the notion of good death is a sign of realism.[54] Instead of denying death, distancing it from the self, and turning it into a taboo that should be hidden, the meaning of the good ending highlights the fact that no one can escape death and offers ways to manage this biological, social, and religious fact. According to the people of al-Zawiya and most Muslims in other places as well, the timing, location, and cause are all predetermined by God. However, one has the ability to shape the type of life one leads and the type of death one deserves. Instead of discouraging acting in the world, as implied in discussions of fatalism, the notion of good death in fact encourages a deep ethical and practical engagement in the life of one's family and community. One's deeds in this life and devotion to religious duties as well as testimonies by family members, neighbors, and friends all shape the experience of death, burial, and the type of afterlife one can enjoy. Being a proper man in this life (through providing for one's family, participating in community life, being kind to one's neighbors, and aiding those who need help), observing one's religious duties, dying when doing the right thing, and the memories that inform people's narratives and testimonies are all important dimensions of the notion of good ending.[55]

It is important to note that people in al-Zawiya are themselves critical of any simplistic, opportunistic, deterministic, and easy road to good death. Perhaps nothing captures what I am saying here as much as an anecdote that was circulated in 2007 and that my interlocutors found very funny. It went something like this:

> A driver was driving late at night when he was stopped by a man who looked a "bit weird." The passenger sat quietly in the back seat for a while and, just before reaching a specific mosque, suddenly screamed at the driver, "Do you know who I am?" The frightened driver said, "No. Who are you?" With a deep voice and absolute authority, the man said, "I am the angel of death and I am here to seize your soul." The driver began trembling with fear and the angel told him, "I see that you are a good man and I will give you the chance to pray one last time. So go to that mosque, pray, and then come back."[56] The driver stopped the taxi and went to the mosque to pray. When he returned, both the car and the angel were gone.

Conclusion
Masculine Trajectories and National Paths

> Yet revolutions are processes and not simply events, and the
> next chapter of this story is only beginning to be written.
>
> Wael Ghonim, *Revolution 2.0*

THIS BOOK ENDS while Egypt is beginning a new era of its modern history. Since the protests of January 25, 2011, much has changed. Mubarak was found guilty of killing peaceful protestors during the revolution and was sentenced to life in prison. His two sons and several of his high-ranking officials are awaiting trial for serious charges, including financial corruption and shooting demonstrators. A constitution was redrafted and a civilian president was voted into office in June 2012.[1] The People's Assembly was elected but was dissolved by the Supreme Council of the Armed Forces in mid-2012 after the Supreme Constitutional Court argued that some elements of the election law violated the constitution.[2] The fate of this assembly is yet to be determined. Over the past two years, I have shared my interlocutors' hope for a better future, worries about the continuities inherited from the old system and the corruption that may not be easily uprooted, doubt about the possibility of real change that would transform in meaningful ways the existing system, anxieties about the deterioration in security and the increase in real and imagined crime, and great expectations about major improvements in housing, education, health care, and political transparency. But above all, ordinary citizens are enjoying a conviction that their opinions and concerns matter and should be central to how politics is done and the country is run. This conviction has been clearly articulated in daily conversations, media reports, and the many protests that continue to take place in several parts of the country.

Making Men and Building a Nation

Most of my interlocutors came to embrace the January 25 Revolution and its goals. Their reactions were framed by their socioeconomic positionality as well as their dreams and hopes for a better future. Almost everyone in al-Zawiya was aware of the brutality of the police, felt the growing pressure on men (and women) to provide for their families, encountered the state's corrupt and inefficient bureaucracy, and suffered marginalization and disempowerment under Mubarak's regime. Every time I visited al-Zawiya, living standards seemed to have further deteriorated. In addition to the chronic problems of housing, traffic, unemployment, and crumbling infrastructure, new problems were emerging and getting worse. In the summer of 2008, for example, people were bitterly complaining about a shortage of bread, increasing prices of construction materials, and lack of subsidized baby formula. By the summer of 2010, the prices of vegetables, meat, chicken, and even macaroni had increased drastically.[3] More important, my interlocutors expressed intensifying anxiety about the future of their children's education, employment, and marriageability. Over the years, I have seen growing promises of a better life stimulated by national policies and global flows of images, ideas, and products. Simultaneously, there has been a noticeable decline in the resources and opportunities that can help children acquire a good education and enable young adults to find jobs with reasonable incomes, obtain adequate apartments close to their relatives and workplaces, and establish happy and healthy families.

All this strongly resonated with the calls of the protestors for freedom and social justice. Yet people in al-Zawiya did not mechanically or uncritically embrace the activists and their calls for political and social change. As my discussion shows, to better understand the Egyptian revolution (and other revolutions, for that matter), scholars need to look closely at the overlaps, redefinitions, and contradictions between existing cultural forms, meanings, and values and emerging political projects, goals, and movements. As Raymond Williams intended with "structures of feeling,"[4] my discussion of notions such as baltaga, gadaʻna, real men, and good ending illustrates how such categories and concepts have shaped the interpretation of significant events and the shifting feelings and views of ordinary Egyptians, many of whom came to strongly support the protests. Knowing about the stigma and illegitimacy attached to acts of baltaga, I understood why people made associations between the attacks in Midan al-Tahrir and the corruption, brutality, and illegitimate violence of the government.[5] Knowing the norms that constitute the meanings of a real man and a gadaʻ, who cares, protects, and supports, I was not surprised to hear about how people came together and collaborated to protect homes, families, and property, or to learn that young men stayed up all night, equipped themselves with household weapons, and took charge of their neighborhood and its protection. This knowledge also helped me to understand how people thought about the future and the type of government they would like to see. Although Egypt, the country and the nation, has often been presented as a woman, who should be cherished, honored, and protected, I have been struck by the parallels people made between a proper government (*hukumah*) and a proper man: protection, support, and provision.[6] This association was clearly reflected in their critique of the previous government and the expectations for the new one as well as how they reimagined the role of the president, the People's Assembly, the police force, and the state more broadly. Both men and women expect the new system to care about ordinary citizens, provide job and housing opportunities, improve the educational system, ensure security, protection, and stability for all, and build a better future for the whole nation.

Looking at such categories as the real man, gadaʻ, and baltagi and how they overlap with events in various locations enables us to capture the lived sense of specific moments of political transformation and how connections established between thoughts and feelings, formed and emerging meanings, past and present experiences, and local and national struggles have been central to the inclusion of most Egyptians in the same political and moral project. Thus, the norms that define a real man, the difference between legitimate and illegitimate uses of violence, and the economic, social, and political marginalization I have described throughout the book all intersect in shaping views and reactions to political change and aspirations for a new future.

As this book has argued, socioeconomic realities are central to the making of bodies and selves. The intersection between class and gender in particular has been central to my analysis. Class, especially in the United States, is often an invisible element of social analysis. As argued by Bettie, given "the U.S. ideology of upward mobility, class is either not a present category of thought at all or is present but understood only as a difference of money and therefore as temporary."[7] In recent years, the same could be said about the Middle East, where the focus on Islam has sidelined serious discussions of socioeconomic disparities.[8]

As my ethnography has shown, one's material, cultural, and social capital are structured and in turn structure (but do not fully determine) the type of opportunities a man has, the daily struggles he engages in, the tastes and dispositions he embodies, and the type of masculine trajectories he is able to materialize. My discussion shows that we should not reify men's actions "in a concept of masculinity that then, in a circular argument, becomes the explanation (and the cause) for the behavior."[9] I agree with the authors who note the damaging aspects of some norms (such as risk-taking, smoking, and refusal to ask for early help) that mold masculine trajectories and who argue that the cultivation of a masculine identity "can be toxic" and that much of "health-damaging behavior may be symbolic, intended to signify capacities to control one's own life, to be invaluable and needless of help, and to be fearless, and hence not easily intimidated by others."[10] I found it important, though, not to rush to "pathologize masculinity as a health risk" and depict masculinity as the cause of all men's poor health.[11] Rather, we need to seriously explore the socioeconomic position of the men we study and interrogate how their location in the social space is intertwined with their embodiment. In fact, there were many moments when I was not able to separate class from gender. Are men like Karim motivated by social norms that link masculinity to providing for one's family, even at the expense of their health, or are they motivated by their class position and their desire for social mobility? Are their injuries and poor health the result of attempts to be real men or the product of a market that consumes (cheaply) certain bodies and disregards them when they age or become sick? Did Samer quit school because of masculine norms that equate manhood with productivity or because of his working-class background and immediate need for money? Are the trajectories I traced in this book related to the reproduction of gender inequalities or class hierarchies? It is unproductive to try to answer these questions by choosing one or the other because one's sense of place and location in the social space is both classed and gendered at the same time. We need to see the two as interconnected from the start and throughout the making of masculine (and feminine) subjectivities and bodies as well as the structuring of access to opportunities and resources in life.

Central to this intersection is the context of the city, which shapes in significant ways access to education, health, and entertainment services as well as economic opportunities and possibilities for consumption. As I have pointed out, urban life is key to understanding masculinity as an ongoing practical achievement. My discussion of Ahmed's childhood—how he was discursively instructed and physically taught how to cross streets, interact with sellers, visit different spaces, and understand diverse urban sounds and sights—shows the important link between the social and spatial knowledge of the city and the construction of gendered identities. One's reputation and standing as a man are linked to one's ability to know the city, enjoy its offerings, manipulate its possibilities, and avoid its risks and menaces. The potentials and restrictions, the inclusions and exclusions, and the expected and unexpected encounters embedded in city spaces, mobilities, and interactions open new ways of being and doing and pose new challenges to men and how they embody gendered norms. As my discussion reveals, the relationship with the city changes over a man's life. Young men tend to enjoy relative freedom of mobility and are encouraged to explore city spaces, enjoy urban offerings, master urban transportation systems, and learn how to handle diverse social groups. While they escape the gaze of their families and neighbors, they become subjected to the gaze of the state and its disciplinary power. While they nurture friendships and ties of solidarity with other young men, they also learn about key (particularly gender and class) inequalities that shape their practices and identities. In contrast, older men become constrained over time by the demands of their families and the requirements of work, which limit their spatial mobilities and freedom to spend money. They are expected to relate to the city as a site for accumulation of economic and social forms of capital but not as a site of leisure and entertainment. To account for the shifting relationships and contextual nature of masculinity, it is important to pay close attention to the specificity of urban life and explore how men negotiate the various spaces, audiences, and expectations that inform their subjectivities and ways of being.

Although some scholars have investigated different masculinities and tried to classify hegemonic, subordinate, complicit, protest, or marginalized masculinities,[12] I have found it more productive to closely look at specific masculine trajectories and how they have shifted over time. This approach enables us to appreciate the changing norms, the multiple contexts, diverse agents, and competing discourses that inform men's daily life and their standing as gendered subjects. My long-term fieldwork in al-Zawiya and ability to trace the important changes that men must negotiate over time has allowed me to see how specific individuals reworked their bodies and selves under a range of circumstances, in various contexts, and for several audiences. Had I told the stories of Ahmed, Zaki, Muhsen, Abu Hosni, and Samer only as they stood in 1993, when I first met them, or only as they stood in 2012, when I last saw them, my ethnography would have been linear and one-dimensional. It would have depicted a stable, complete, and secure type of identity that would not have reflected the many negotiations men engage in everyday life. Examining their masculine trajectories and how they shifted over an extended time has allowed me to capture how they have negotiated changing social expectations, economic opportunities, disciplinary systems, and consumption patterns in the making of their bodies and subjectivities.

My methodology and positionality have allowed me to trace the different agents who shape masculine trajectories. As a collective project, the study of masculinity should include not only the words and deeds of men but also the actions, instructions, and views of people around them. The role of women in the making of proper men has been especially important for me to account for and analyze. My ethnography shows that women are not merely an oppositional mirror against which men define themselves. Rather, mothers, sisters, and wives actively work to materialize the notion of real men and contribute in numerous ways to the standing of their male relatives both in private and public. It is through the interaction between men and women as well as their separation and opposition that gendered identifications are elaborated and reproduced.

Looking at how several trajectories have shifted over time reveals that, although one could argue that they have similar starting points, their directions are not clearly defined, predetermined, or guaranteed. Rather, they are shaped by the interplay between individuals' lives and experiences and many local, national, and global socioeconomic, political, and religious forces that can take men in different directions. My discussion also shows that even death does not represent a simple or clear ending point. How a young man's death is interpreted and related to his life and standing as a man and expected status after life complicates any simple way of seeing death as an end to a masculine trajectory. Contextualized by these complexities, men work and are supported by others to cultivate a sense of coherence that secures the social recognition supporting their identifications as proper men. This coherence may become more pronounced over a man's life, but it has to be fostered and produced through a continuous process of actualization of specific norms in various spatial and temporal settings.

Rather than representing distinct masculinities, the trajectories I have traced in this book are ways of materializing hegemonic norms that define a proper man. As argued by Hearn, "analysing multiple masculinities brings dangers of relativism, and infinite regress of multiple permutations."[13] This idea also implies the existence of discrete types of masculinity that can be "selected" and performed.[14] To avoid these assumptions, my analysis has aimed to maintain the strong connections, tensions, mismatches, and overlaps between a set of loosely defined social norms and enactments of manhood. I have endeavored to account for the promises and gaps between the expected and the possible, conduct and judgment, the desirable and the achieved, and the ideal and the actual. The masculine trajectories I have described show that few (if any) are able to fully exemplify the norms that define a proper man. This inability should not be viewed as failure. Rather, it is an inherent part of the social logic that sustains gender distinctions. The promise to measure up to the norm engages individuals' feelings and desires and ensures that they spend time and energy working on themselves and helping others to master norms that define the ideal man (and woman). There is a process of "normalization" that both homogenizes, hence we have the category of the "real man," and individualizes, hence we have techniques and agents who continuously observe, instruct, measure gaps, correct, and (at least occasionally) coerce men, especially boys and young men, to make sure they master certain norms and refine their conduct.[15]

This oscillation between homogenization and individualization and the central role others (especially women) play in defining and recognizing proper men leave me unconvinced of the "generalized instability" and unlimited fluidity of gender identifications emphasized by some scholars.[16] Even though recent approaches have broadened our horizon beyond the binary oppositions (body/mind, individual/society, and nature/culture) that shaped earlier approaches to gender and opened spaces for us to see competing forms of masculine identification, I believe that the number of possibilities is not infinite, especially in working-class contexts. As argued by Connell, "the idea of generalized instability of categories seems to have arisen in the global metropole, and perhaps captures something important about social life in the neoliberal rich countries."[17] One should also add that this view might be true for specific classes in neoliberal affluent societies but does not capture how gender is constructed across different national spaces and class formations. My research shows how fluidity and fixity, instability and stability, the emerging and the established, ambiguities and clarities, uncertainties and certainties all shape a masculine trajectory. Without recognizing how these contradictory tendencies coexist and how they are negotiated in daily life in various situations, we would not be able to understand how masculine identifications are produced, challenged, and legitimized. We as analysts may be eager to account for flexibility, instability, and incoherence, yet for our interlocutors a sense of coherence, stability, and continuity has to be nurtured and sustained over a masculine trajectory to secure the social recognition and credibility that define a real man. A proper man is produced through an elaborate differentiation between various modes of doing and being. Thus, our ethnographies should elaborate on the flexible as well as not-so-flexible and the durable as well as not-so-durable aspects of the construction of gendered identifications and how their interplay shapes masculine trajectories.

Writing to Humanize

Historically, gender inequalities have played an important role in legitimizing Western political and social projects in the Middle East. Since the beginning of the colonial interest in the region, specific aspects of Middle Eastern women's lives such as veiling and segregation were used by political figures to offer moral justification and support for their control and domination of the Middle East.[18] More recently, women's "oppression" (largely signaled by veiling and limited access to education and employment) and male "domination," both of which violate liberal views of equality, have been widely mentioned in Western media and deployed by politicians as important reasons for "liberating" various Muslim countries and communities. Several scholars have critiqued and challenged these representations of women and Islam in American and other Western media.[19] They have forcefully questioned the assumptions that structure ideas about liberation, freedom, equality, and human rights, and have cautioned against simple assumptions and interventions to "liberate" or "free" Muslim women. Most recently, public discourses of "men in crisis" structured much of American media coverage of uprisings and revolutions in the Arab world.[20] Various media have used notions about "the sexually frustrated," "undisciplined male aggression," "paternalism," and "ruthless masculinity,"[21] which simplifies and depoliticizes the massive mobilization of Arabs against dictators in Egypt, Libya, Yemen, and other Arab countries.

I have aimed to contribute to current studies on gender by looking at men, an often taken-for-granted category. My ethnography has offered a thick sense of the various social norms that inform masculine trajectories and how they are embodied in daily life. Through tracing specific trajectories and concrete experiences, this book counters the prevalent disembodiment and dehumanization of Middle Eastern men. When the media homogenize, stereotype, and stigmatize, I cannot help but think of the many hardworking, sincere, and decent men I met in al-Zawiya and other parts of the Middle East. I think of men like Karim, who died while trying to provide for his family. I think of Zaki, who is struggling to marry the woman he loves. I think of Samer, who is eager to become a father and is anxiously waiting for his wife to become pregnant. Seemingly simple stories about men caring about their hair, shoes, and style of dress, falling in love, finding a spouse, securing a home, educating their children, and providing for their families involve mundane issues that are important to write about to counter stereotypes and generalizations about Middle Eastern men.

The dehumanization of men should not be countered by either essentializing or romanticizing them. Writing to humanize does not mean presenting men as flawless. It does not mean claiming that all men are caring, responsible, or affectionate or that they are all eager to challenge patriarchal structures or redefine gender distinctions. It does not mean smoothing over the inequalities that structure male/female or old/young relationships. Rather, it means addressing men as embodied beings who are both the subjects and the objects of systems of power. It means looking not only at "masculine domination" but also at vulnerabilities, dependencies, and disempowerments.[22] It means engaging men's concrete realities and accounting for the social and political hierarchies that configure their bodies and subjectivities. It means being sensitive to their daily struggles, frustrations, achievements, failures, and successes. It means countering simplification with complexity, stereotypes with concrete realities, and abstractions with specific experiences. It means understanding men as embodied agents, who pay attention to their bodily presentations and worry about their appearances, who work hard to make families and provide for their children, who inflict but are also subjected to violence, and who get sick and die.

My book has sought to elaborate on a main paradox embedded in the intersection between patriarchy and capitalism, which grounds gender distinctions in biological differences and at the same time negates the importance of the materiality of the male body in daily life. While the male body is physical capital that could (and should) be converted to other forms of capital, its needs, passions, and emotions are expected to be regulated, denied, and controlled. While the corporality of the body is recognized as the grounds of social difference and incommensurable distinctions between men and women, it is denied and conquered when it comes to the production of a working body that is both economically productive and politically obedient. While the over-embodiment of women has led to their objectification, alienation, and fragmentation, the disembodiment of men has led to their dehumanization, the suppression of their emotions, and the subordination of their bodies to patriarchal and capitalistic demands. When we humanize and elaborate on the embodiment of men we open spaces for questioning patriarchy, which continues to reproduce itself largely by equating the man with mind, reason, and culture, and the woman with body, desire, and nature. The trajectories I have traced in this book illustrate that looking at men as embodied social agents helps us make the gender of men visible and moves us beyond viewing them as superhumans, whose domination is granted by their transcendence over the body. As Kimmel argues, "even when we acknowledge gender, we often endow manhood with a transcendental, almost mythical set of properties that will keep it invisible."[23] Rather than continuing the negation, which denies similarities between boys and girls and exaggerates differences that make men and women seem to be distinct species or inhabit separate planets, looking at the embodiment of men could help us shift the attention to some of the common forces that configure the lives of men and women and the joint struggles they have to engage in daily. The recognition of the mutual economic and political challenges and the physical and emotional vulnerabilities that men and women share could contribute to questioning gender inequalities.[24]

We got a glimpse of this recognition during the eighteen days the protestors spent in Midan al-Tahrir, when millions of men and women (young and old, Muslim and Copt, rich and poor, religious and secular) came together and saw each other as fellow citizens, with similar concerns, aspirations, and goals. They chanted, ate, cleaned, and prayed together. They shared moments of horror and despair and moments of joy and triumph. They protected each other from the brutality of the police and the violence of baltagiyya. The feelings generated during these times were aptly captured by Maha, a 20-year-old college student, who was involved in the protests from the beginning. Like her deceased father, she belonged to the Nasserite Party and participated in the planning and organizing of the demonstrations. She was in Tahrir on January 25 but did not sleep there until the next day, when she took her younger brother with her. She knew that neither her mother nor her neighbors would approve of a single young woman like herself sleeping outside without the presence of a male relative or an older female relative. She described with pride what she called the "manhood of Liberation Square" (*ruguulit*

Midan al-Tahrir), noting that no woman was harassed during the eighteen days they spent protesting. Women had a designated space to sleep in the middle to be fully protected and it felt like "when people are in the hajj, doing *tawaf* [circumambulating the Kaaba]. It didn't matter who was standing next to you. What mattered was the purpose and unity of goal." She raved about how men and women worked together to improvise ways to solve problems and support each other.[25] During this time, men saw that not only their sisters, mothers, and wives but also women as a collectivity are strong, resourceful, and supportive. Women saw that not only their fathers, sons, and brothers but also other men could be vulnerable and need care, protection, and support. Such feelings could be an important step toward poking holes, creating new cracks, and expanding the rip in the fabric of patriarchal hegemony.

Yet, we have learned from history and many feminist and anthropological studies that this recognition and such feelings are not enough to transform gender inequalities. Maha herself was quickly disillusioned with how things were changing in the country. In the summer of 2011, she commented with bitterness on how the faces of protestors in Tahrir had changed, how the unity of the protestors was fragmented, and how many of the men and women who were the driving force behind the revolution have been increasingly excluded from the political system. Women were quickly excluded from important committees (such as the Council of Wise Men, organized by the protestors to start negotiations with the Supreme Council of the Armed Forces and the Committee on Constitutional Reform) formed after the resignation of Mubarak to plan for the future of Egypt.[26] Most recently, women have been largely excluded from the drafting of Egypt's new constitution. There are strong indications that even female activists like Asma Mahfouz, who got a great deal of credit for igniting the revolution, have been increasingly marginalized and viewed by many Egyptians as instigators of the continuous protests and as deliberately "sowing discord between the people and the army" to ruin the country.[27] Thus, the recognition I have underscored here is only one step toward redefining gender constructions. At this moment in Egypt's history, it is important to think of how legal, social, economic, and political reform could help support creative ways of rethinking gender inequalities.

However, stopping here to recognize and emphasize only the marginalization of women risks us becoming complicit in the same discourses that I have been critiquing in this book. We risk missing the crucial point that men represent a diversified category that encompasses a wide range of individuals who are positioned very differently in Egypt's economic, political, and social landscape. We risk missing the point that many men, including those who initiated the revolution, have been also marginalized and excluded from the political process. We risk missing the point that men like Samer, who wholeheartedly supported the protests from the beginning, are not included in discussions about the future of the country either. But more important, we risk reproducing the unproductive assumptions that depict men and women as oppositional groups with no common interests, values, and goals. As this book has sought to demonstrate, both men and women are mindful embodied agents who are constrained by economic demands, shaped by social norms, subjected by political systems, regulated by security forces, and disciplined by religious discourses. If we are to capture how gender is constructed and reconstructed over time and how it could be transformed and reimagined, we must critically account for differences and similarities, inequalities and commonalities, and strengths and vulnerabilities that structure male and female bodies, practices, and subjectivities.

As the trajectories discussed in this book show, masculinity is a contextual, relational process of becoming. It is contingent and open for new possibilities and transformations. Men re-create their masculine identifications under changing circumstances and for diverse audiences. Thus, the new political system that will emerge, the constitution that will be operationalized, the economic policies and opportunities that will be pursued, the political forces that will frame public debate, and the social divisions that will be highlighted and politicized will shape the meaning of masculinity and how it is embodied in daily life.

Reference Matter

Notes

Introduction

Parts of the this book were originally published in "Mobility, Liminality, and Embodiment in Urban Egypt," *American Ethnologist* 38, no. 4 (November 2011); and "Meanings and Feelings: Local Interpretations of the Use of Violence in the Egyptian Revolution," *American Ethnologist* 39, no. 1 (February 2012).

1. Different words are used to refer to the recent events that have been transforming Egypt and the Middle East at large. Here I use the word "revolution" (*sawra*, from the Arabic root *thar*, to rise up or rebel), the word most frequently used by Egyptians, including the activists who initiated the protests. This word captures both the significance of the protests that have led to major changes in Egypt's political system and also, more importantly, the feelings and aspirations of most of my interlocutors in al-Zawiya al-Hamra about the future they expect and hope for.

2. www.youtube.com/watch?v=SgjIgMdsEuk (accessed Mar. 6, 2011).

3. The full name used to refer to the neighborhood is al-Zawiya al-Hamra but often people drop the second word and simply use al-Zawiya. Hence, I follow their use and often refer to the area simply as al-Zawiya. A more detailed discussion of the name and the history of the area can be found in Ghannam (2002).

4. Williams (1977).

5. Ibid., 132.

6. Not only the Egyptian government and the United States administration but also the activists themselves were surprised by the scope, effectiveness, and outcome of the protests.

7. I am well aware of the criticisms (especially against assumptions about the unity and coherence of individual and collective identities) that have been directed at the identity concept. See, for example, Hall (1995), Jenkins (2008), and Connell (2009). Rather than dismissing this concept entirely, I follow the lead of Hall (1995) and Jenkins (2008) in emphasizing that identity and identification should be conceptualized as a process of becoming that is never complete, fixed, or fully established.

8. On "collective projects," see Connell (2009).

9. West and Zimmerman (2010), Butler (1993, 1999), Moore (1999).

10. See, for example, Bourdieu (1966), Gilsenan (1996).

11. Mernissi (1987), MacLeod (1991), Boddy (1997), Chamberlin (2006).

12. Inhorn (2009: 253).

13. I use "distracted" in Taussig's (1992) sense of the word. Susan Bordo (1999) credits the gay movement and the discovery of men as consumers for making the male body "visible" in the media and an object of growing scholarly attention. In Egypt, religious activists have been working to discipline the male body and have presented certain ways of inhabiting the body as key to the cultivation of ethical selves. For more on this, see Hirschkind (2006).

14. For a historical look at these stereotypes and their circulation in Hollywood movies since the early twentieth century, see Shaheen (2001). The author shows that many movies "link the Islamic faith with male supremacy, holy war, and acts of terror, depicting Arab Muslims as hostile alien intruders, and as lecherous, oily sheiks intent on using nuclear weapons" (Shaheen 2001: 9). See also Said (1978) for an analysis of the broader discourse of orientalism, which continues to structure the writings and representations of the Middle East and its peoples. For a discussion of the continuities between the historical discourses discussed by Said and current representations of Arab men, see Inhorn (2012).

15. These negative assumptions are also common in European countries. Archer (2009: 74), for example, argues that "British Muslim young men occupy a sensationalised and demonised position in contemporary British society—indeed, we might describe them as the new folk devils of the British imagination." In Germany, as Ewing shows, the Turkish Muslim man is associated with oppressive gender practices and is "recognized as seeking honor and respect primarily through violence and the oppression of women, means that are incompatible with the ethical subject of a democracy" (2008: 4).

16. Geertz (1979), Gerholm (1977), Gilsenan (1982), Crapanzano (1980), Evans-Pritchard (1958), Dresch (1989), Caton (1990), Lancaster (1997).

17. Such scholars include Nelson (1974), Fernea and Bezirgan (1977), Beck and Keddie (1978).

18. Eickelman (1984), Altorki (1986), Mernissi (1989), Ahmed (1992), Abu-Lughod (1993a, 2002), Early (1993), Najmabadi (1998), Meneley (1996, 2007), Al-Ali (2000), El-Kholy (2002).

19. Ouzgane (2006), Ghoussoub and Sinclair-Webb (2000), Inhorn (2009, 2012), Ali (2002), Peteet (2000), Kanaaneh (2005), Ismail (2006), Amar (2011a). Historians have generated fascinating studies of the history of gendered projects and subjectivities. See, for example, Jacob (2011), and El Shakry (2007). Another recent exciting area of inquiry has been in literary criticism. El Sadda (2012) offers an intriguing analysis of literary masculinities in Egyptian novels, and Aghacy (2009) offers a discussion of masculinity in the literature of the Arab East, including Lebanon, Jordan, Syria, Iraq, and Palestine.

20. Thomas (1996), Bordo (1999), Luciano (2001), Lehman (2001), Forth (2008), Chapman and Grubisic (2009).

21. Abu-Lughod (1986), Kapchan (1996), Meneley (1996), Mahmood (2005), Deeb (2006).

22. Although in the rest of the book, the phrase "real man" will not appear within quotation marks, I urge the reader to imagine them all the time. Their original goal is to remind the reader of the shifting, contested, and ambiguous social meanings of this notion.

23. For a critique of the life cycle notion, see Hockey and James (2003), Johnson-Hanks (2002).

24. Connell and Messerschmidt (2005: 832).

25. Hearn (2004: 58).

26. Connell (2000). For a critique of the concept of hegemonic masculinity, see Whitehead (2002), Hearn (2004), Connell and Messerschmidt (2005), and Messerschmidt (2010). See Inhorn for a critical discussion of "hegemonic masculinity, Middle Eastern-style" (2012: 48) and her alternative concept, "emergent masculinities," which aims to understand "new forms of masculinity in interaction with new forms of medical technology" (40), and to embrace "social history and new forms of manhood in a way that 'hegemonic masculinity' does not" (60).

27. Inhorn (2012: 45).

28. Foucault (1979: 304).

29. Nash (2008), Lutz et al. (2011), Crenshaw (2011), Taylor et al. (2011).

30. Taylor et al. (2011: 38).

31. Vaid (2009), Thomas (2009), Glenn (2009a).

32. Glenn (2009b: 166).

33. It is important to note that the darker color could also be equated with attractiveness and desirability. In fact, there is folk poetry and many popular songs by famous singers like Abel Halim Hafiz that highly celebrate the beauty and charm of el-asmar (a dark complexion).

34. It is important to note that "the urban" appears in most studies either as a mere site for the discussion of men or as the context of specific problems such as drugs, poverty, violence, and homelessness and their impact on men (Barker 2005, Holzer 2009, Martino et al. 2009, Seal and Ehrhardt 2007).

35. Herzfeld (1985), Bourdieu (1966, 2001 [1998]), Gilsenan (1996), Caton (1990), Gilmore (1990), Herdt (1994).

36. I use "rules of the game" in Bourdieu's (1990, 2001 [1998]) sense.

37. If you go to Google Maps, a search for "el-Zawya el-Hamraa, Cairo Governorate" will quickly locate the neighborhood.

38. One of these projects was built in the 1960s and the second in the early 1980s. The differences between public housing and privately constructed homes and the sociocultural meanings attached to them are discussed in my earlier work (Ghannam 2002).

39. It is important to note that this book is largely based on interactions with Muslims. For more on the relationships between Muslims and Christians and the limitations my religious identity imposed on my research, see Ghannam (2002).

40. Cultural capital includes different forms of cultural knowledge such as education, speaking skills, writing styles, familiarity with foreign languages, and aesthetic preferences.

41. Bourdieu (1984).

42. See Samer Shehata (2009: 183) for an interesting study of Egyptian factory workers and "the role of social organization of production" in the formation of their class identity.

43. Bourdieu (1984, 1990, 2001 [1998]). For a critique of Bourdieu's work, see Certeau (1988), Collins (2000), Shilling (2002), Mahmood (2005), Elyachar (2011).

44. Bourdieu (1990, 2001 [1998], 1984: 107).

45. As argued by Ismail (2006).

46. Ironically, and as stated by several people in al-Zawiya, disrupting phone services, which aimed to restrict the planning and mobilization of young people, led to more men and women moving physically (and some even going to Midan al-Tahrir) to check on the safety of relatives and friends.

47. Many believe that Mubarak's government orchestrated the escape of these criminals to spread chaos and reinforce the need for its disciplinary power to maintain order.

48. Ghannam (2002).

49. Since I started my research as a new bride ('arusa), women waited for me to announce my pregnancy, and when that did not happen, they urged me to see a doctor, recommended some local methods that could help cure infertility, and showered me with prayers asking God to help me conceive a child. Thus, having a child after eight years of marriage was particularly welcomed and celebrated.

50. I also did a textual analysis of several Egyptian daily newspapers, weeklies, and magazines. In addition, I have followed some TV programs. In particular, I followed al-Naas channel, which was established in 2005 and was very popular in Cairo in 2006–2007. Although I do not make extensive use of this material in this book, the preliminary textual analysis I did contextualizes my understanding of life in al-Zawiya.

51. Scheper-Hughes and Lock (1987), Csordas (1990), T. Turner (1995), Shilling (2002), Reischer and Koo (2004), Connell (2009), B. Turner (2009).

52. Connell (1987), Messerschmidt (2010), Elyachar (2011).

53. Connell (2009: 67; italics in original); see also T. Turner (1995).

54. I am referring here to the controversial book by John Gray (2004), *Men are from Mars, Women are from Venus: The Classic Guide to Understanding the Opposite Sex*, which was first published in 1992, has sold over 50 million copies, and has been published in 40 languages.

55. Examples include Ghoussoub and Sinclair-Webb (2000), Peteet (2000), Kanaaneh (2005), and Inhorn (2005, 2009, 2012).

56. See also Herzfeld (1985), Connell (2000, 2005), Gutmann (2007), Kimmel (2011).

57. Susan Bordo (1999) for example, spends most of her book, *The Male Body*, talking about the meaning of the phallus, the importance of the penis size, and Viagra and its consumption. While she addresses other topics such as hair, clothes, and muscles, these topics remain marginalized compared to the sexual meanings that end up equated with masculinity.

58. For a discussion of the relationship between infertility and "sexual dysfunction" in Egypt, see Inhorn (2005: 290).

59. *Bango* is a strain of marijuana.

60. See Peterson (2011) for a discussion of the old traditional coffeehouses and the more recent cafés that are spreading in upper- and upper-middle class neighborhoods and their role in the construction of gendered identities.

61. See, for example, the analysis of Bourdieu (1966), Herzfeld (1985), Gilmore (1990), Gilsenan (1996).

62. Hearn (2004: 50).

63. On "thick description," see Geertz (1973).

64. Geertz (1988).

65. Amar (2011b: 302). For an illuminating discussion of the damaging consequences of equating Muslim men with violence and the oppression of women, see Ewing's (2008) study of Turkish immigrants in Germany.

66. Hirschkind (2008).

67. On "visions and divisions," see Bourdieu (2001 [1998]).

68. Bourdieu (1977, 2001 [1998]).

Chapter 1

1. The same connotations often extend to the more sophisticated concept of performativity, which is furthermore limited by its tendency to focus mainly on the discursive aspects of the construction of gender.

2. Beauvoir (1964).

3. The situation is somewhat different in Cairo, where women are also eager to have girls and pity a mother who only has boys. A girl is viewed as the source of tremendous (especially moral) support for her parents and siblings. This support becomes especially important during old age, when girls are the main caregivers for their aging parents.

4. Connell (1987).

5. Butler (1993: 8).

6. Girls are also circumcised in al-Zawiya, usually when they are 6–10 years old and not during infancy, as is the case with most boys.

7. Earrings, for example, are one of the most important gender markers. Female infants are given earrings during the first few weeks of their life. Even when she was wearing a dress, my daughter was sometimes mistaken for a boy because she did not have a pair of earrings to signify her gendered identity. That lack coupled with her short hair promoted some people to think that she was really a boy dressed like a girl to protect *him* from the evil eye.

8. The first week of a baby's life is marked by an elaborate celebration (called *subu'*). While the songs and overall structure of the celebrations are often similar, there are variances in the amount and quality of food offered and the decorations that mark the gender of the baby.

9. Since the January 25 Revolution, the relationship between the police, government, and ordinary citizens has become the subject of intense debates and attempts to restructure it.

10. When his grandmother was in a hurry, she would ask Ahmed to stand in the men's line. Other mothers also told me about times when they were in a rush to buy bread and noticed that the men's line was shorter and quicker so they would claim a turn in that line for their male infants or toddlers. If anyone objected, they would playfully say "Why, is not he a man?" Usually men smiled or nodded and let the little boy get the bread when it was his turn.

11. In the summer of 2011, Ahmed seemed to have forgotten that he used to stand in the women's line and claimed that he always stood in the men's line.

12. My daughter, raised in the relative affluence of American middle-class Swarthmore, was stunned to see how much Ahmed and other children worked. At the age of six, she was disturbed to see how grownups were "bossing the children around" and did not see the logic of working them so hard. My attempts to explain that children are part of the household and are expected to also work to aid their families, especially in a working-class context, did not resonate very well with her. See Zelizer (1985) for a discussion of how, between 1870 and 1930, children in the United States shifted from being objects of utility, who contributed economically to their families, to objects of sentiment, worthless economically but priceless emotionally.

13. Habitus is a set of internalized dispositions that are structured by one's location in the social space and that structure one's practices, views, and systems of classification (Bourdieu 1977, 1984, 2000 [1997], 2001 [1998]).

14. On bodily learning, see Bourdieu (2000 [1997]: 141).

15. Ramadan in the summer of 2012 started in the second part of July, the hottest month in Egypt. The fasting day was long, lasting around sixteen hours (from sunrise until sunset).

16. Virtual and real pool games have become very popular in the area in recent years. Ahmed loved to go to a nearby place that was created by one of his neighbors, who fenced and roofed part of the shared space between their buildings and charged boys and young men for playing table tennis and pool.

17. Inhorn (1996, 1994, 2009). In a recent study, Inhorn shows that infertile Arab men are "rethinking what it means to be a man" and that a "notion of 'manhood beyond fatherhood' is emerging" (2012: 30, 89). I have not noticed such a tendency in al-Zawiya, where fatherhood continues to be highly regarded and desirable. Yet, it would be interesting to further explore how the meaning of fatherhood could be shifting over time in a working-class context.

18. I personally experienced part of the intense pressure people exert on newlyweds to get pregnant as soon as possible. As stated in the Introduction, since I started my research as a bride ('arusa), women waited for me to announce my pregnancy and when that did not happen, they urged me to see a doctor, recommended some local methods

that could help cure infertility, and showered me with prayers asking God to help me conceive a child.

19. See Lancy (2008) for a comparative look at the roles of fathers in different cultures and societies.

20. See Roberson (2003) for a similar description of working-class fathers in Japan.

21. Hoodfar (1996) offers an excellent discussion of similar issues in relation to the absence of fathers due to labor migration.

22. Bourdieu (1990).

23. His daughter was born when he was in Saudi Arabia and he died before ever seeing her.

24. Hiba's husband left her no money. She received no pension or compensation from his employers in Saudi Arabia. However, because of her status as a widow, she managed to retrieve part of her deceased father's pension. In 2011, she was earning the equivalent to $50 a month. She was occasionally offered small amounts of money and gifts from relatives and close friends.

25. The older his sister became, the more chores she was asked to do. She was limited though to outings close to the home during the day (but never at night) and Hiba monitored her whereabouts very closely.

26. Montgomery (2009: 158).

27. Hiba's older sister was also a main caregiver for Hiba and her younger siblings, and all of them (boys and girls) describe the terror she inflicted on them. Even Hiba's mother described how strict Mirvat was with the whole family and how the neighbors referred to this eldest daughter as the mother's co-wife to capture the power she exerted over her parents and siblings.

28. As noted by El-Kholy, the word *aytaam* (plural of *yatiim*) refers to "children who lost their fathers, which is different from the standard dictionary definition of an orphan as an individual who lost both parents to death" (2002: 56). Religious teachings and social norms strongly encourage people to be kind, caring, and supportive (financially and emotionally) of orphans.

29. See Joseph (2002) for a similar discussion of her childhood while growing up in Lebanon.

30. hooks (2004: 145, 137).

31. As in many other places (Matthews 2003), in al-Zawiya *el-shari'a* (the street) is a metaphor for most spaces outside the housing unit.

32. This parallels the description given by Wikan in her study of a poor neighborhood in Cairo. She states that for many mothers, "the home stands for everything good: polite language, good manners, neatness, and compassion, whereas the street embodies the evils of impudence, filthiness, rudeness, and ugliness" (1996: 160). Yet parents clearly recognize the importance of the street in shaping masculine trajectories, a topic that will be discussed in this chapter and the next.

33. Ahmed senses the difference between the city and countryside when he travels to visit his father's family in Upper Egypt. In their little village, he can play with his cousins for long hours. There are few chores he is expected to complete. Children of his age in the village work hard with their families (such as helping in the field, taking care of animals, and looking after younger siblings), but Ahmed himself is exempted because he is a "guest." He can ride his bike, which he cannot do in al-Zawiya because of congestion and traffic, and kick the ball with his cousins for many hours without worrying about fights that could strain relationships with others.

34. One time when we visited, my daughter, who was five at the time, looked down from the balcony and saw the children collect dry branches and start a little fire as part of their play. Having been trained in the United States to think of fire as a danger, she started yelling very loudly asking the children to put the fire out. My attempts to assure her that nothing would happen did not soothe her worries and only when the children ended their play with the fire did she relax.

35. His mother did not want him to watch TV either. The TV was shared with the rest of the family, who wanted to watch programs other than the cartoons favored by Ahmed. His religiously devout grandmother, for example, preferred to watch religious programs and one of his uncles wanted to watch movies and video clips at night, and both often felt frustrated when Ahmed wanted to watch hours of cartoons.

36. Bourdieu (1989: 19).

37. Ants are a major problem for many families during the summer. They are seen crawling everywhere and getting rid of them is very challenging.

38. Nicknames often relate to the size and shape of the body. One woman who was overweight was called Fara ("female mouse") and a man in his late forties was called il-Iswid ("the black one"). He proudly accepted the nickname and used it to refer to himself. As he explained, the name was conferred on him at an early age, when he was working with another man with the same name. To differentiate them, their co-workers nicknamed him Iswid and the other Abyad (white). Similar examples can be found with other adults and I would not be surprised if Ahmed eventually accepts his nickname and uses it in the future.

39. I have seen many other photos that were digitally manipulated to make the skin lighter and clearer and the eyes green, two of the main qualities that define beauty in al-Zawiya.

40. Close family members also tease Ahmed about his dark skin and some joke about it by saying things like "Why are you so dark? Did they [meaning his parents] forget you in the oven?"

41. Body idiom is "body symbolism" and "embodied expressive signs," which consist of "appearances and gestures that tend to call forth in the actor what it calls forth in the others, the others draw from those, and only those, who are immediately present" (Goffman 1959: 33–34).

42. Certeau (1988); Foucault (1979).

43. American wrestling continues to be one of Ahmed's favorite TV shows and it is widely enjoyed by many men in al-Zawiya. In the summer of 2012, Ahmed quizzed me on some of the wrestlers whom he liked and asked me about the possibility of buying him a mask like the one worn by one of the wrestlers he adored.

44. Despite his mother's attempts to make sure he grows stronger and fatter, a combination of lots of physical activities, limited access to healthy food, and occasional infestation with intestinal parasites has left him very thin.

45. Transcendence refers to the transformation of the body in ways to substantiate social ideas about physical differences between male and female. For example, assumptions that men should have muscular and strong bodies prompt parents to encourage their sons to engage in sports and physical training, which in effect produces muscles and bodily shapes that are increasingly equated with masculinity. For more, see Connell (1987), and Shilling (2002).

46. Durkheim (2002).

47. Bourdieu (1977).

48. El-Messiri (1978: 49).

49. Elyachar (2005: 138).

50. El-Messiri (1978: 82).

51. As stated by Nakamura and Matsuo, "one of the greatest tragedies of post-Freudian society in the United States is the sexualization of all human relations from mother-infant onwards," which has essentially prevented scholars from seeing "the possibility of asexualized relations or the transcendence of gender in non-Freudian societies" (2003: 61).

52. Singerman (1995: 100).

53. Lane (1978).

54. Jacob (2011: 178).

55. The most common criticisms and insults directed at women are focused on sexual impropriety and incompetence in household work.

56. Some of these words, such as *khawal*, are never used to refer to women while some, such as *'ayyil*, have feminine forms that are used to refer to women who do not behave properly.

57. Mahmood (2005: 8); see also Strathern (2010).

58. Bourdieu (1966, 1977, 2001 [1998]).

59. Bourdieu (1990).

Chapter 2

1. I have known Samer since 1995, when he was twenty-five years old. This section draws on conversations we had when he was thirty-six. Later in the chapter, I draw on his life experiences before and after this age and then focus on the challenges that faced him at the age of forty.

2. According to him and his family, even the firemen did not want to go upstairs to bring the cylinder down.

3. While older men refrain from carrying it, young men often carry a pocketknife but rarely use it. Displaying the knife and the threat it poses is often all is needed to assert one's power. As explained by a man in his late forties, the click made by the pocketknife of his youth was often enough to scare off an opponent.

4. On bodily hexis, see Bourdieu (1977: 93).

5. Ibid., 76, 72 (emphasis in the original).

6. Bourdieu (1984: 190, 193).

7. Ibid., 190 (emphasis in the original).

8. Bourdieu (2000 [1977]: 93; emphasis in the original).

9. Ibid., 94 (italics in the original).

10. Bourdieu (1984).

11. See Schielke (2008), Mahmood (2005), Ghannam (2004, 2011), Starrett (1995).

12. Mahmood (2005: 139); Starrett (1995: 953).

13. Mahmood (2005: 139).

14. Ibid., 139.

15. Ibid., 30–31.

16. Ibid., 126.

17. For more on this issue, see Ghannam (2002).

18. On disciplinary power, see Foucault (1979).

19. Willis (1981).

20. A similar pattern was also documented by Roberson's (2003) work in Japan.

21. In Bourdieu's sense.

22. Youth is a social category linked to age but cannot be reduced to it. As argued by other anthropologists (Durham 2000, Johnson-Hanks 2002), "youth" should not be seen as a universal phase of the life cycle or a simple transitional period between childhood and adulthood. Rather, we should always explore how this category is created, contested, and materialized in various cultures and how youth negotiate competing demands, conflicting social expectations, and surveillance regimes and disciplinary techniques that seek to regulate their bodies, minds, and selves.

23. Men's practices, like women's, are increasingly informed by new ideas (about beauty and fertility), spaces (such as the gym), and products (lotions, pills, and herbs). Gyms in particular are becoming important sites for the shaping of the young male body.

24. On malls and how they cater to different classes in Cairo, see Abaza (2001).

25. For more on this topic, see Ghannam (2011).

26. Merry (2001).

27. Ibid., 6.

28. Ismail (2006).

29. Other important signs of beauty are green eyes, light skin, and blond hair.

30. Even if they want to, older men do not have the time to frequent the gym. As a working man in his thirties said, "The gym is for people who have free time but working men like me have no time for such things. I only went to the gym three times in my life but had to stop because of a lack of time." Most of those who frequented the gym were college students and young men not engaged in manual labor.

31. Although people are generally positive about the Egyptian army, military service is often considered a burden that young men have to endure to acquire the documents that would allow them ease of mobility inside and outside Egypt. In addition to the length of service (men like Samer who do not have a high school diploma are expected to serve for three years, but college graduates for only one year), hardships include meager pay, demeaning chores, and harsh conditions of service. Thus, men who evade military service are not stigmatized or looked down upon but they do face some institutional obstacles that could prevent their access to certain jobs and to travel abroad.

32. Over the past two decades, I heard of a couple of rumors about young men who had sexual relations with other men but I have never encountered anyone in al-Zawiya who openly defined himself (or was identified by others) as anything but heterosexual.

33. For a critique of the idea of a crisis and a historical look at a so-called marriage crisis in Egypt during the early twentieth century, see Kholoussy (2010).

34. Aging is socially defined and may indicate various things in diverse cultures. Many in al-Zawiya think of people as old when they approach their forties.

35. See Ismail (2006) and Kandiyoti (1994).

36. He was especially unhappy that she tended to issue "commands" and to cry whenever he did not respond quickly and positively.

37. Many men suffer from health problems (such as constipation, hemorrhoids, and high blood pressure). These problems are deeply connected with the nature of their work as well as the quality of life in Cairo.

38. In particular, Samer (encouraged by his mother, who sees herself as dark but always declared that she preferred light skin) was determined to marry a light-skinned woman. Because he had a dark complexion himself, he explained, it was particularly important to have a light-skinned wife to avoid having children who are too dark. Samer always emphasized that the beauty of the face, which he would be seeing every morning and evening, was the most important part of the physical attributes of his future wife. In addition to nicely proportioned features, whiteness was an important part of his view of the beauty of the face.

39. Since he did not use any sunblock, Samer indeed came back with lots of burns that bothered him for days.

40. On liminality, see V. Turner (1967).

41. I remember one time when Samer told me about the death of one of his Egyptian co-workers, who lived and worked in Libya for several years. The man died suddenly and left his children and wife abroad without much support. The widow asked Samer to help with the paperwork needed to transport the body to Egypt. He described his deep frustra-

tion with the reluctance of the officials at the embassy to offer any help and he almost had a fistfight with them. He described other times when Egyptian workers would be insulted and assaulted by Libyans and found no support whatsoever.

42. Mahmood (2005: 89, 116).

43. Starrett (1995).

Chapter 3

1. Khal (2000: 31).

2. Ghoussoub and Sinclair-Web (2000: 19).

3. Khal (2000: 30).

4. Moore (2007: 117); see also Butler (1993, 1999) and Reeser (2010).

5. Gregory (2007: 148), Messerschmidt (2010: 21); see also Brod (1994).

6. Moore (2007).

7. Kimmel (2006: 5).

8. Nelson (1974), Altorki (1986), Meneley (1996), Lancaster (1997), Ghannam (2002). See Ghannam (2005) for a review of the literature on the split between public and private and how it has shifted over time.

9. Joseph (2001: 234); see also Joseph (1999).

10. Joseph (2001: 229).

11. Ibid., 34.

12. Ibid., 250.

13. Altorki (1999: 216).

14. Ibid.; Foucault (1979).

15. Foucault (1982: 18; emphasis added).

16. Herzfeld (19 85: 16; emphasis in the original).

17. In few cases, instead of providing for their families, men spent most of their income on drugs, gambling, or affairs with women.

18. See also Ghannam (2011).

19. The link between providing and claims over others has been also observed by El-Messiri (1978), Wikan (1996), El-Kholy (2002), and Ismail (2006).

20. Muhsen worked in Kuwait for eight years. He and Manal were engaged for three years before he returned to finalize the marriage and fully settle down in al-Zawiya.

21. Muhsen also makes a point of not asking Manal to spend any of her salary on their home. While she herself may use some of her monthly income to buy things her home needs, he always gives her a weekly allowance to cover their household expenses.

22. They also recognize Manal's skills as a good housewife and her wise ways of managing her husband's feelings and preferences but often give more credit to Muhsen and his ability to assert his views and inclinations.

23. Ironing is one of the most gendered chores that changes over time and reflects the status of a man. Mothers and sisters take care of this time-consuming chore for their

young male relatives. Once a young man starts working, he is expected to spend part of his money on getting his clothes professionally pressed. Upon marriage, ironing becomes the exclusive task of the wife and her husband's wrinkle-free clothes reflect positively on her skills as a homemaker.

24. In general, mothers-in-law are influential in the making or breaking of a marriage. Their mediating role, their support, or meddling in the couple's affairs could be the source of either stability or tension between the couple and could have a serious impact on their relationship.

25. Umm Ali (mother of Ali) and Abu Ali (father of Ali) are labels that reflect the custom of naming the parents after their first born child, especially if it is a boy.

26. See Ghannam (2008b) for more on how they built their home.

27. Divorce is complicated financially and socially and is considered undesirable except in rare cases.

28. Safwat was excited to describe to me and to others in detail the teas and instruments that he used in Kuwait to get rid of his belly fat and become slimmer.

29. See Inhorn (2012: 49) for a critical discussion of Western constructions of Middle Eastern hegemonic masculinity.

30. Ismail (2006: 96).

31. Ibid., 113.

32. Morgan (2006: 112).

33. Ismail (2006). Polygamy is very limited in al-Zawiya. While the possibility is there, very few men want or can afford to have more than one wife.

34. As presented by Kandiyoti (2005).

35. Ibid., 29.

Chapter 4

1. There is little stigma attached to going to prison per se. The cause of imprisonment, however, is important and could be a sign of distinction or stigma. A man who is falsely accused of a crime or who lands in jail because he was trying to help or protect others could acquire symbolic capital while someone who is jailed for bullying or socially unacceptable crimes such as rape could be negatively viewed.

2. The transgression of having an affair with a married women is extremely rare and socially unacceptable. To make such an affair public makes the act even more abhorrent.

3. Many men experiment with *birsham* and other mild narcotics during their youth, but very few continue to use it beyond their early twenties.

4. Neighbors said that two other public hospitals refused to admit the fatally wounded brother. I heard of a few other incidents where people who were badly hurt in an accident or who were having massive heart attacks were not admitted to a specific hospital because administrators claimed they did not have the resources and directed the relatives to other hospitals that could be better equipped to take care of the patient. People explain

otout

this refusal by the hospital administration's fear that the victim would die on its premises and would be counted against them by the government. This issue, however, needs more investigation.

5. The policeman, people believe, was either paid or expected a payment from Atif's family. Alternatively, the policeman may have been tired of Kirsha and his conduct. Earlier, the police tried to incite people to do something to stop Kirsha and it was reported that an officer asked publicly, "Are there no men (*mafish rigaala*) in this area to put an end to his [Kirsha's] acts?" This question is usually understood as a provocation to pressure or encourage the men in the area to act quickly to correct a wrongdoing.

6. I have heard of similar stories when people inflicted self-injury to counter the claims of the other party or initiate a formal complaint in the police station to have some leverage that may allow them to pressure the other party to retract their allegations. In one case, a teenager (along with his cousin) fought with another boy and managed to leave a deep cut on his face. Realizing that her son and nephew were in the wrong and could face serious charges, the mother slashed her head with a knife and went to the police station claiming that the family of the injured boy caused her injury. This gave her leverage in negotiating with the other family, who eventually agreed to work out a deal that avoided formal venues (such as courts) in favor of an informal settlement that included the payment of the medical expenses of the treatment of boy's face to avoid any permanent scars.

7. *Al-Hawadith al-'Arabiyya*, July 19, 2010, p. 9.

8. When I asked about the raped woman and what happened to her, I was told that she was still living in the area with her husband. One man suggested that the reason the husband did not do anything about his wife's alleged transgressions could have been because he did not know about her affair with Kirsha, that he was not a real man and did not mind, or that he was just a poor soul (*ghalbaan*) who lacked the ability to discipline his wife and is just trying to get by.

9. Herzfeld (1985), Kandiyoti (1994), Connell (2000, 2005), Gilsenan (1996), Gilligan (2004), Barker (2005), Kimmel (2011).

10. Connell (2002: 95).

11. See Elyachar (2011) for an interesting discussion of gesture in Cairo.

12. One mother described how she never really wanted to beat her children and always announced her intention very loudly to make sure they hid or ran to the neighbors before she got to them.

13. V. Turner (1982: 10).

14. Ibid.

15. V. Turner (1982).

16. V. Turner (1980: 149).

17. In some cases, a young man may take his shirt off to indicate that he is not afraid of anything and that he is so determined to fight that he will not allow others to restrain him through taking hold of his clothes.

18. One has to be selective when to become loud. In the right context, it is considered a sign of fearlessness, but it could also be seen as vulgar and bad manners, especially in women. Educated women and respectable families would assert their status in statements such as "no one ever hears our voices" to indicate that they do not engage in fights inside or outside the house.

19. Watching and evaluating the performances of both sides is an important aspect of these dramas. The judgment of the observers and the stories circulated about the events could make or break reputations after the exchange is over. Even total strangers are expected to intervene to end a fight in the street. In more semi-private spaces (such as alleyways and shared spaces in front of apartment houses), only those who are related to one of the sides are expected to appear to help or make amends. The immediate interference of others often prevents fights from escalating beyond the exchange of a few verbal insults.

20. Like what Gutmann describes in Mexico City (2007), as the main caregivers, mothers in al-Zawiya tend to use physical punishment in disciplining their children more often than fathers do.

21. Over the past ten years, video clips of policemen beating men in custody widely circulated via mobile phones and the Internet. They have been used by different groups to document the brutality of the police. In al-Zawiya, such clips sometimes seemed to assert the power of the state in daily life and offered a visible warning, especially to young men, to avoid confrontation with the police. When in 2007 a man in his mid-forties was showing me the clip of a policeman repeatedly slapping a man, I asked him how he felt when viewing such clips. He answered: "I feel I should mind my business (*khalleeni fi haali*) and avoid any situation that could allow this [the beating] to be inflicted on me." At other times, these clips outraged the viewers and generated condemnation of police brutality.

22. A 2008 study by CAPMAS (the Centre for Public Mobilization and Statistics) revealed that 47 percent of Egyptian women between fifteen and forty-nine had been victims of domestic violence. *Al-Ahram Weekly*, Dec. 24– 30, 2009; http://weekly.ahram .org.eg (accessed Dec. 22, 2010).

23. It is important to look at how notions of love, care, solidarity, and modesty are tightly linked to the use of violence and its legitimization. For more on this, see Joseph (2001) and Ghannam (2002).

24. Many of these poorly maintained vans are driven by reckless teenagers, who may not have a driver's license and are known for quarrels among themselves and with passengers.

25. Schrock and Schwalbe (2009: 285).

26. The famous "Egypt: Demographic and Health Survey 1995," administered by the National Population Center, found that 35 percent of women (ages 15–49) had been beaten at least once after getting married. Most women believed "violence was justified" if a woman "talked back" to her husband and that it was a "legitimate form of punishment for disobedience" (www.hrw.org/reports/2004/egypt1204/2.htm; accessed Nov. 27, 2010).

27. Very rarely did I hear of someone beating his/her mother. Such an act is highly stigmatized. In the case referred to here, the son was spoiled by his mother, as the neighbors say, because he was the only boy and grew up to be violent and a drug addict.

28. On "misrecognition," see Bourdieu (1977). A similar example is that of fertility, which is credited to men while infertility is usually blamed on women, even when medical tests reveal the man is infertile (Inhorn 1994).

29. See Paul Amar (2011a) on how female activists have been targeted over the past decade by the authorities to limit their role in public protests and opposition and discourage the mobilization of other women.

30. Herzfeld (1985), Herdt (1994), Bourgois (1995), Connell (2005), Gutmann (2007), Kimmel (2006, 2011).

31. Young women are occasionally verbally harassed by men. Most women choose not to respond to avoid a prolonged exchange with the offending man that could turn into a conflict. However, if he physically touches her, a woman usually retaliates either verbally or physically (I have seen women use their sandals to beat their harassers). Others, including men, often rush to help the woman and punish (either verbally or physically) the offender.

32. This is also true in the context of the home. As aptly put by a man in his late fifties, "a real man knows how to run his household using his brain, not his arm."

33. The category of "older men" is flexible and shifts but, in this context, it tends to include men in their early thirties and over.

34. The meaning of the word *sayyaa'a* can shift from one context to the other. Most often, it has negative connotations. The verb *saa'*, for example, means being a bum or going around hassling people, and the noun, *saaye'*, implies a worthless or useless man. But, it could also refer to eclectic knowledge of ways of doing and being that is earned by not adhering to social norms and proper manners, but is ultimately used for good ends.

35. Some people were sympathetic to Atif's acts because they thought he may have been fundamentally challenging Kirsha's attempts to be a thug who would use excessive violence to coerce people to comply with his wishes.

36. Unlike other regions, such as Palestine, where physical injuries could be seen by others as signs of sacrifice that reinforce the social standing of a man (Peteet 2000), facial scars in al-Zawiya are negatively viewed and young men try to avoid getting them.

37. Elyachar (2005: 138).

38. El-Messiri (1978: 49).

39. According to El-Messiri, "essentially *gad'a* means 'young man'" (1978: 82). In the early twentieth century, the term referred to men "who were known for their excellence in beating and fighting and who specialized in protecting those who sought their help. The police used to fear them, and prison for them was an honor that they could boast of" (ibid.).

40. Over the past two decades years, I have heard the word used on a couple of oc-

casions to refer to women who used violence to intimidate others, but most of the time, the label was used to refer to men.

41. "Baltagiyya between the Past and the Present," *Al-Masry al-Youm*, July 19, 2011: 12.

42. Ismail (2006: 122).

43. Ibid., 140.

44. Ibid., 139.

45. The emergency law granted the police the right to detain Egyptians for up to six months without probable cause, a warrant, or legal representation (Ghonim 2012: 2).

46. Amar (2011b: 308).

47. Unlike the *singa*, which is visibly displayed, the pocketknife is discreetly carried by young men and is displayed only when there is a need.

48. Tharwat (2011) adds two other "facial characteristics" that Egyptians identify with a baltagi: "a messed up hair" and "a missing tooth." These two bodily features, however, were not highlighted in people's descriptions in al-Zawiya.

49. Because most of them are not Facebook or Twitter users, my only connection with my interlocutors in al-Zawiya during January and February was the phone, a technology that, as I said in the Introduction, has increasingly become important to my research over the past two decades. While I was in the United States, the phone enabled me to keep track of the changing feelings and views of several of my close friends in al-Zawiya, thereby allowing me to see how some of the events were linked to cultural meanings and categories that inform the daily life of people in that neighborhood.

50. Many families in the neighborhood have access to satellite TV. Early in the protests, though, the Egyptian regime managed to disable channels deemed anti-Mubarak (most important, al-Jazeera), forcing the people to rely on news that mainly promoted the views of the government.

51. Kentucky Fried Chicken, which has a restaurant in Liberation Square, was highlighted as a symbol of the external forces said to be inciting (and bribing) youth to protest to undermine order and security in Egypt.

52. On the history of Midan al-Tahrir and its contemporary spatial significance, see Ghannam (2011).

53. Currently, these events are widely known both in the media and in al-Zawiya as *Mawqi'at el-Gamal*, or the Battle of the Camel. This name is reminiscent of the first armed confrontation among Muslims in 656. In both cases, camels figure prominently in the events and how they unfolded.

54. Most of these officials are now in custody awaiting trial.

55. Adel Iskandar (2011) is right in reminding us that the attackers could have been "poor, desperate and misinformed camel and horse riders" who were turned into baltagiyya with "food, money, and the instructions to attack what they were told was a demonstration responsible for the tourism slump that cost them their livelihoods."

56. The news that thousands of criminals either escaped (according to the govern-

ment) or were released deliberately (according to most Egyptians) generated fears in different parts of Egypt, including al-Zawiya. Although families in the neighborhood initially believed the stories of looming attacks by baltagiyya from a nearby community, even children eventually realized that they were rumors generated and circulated by the government and its agents to highlight the need for police to maintain order and security. Residents of al-Zawiya were amused to discover, after the fact, that the people in the other community were equally fearful of impending attacks by baltagiyya from al-Zawiya.

57. A figure like Wael Ghonim, totally unknown in al-Zawiya before February 2011, who appeared crying to TV while describing his detention for twelve days and his sorrow for the lives that were lost during the protests, deeply moved people and became (at least temporarily) a highly respected hero. I say temporarily because Ghonim and some other prominent leaders of the protests have been redefined over time and some have been increasingly attacked and stigmatized by their political opponents and government officials in different media.

58. Certain bodily hexis such as their dress style (jeans and t-shirts) and consumption patterns (for example, they drank soft drinks from expensive cans) as well as their Western education (reference was made to the American and German universities) were class-based signs mentioned by some people in al-Zawiya to distinguish the protestors from baltagiyya and highlight their dedication to positive social and political change.

59. Several people in al-Zawiya joked that they were safe from kidnapping because no one would pay any ransom to get them back, yet there were deep concerns about issues of security and safety. For example, not only did my "adopted family" in al-Zawiya insist on meeting me at the airport when I arrived and on taking me back when I was leaving the country, something they had never done before, but I also noticed other issues that indicated fear and insecurity such as new metal gates added to housing blocks and double locks added to the doors of apartments.

60. Tharwat (2011; italics in the original).

61. Iskandar (2011).

62. While originally distancing themselves from the notion of baltaga and presenting themselves as gid'aan, some of the protests mocked the politicization of baltaga by using it to refer to themselves. This move could be productive in certain circles (among progressive, liberal, and middle/upper middle classes), but it risks generating the opposite results in working-class neighborhoods like al-Zawiya.

63. This concept has been widely circulated and is now being used in many Arab countries, such as Jordan, Syria, Yemen, and Lebanon.

64. Zuckerhut (2011: 22, 23); see also Whitehead (2004).

65. I never heard of a wife beating her husband in al-Zawiya. In another part of Cairo, however, there was a widely publicized case of a TV broadcaster killing his wife. He claimed that she not only verbally insulted him but also slapped him. Several of the

people (including women) I know in al-Zawiya sympathized with him and found him justified in killing his wife because she physically attacked him.

66. As I said in Chapter 1, people in al-Zawiya often use the word *hukumah* (which means government) to refer also to the police, in the process equating the two.

67. See Dorsey (2012), El Amrani (2012), and Azeb (2012) for a discussion of the Ultras (strong fans and supporters of Egyptian soccer teams, including al-Ahly), their history, and relationship to the Egyptian political system.

Chapter 5

1. Ghonim (2012: 59).

2. Ibid.

3. Foucault (1979).

4. I call him Karim (literally, "generous") to capture the spirit of generosity he has been credited with by all his acquaintances.

5. Courtenay (2009: 24). See also Martin (1992) for an anthropological critique of the medical discourse and how it systematically devalues the female body and its reproductive functions.

6. Martin (1992), Rosenfeld and Faircloth (2006).

7. Sabo and Gordon (1995), Courtenay (2009, 2011), Broom and Tovey (2009b), Aguirre-Molina, Borrell, and Vega (2010b).

8. Rosenfeld and Faircloth (2006).

9. Ibid., Riska (2003).

10. Broom and Tovey (2009a: 1).

11. Petersen (2009: 209).

12. Rosenfeld and Faircloth (2006: 15).

13. See Hamdy (2008) for a thoughtful analysis of the inequalities that shape disease and its distribution in Egypt.

14. For more on this topic, see Ghannam (2002).

15. Up to that time, he had suffered from diabetes and hypertension.

16. Daily group trips, usually to beaches, are common during the summer. Participants collaborate with other neighbors and residents to plan for the outing. Each participant pays a little money to cover the expenses of a big bus and each family or group takes its own food and drinks.

17. Anger is considered the cause of many health problems in al-Zawiya and people often relate serious illness (such as diabetes and strokes) to specific moments of anger.

18. Bourdieu (1984: 167).

19. This trend is of course not limited to Egypt but exists also in other societies, including the United States (see, for example, Courtenay 2011).

20. Umm Hosni resented the fact that they continued to share the little apartment and bathroom with the neighbors. She sometimes hinted that they could afford to move

to another apartment but they (especially her husband) hesitated about moving because of the high rent they would have to pay. They also hoped that the neighbors would eventually leave and that they would end up with the whole unit.

21. For example, a catheter was continuously attached to collect his urine.

22. A similar pattern has been reported in other countries including the United States. See Courtenay (2011), Broom and Tovey (2009b), and Watson (2000). Statistics indicate that life expectancy at birth for men in Egypt was 70.85 in 2009 (compared to 45 in 1960), and for women 74.7 in 2009 (compared to 45 in 1960). These numbers, however, do not account for differences based on class and place of origin (http://data.worldbank.org/data-catalog/health-nutrition-and-population-statistics; accessed Mar. 19, 2012).

23. It is important to note that while women may live longer than men, they do not necessarily live better (Lorber 2000).

24. See Robben (2009) for a survey of anthropological research on death.

25. Catedra (2004: 78).

26. Lock (2000).

27. Firth (1989: 70).

28. Palgi and Abramovitch (1984: 412).

29. His mother, after his death, emphasized that he left school because he felt sorry for her, since she was left without help after the marriage of her two oldest daughters. He wanted to support her, especially in the field and with the livestock she kept.

30. Shilling (2002).

31. There was usually a sense of tension and jealousy between them because Karim was less educated than his brothers yet was able to earn much more. This tension was especially clear between Saed and Karim because of their proximity in age.

32. Bourdieu (1984: 218).

33. Ali (2002: 128).

34. See Ghannam (forthcoming) for a discussion of the mourning of his male and female relatives.

35. Since children are considered sinless and are not subjected to the same obligations and judgments as adults, many thought that having a boy in Karim's arms would guarantee that he would be treated the same way as the boy. Some sheiks have contested this idea and argued that one is accountable for one's own deeds and will be judged individually no matter where and with whom one is are buried.

36. Most devout Muslims believe that after death two angels appear in the grave to punish or reward the deceased. A person who led a good and pious life will enjoy many rewards while a nonbeliever could suffer horrible torture. All people will come alive again on the Day of Judgment, when God will evaluate their deeds and make a final judgment that will admit the pious to heaven and banish the non-pious to hell. For more on this, see Muwahidi (1989).

37. In crowded Cairo, a speedy ride to the cemetery and a quick burial are taken as a

clear sign of a good ending. To be able to overcome Cairo's congested streets and its hectic traffic indicates the eagerness of the deceased to be buried as quickly as possible.

38. V. Turner (1967).

39. Some of the social explanations for the general preferences for quick burial included the need to avoid any desecration of the corpse and the need to ease the pain and suffering of the family.

40. After washing and shrouding the corpse, it is taken to a nearby mosque for a special prayer before it is transported to the cemetery for burial.

41. Participation in managing the corpse, funeral prayer, and burial are all good and pious acts that will be rewarded by God.

42. I am here referring to the ferryboat *al-Salam*, which sank in February 2006. It is believed that at least a thousand men, women, and children (mainly Egyptians) perished.

43. Visiting relatives and sick people is both socially and religiously sanctioned and rewarded.

44. Elias (1993), Shilling (2002).

45. "On the Friday of Rage: 14 Martyrs from al-Zawiya" (http://digital.ahram.org.eg/articles.aspx?Serial=445996&eid=14839; accessed April 25, 2011).

46. According to *al-Ahram*, the only woman killed was an 18-year-old who was shot by a policeman while she was on the roof of her building using her mobile phone to document what was taking place in the nearby police station.

47. Elias (1993), Shilling (2002).

48. Ariès (1974: 94), Giddens (1991), Shilling (2002).

49. Palgi and Abramovitch (1984: 404). See also Ariès (1974), Firth (1989), Giddens (1991), Elias (1993), Shilling (2002).

50. Ariès (1974: 85).

51. Palgi and Abramovitch (1984: 408).

52. Hirschkind (2006: 176); see also Hirschkind (2008).

53. Hirschkind (2008: 41).

54. See Hamdy (2009) for a perceptive refutation of the tendency of Western scholars and media to depict Muslims as "fatalistic."

55. It would be important to explore how the death of young women is conceptualized and relates to but differs from the death of young men. This is a topic beyond the scope of this book.

56. Dying while or immediately after praying is considered one of the best things that could happen to a person and it signals a good death.

Conclusion

1. In June 2012, Muhammad Morsi, candidate of the Freedom and Justice Party (with strong links to the Muslim Brotherhood), won 51.7 percent of the total votes and became the president of Egypt.

2. Many participated in the election for the People's Assembly. Due to some violations, these elections were reheld in the district that included al-Zawiya. I was not there to see for myself, but one of my close interlocutors described the excitement people felt and how many men and women voted in the first round. She described how even old and sick people were carried or physically supported to be able to reach the election centers. Part of the reason for this impressive turnout, she argued, was a rumor that those who failed to vote would be fined 500 Egyptian pounds (around $83), a substantial amount for many people in al-Zawiya.

3. I say "even macaroni," because when all else fails, women resort to frying macaroni in lots of oil and serve it with tomato sauce to their families. So statements by low-income housewives that "even macaroni" was expensive and beyond their reach indicated the seriousness of the situation and the threat posed by not being able to fill the stomachs of their children.

4. Williams (1977).

5. The financial corruption of the government was aptly captured by a joke told to me by a 12-year-old boy in the summer of 2011. Obama sent one million dollars to Mubarak to pass along to an Egyptian beggar Obama heard about. Mubarak called the minister of interior and gave him half a million to pass along to the beggar as a gift from Obama. The minister called the head of the district and gave him 250,000 dollars. The head of the district called the person below him in the hierarchy and handed him half of the amount . . . until eventually the chain reached a simple policeman, who went to the beggar and told him: "Obama says 'may God provide for you' [*Allah yihannin 'alik*, literally "may God make people kind to you"]," a phrase usually said to beggars when one does not want to give them anything.

6. See Baron (2005) for a discussion of Egypt as a woman. It is worth noting that although women are often "designated symbols of the nation, the mothers of the nation, the bearers of traditional values and heritage," they are still "accorded limited national agency" (El Sadda 2012: xxxiii).

7. Bettie (2003: 195). See Taylor et al. (2011: 38) for a critique of how class is also often "sidelined and absent in researching and theorising sexuality."

8. Elyachar (2011).

9. Connell and Messerschmidt (2005: 849).

10. Schrock and Schwalbe (2009: 289); see also Courtenay (2000), and O'Brien et al. (2005).

11. Rosenfeld and Faircloth (2006: 14).

12. Connell (2000, 2005), Ismail (2006), Messerschmidt (2010). See also Inhorn (2012) for a thoughtful critique of this tendency to reify specific types of men and how this limits our understanding of men's lived experiences.

13. Hearn (2011: 91).

14. As argued by Petersen, both academic research and the media continue to re-

inforce the idea that "gender identity is a matter of 'consumer choice' . . . [a view that] serves to divert attention from the social structures and values that shape (although do not determine) individual beliefs and actions" (2009: 210).

15. On normalization, see Foucault (1979: 184).

16. Connell (2009: 90). See also Reeser (2010), and Watson and Shaw (2011).

17. Connell (2009: 90).

18. Ahmed (1992).

19. See for example, Abu-Lughod (2002), Hirschkind and Mahmood (2002), Mahmood (2005), Ewing (2008).

20. Amar (2011a).

21. Ibid., 37–38.

22. Bourdieu (2001 [1998]).

23. Kimmel (2006: 3).

24. For example, and as argued by Courtenay (2009: 27), "naming and confronting men's poor health status and unhealthy beliefs and behaviours may well improve their physical wellbeing, but it will necessarily undermine men's privileged position and threaten their power and authority in relation to women."

25. Maha did not agree with the politics of the Muslim Brothers, but she gave them credit for the protection they offered the protestors, especially when the horses and camels attacked Midan Square. The Muslim Brotherhood, she argued, was the only organized political group that had some training in dealing with the police. They divided themselves into several groups that broke up the pavement and passed stones to those in the front lines to throw at the attackers.

26. Hafez (2012).

27. *Al-Hayat*, Dec. 29, 2011: 19.

Glossary

aaya sughra: a minor sign signaling the Day of Judgment
Abu: father of
abyad: white
'aql: mind
asmar: dark skin
'ayyil: child *or* childish
bahdala: humiliation
baltaga: thuggery
baltagi: thug, bully
baltagiyya: thugs, bullies
bango: a strain of marijuana
bi 'aql: with reason
bi dima'ah: a crybaby
birsham: drugs consumed orally
btihtirim nafsaha: respects herself
el-nizam: the system
el-sha'b: the people
el-shari'a: the street
el-suwwaar (*alternative spelling,* thouwar): the rebels
er-ruguula mawqif: manhood as an attitude *or* a stand
gada': the honest, brave, and capable man
gad'a: *feminine of* gada'
gada'na: a mix of gallantry, generosity, and strength
gariimat sharaf: honor crime
ghabaawa: social incompetence
ghabi: a man who displays ghabaawa
ghalaba: ordinary Egyptians

ghalbaan: a humble individual; a poor soul

gid'aan: *plural of* gada'

haagaat hayfa: trivial things

haayif: trivial

hafa': insignificant

hafiyya: nobody; insignificant

haqaaniha: fair-minded

haqqak 'alayya: I owe you an apology, *or* Let me apologize to you

himish: tough and strong

hinayyin: tender; kindhearted

hiniyya: tenderness

hukumah: government; police

husn el-khaatimah: good ending

illi bye'mil raagil: one who pretends to be a man

illi fi geebu mish lih: too generous

i'mel raagil: Make a man of yourself

iswid: black, dark

kaseeb: good earner

khafeef: not serious, talks too much

khalleek raagil: Be a man

khawal: submissive

kheekha: weak *or* sissified

khushuuna: toughness

laff we daar: He roamed the city, *lit.* "He went around in circles"

ma bikabruish had: not deferring to any person, *lit.* "They do not make anyone big"

ma byisma'sh il-kalaam: being spoiled and not listening

maluush fil-khinaaq: a man who deliberately avoids physical confrontation

mawqif: position *or* stand

mawaaqif: *plural of* mawqif

mibarshim: taking birsham, drugs consumed orally by some men

midardah: educated in city ways; street savvy

min gheer ma yiftiru 'ala hadd: without oppressing others

mirakhrakh: weak, soft, and spineless

mish raagil: not a man

mistargila: a biological woman who adopts the conduct and dress code of men

moota kwaisa: good death

moota tisharaf: honorable death

muftari: unjust and brutal

nakhwa: honor

nas muhtarama: respectable people

nour: special light

qillet adab: lack of good manners

raagil: a man

raagil bi saheeh: a real man

raagil fi hayaatu, shaheed fi mamaatu: A man in his life, a martyr in his death

ruguula: manhood

saaye': worthless, or good-for-nothing

sai'at: bad deeds

san'a: a manual occupation

sanaay'i: a skilled worker, or an artisan

sawra: revolution

sha'bi: popular

shahid: a martyr

shideed: tough

singa: a long knife usually carried visibly to intimidate others

sitt bi meet raagil: a woman who equals a hundred men

sua' el-khaatimah: bad ending

tahara: purity

tarbiyyet niswaan: raised by women

tari: soft or weak

ummra: an abbreviated form of the pilgrimage ceremonies

umm: mother; mother of

unusa: femininity

usta: a master of a trade

warsha: a workshop

wazeefa: a white-collar job

Bibliography

Abaza, Mona. 2001. "Shopping Malls, Consumer Culture and the Reshaping of Public Space in Egypt." *Theory, Culture and Society* 18, no. 5: 97–122.

Abu-Lughod, Lila. 2002. "Do Muslim Women Really Need Saving? Anthropological Reflections on Cultural Relativism and Its Others." *American Anthropologist* 104, no. 2: 783–90.

———. 1993a. *Writing Women's Worlds: Bedouin Stories.* Berkeley: University of California Press.

———. 1993b. "Islam and the Gendered Discourses of Death." *International Journal of Middle Eastern Studies* 25, no. 2: 187–205.

———. 1986. *Veiled Sentiments: Honor and Poetry in a Bedouin Society.* Berkeley: University of California Press.

Aghacy, Samira. 2009. *Masculine Identity in the Fiction of the Arab East since 1967.* Syracuse, NY: Syracuse University Press.

Aguirre-Molina, Marilyn, Luisa N. Borrell, and William Vega. 2010a. "Introduction: A Social and Structural Framework for the Analysis of Latino Male's Health." In Aguirre-Molina, Borrell, and Vega, eds. (2010b), pp. 1–16.

———, eds. 2010b. *Health Issues in Latino Males: A Social and Structural Approach.* New Brunswick, NJ: Rutgers University Press.

Ahmed, Laila. 1992. *Women and Gender in Islam.* New Haven, CT: Yale University Press.

Al-Ali, Nadje. 2000. *Secularism, Gender and the State in the Middle East: The Egyptian Women's Movement.* Cambridge, UK: Cambridge University Press.

Ali, Kamran Asdar. 2002. *Planning the Family in Egypt: New Bodies, New Selves.* Austin: University of Texas Press.

Altorki, Soraya. 1999. "Patriarchy and Imperialism: Father-Son and British-Egyptian Relations in Najib Mahfouz's Trilogy." In *Intimate Selving in Arab Families,* ed. by Suad Joseph, pp. 214–34. Syracuse, NY: Syracuse University Press.

———. 1986. *Women in Saudi Arabia: Ideology and Behavior among the Elite.* New York: Columbia University Press.

Amar, Paul. 2011a. "Middle East Masculinity Studies: Discourses of 'Men in Crisis,'

Industries of Gender in Revolution." *Journal of Middle East Women's Studies* 6, no. 3: 36–70.

———. 2011b. "Turning the Gendered Politics of the Security State Inside Out?" *International Feminist Journal of Politics* 13, no. 3: 299–328.

Archer, Louise. 2009. "Race, 'Face' and Masculinity: Identities and Local Geographies of Muslim Boys." In *Muslims in Britain: Race, Place and Identities*, ed. by Peter Hopkins and Richard Gale, pp. 74–91. Edinburgh: Edinburgh University Press.

Ariès, Philippe. 1974. *Western Attitudes toward Death: From the Middle Ages to the Present*. Baltimore: Johns Hopkins University Press.

Asad, Talal. 2007. *On Suicide Bombing*. New York: Columbia University Press.

Azeb, Sophia. 2012. "Why SCAF to Be Blamed?" *Soccer Politics / The Politics of Football*, Feb. 2. http://sites.duke.edu/wcwp/2012/02/02/ (accessed Mar. 3, 2012).

Barker, Gary T. 2005. *Dying to be Men: Youth, Masculinity and Social Exclusion*. New York: Routledge.

Baron, Beth. 2005. *Egypt as a Woman: Nationalism, Gender, and Politics*. Berkeley: University of California Press.

Beauvoir, Simone de. 1964. *The Second Sex*. New York: Knopf.

Beck, Lois, and Nikki Keddie, eds. 1978. *Women in the Muslim World*. Cambridge, MA: Harvard University Press.

Bettie, Julie. 2003. *Women Without Class: Girls, Race, and Identity*. Berkeley: University of California Press.

Boddy, Janice. 1997. "The Womb as Oasis: The Symbolic Context of Pharaonic Circumcision in Rural Northern Sudan." In *The Gender/Sexuality Reader*, ed. by Roger Lancaster and Micaela di Leonardo, pp. 309–24. London: Routledge.

Bordo, Susan. 1999. *The Male Body*. New York: Farrar, Strauss and Giroux.

Bourdieu, Pierre. 2001 (1998). *Masculine Domination*. Stanford, CA: Stanford University Press.

———. 2000 (1997). *Pascalian Meditations*. Stanford, CA: Stanford University Press.

———. 1990. *The Logic of Practice*. Stanford, CA: Stanford University Press.

———. 1989. "Social Space and Symbolic Power." *Sociological Theory* 7, no. 1: 14–25.

———. 1984. *Distinction: A Social Critique of the Judgement of Taste*. Cambridge, MA: Harvard University Press.

———. 1977. *Outline of a Theory of Practice*. Cambridge, UK: Cambridge University Press.

———. 1966. "The Sentiment of Honour in Kabyle Society." In *Honour and Shame*, ed. by J. G. Peristiany, pp. 191–241. Chicago: University of Chicago Press.

Bourgois, Philippe. 1995. *In Search of Respect*. Cambridge, UK: Cambridge University Press.

Brod, Harry. 1994. "Some Thoughts on Some Histories of Some Masculinities: Jews and Other Others." In *Theorizing Masculinities*, ed. by Harry Brod and Michael Kaufman, pp. 82–76. Thousand Oaks, CA: Sage.

Broom, Alex, and Philip Tovey. 2009a. "Introduction: Men's Health in Context." In Broom and Tovey, eds. (2009b), pp. 1–8.

———, eds. 2009b. *Men's Health: Body, Identity and Social Context.* Oxford: Wiley-Blackwell.

Butler, Judith. 1999. *Gender Trouble: Feminism and the Subversion of Identity.* New York: Routledge.

———. 1993. *Bodies That Matter: On the Discursive Limits of "Sex."* New York: Routledge.

Catedra, Maria. 2004. "Kinds of Death and the House." In Robben, ed. (2009), pp. 77–90.

Caton, Steven C. 1990. *"Peaks of Yemen I Summon": Poetry as Cultural Practice in a North Yemeni Tribe.* Berkeley: University of California Press.

Certeau, Michel de. 1988. *The Practice of Everyday Life.* Berkeley: University of California Press.

Chamberlin, Ann. 2006. *A History of Women's Seclusion in the Middle East: The Veil in the Looking Glass.* New York: Haworth.

Chapman, David L., and Brett Josef Grubisic. 2009. *American Hunks: The Muscular Male Body in Popular Culture, 1860–1970.* Vancouver, BC: Arsenal Pulp.

Collins, Randall. 2000. "Situational Stratification: A Micro-Macro Theory of Inequality." *Theory: A Journal of the American Sociological Association* 18, no. 1: 17–43.

Connell, R. W. 2009. *Gender.* Cambridge, UK: Polity.

———. 2005. *Masculinities.* Berkeley: University of California Press.

———. 2002. "On Hegemonic Masculinity and Violence: Responses to Jefferson and Hall." *Theoretical Criminology* 6, no. 89: 89–99.

———. 2000. *The Men and the Boys.* Berkeley: University of California Press.

———. 1987. *Gender and Power.* Cambridge, UK: Polity.

Connell, R. W., and James Messerschmidt. 2005. "Hegemonic Masculinity: Rethinking the Concept." *Gender and Society* 19, no. 6: 829–59.

Courtenay, Will. 2011. *Dying to Be Men: Psychosocial, Environmental, and Biobehavioral Directions in Promoting the Health of Men and Boys.* New York: Routledge.

———. 2009. "Theorising Masculinity and Men's Health." In Broom and Tovey, eds. (2009b), pp. 9–32.

———. 2000. "Constructions of Masculinity and Their Influence on Men's Wellbeing: A Theory of Gender and Health." *Social Science and Medicine* 50, no. 10: 1385–1401.

Crapanzano, Vincent. 1980. *Tuhami: Portrait of a Moroccan.* Chicago: University of Chicago Press.

Crenshaw, Kimberle. 2011. "Demarginalising the Intersection of Race and Sex: A Black Feminist Critique of Anti-discrimination Doctrine, Feminist Theory, and Anti-racist Politics." In *Framing Intersectionality: Debates on a Multi-faceted Concept in Gender Studies,* ed. by Helma Lutz, Maria Teresa Herrera Vivar, and Linda Supik, pp. 25–43. Farnham, UK: Ashgate.

Csordas, Thomas 1990. "Embodiment as a Paradigm for Anthropology." *Ethos* 18, no. 1: 5–47.

Dorsey, James. 2012. "Ultra Violence: How Egypt's Soccer Mobs Are Threatening the Revolution." *Foreign Policy*, Feb. 12. www.foreignpolicy.com (accessed Feb. 20, 2012).

Deeb, Lara. 2006. *An Enchanted Modern: Gender and Public Piety in Shi'i Lebanon.* Princeton, NJ: Princeton University Press.

Dresch, Paul. 1989. *Tribes, Government, and History in Yemen.* Oxford: Oxford University Press.

Durham, Deborah. 2000. "Youth and Social Imagination in Africa: Introduction to Part 1 and 2." *Anthropological Quarterly* 37, no. 3: 113–20.

Durkheim, Emile. 2002. "The Rules of Sociological Method." In *Classical Sociological Theory*, ed. by Craig Calhoun, pp. 109–27. Malden, MA: Blackwell.

Early, Evelyn. 1993. *Baladi Women of Cairo: Playing with an Egg and a Stone.* Boulder, CO: Lynne Rienner.

Eickelman, Christine. 1984. *Women and Community in Oman.* New York: New York University Press.

El Amrani, Issandr. 2012. "In Port Said." *LRB Blog*, Feb. 2. www.lrb.co.uk/blog/2012/02/02/issandr-el-amrani/in-port-said (accessed Mar. 10, 2012).

Elias, Norbert. 1993. *The Civilizing Process.* Oxford: Blackwell.

El-Kholy, Heba. 2002. *Defiance and Compliance: Negotiating Gender in Low-Income Cairo.* New York: Berghahn.

El-Messiri, Sawsan. 1978. *Ibn al-Balad: A Concept of Egyptian Identity.* Leiden, Netherlands: E.J. Brill.

El Sadda, Hoda. 2012. *Gender, Nation, and the Arabic Novel: Egypt, 1892–2008.* Syracuse, NY: Syracuse University Press.

El Shakry, Omnia 2007. *The Great Social Laboratory: Subjects of Knowledge in Colonial and Postcolonial Egypt.* Stanford, CA: Stanford University Press.

Elyachar, Julia. 2011. "The Political Economy of Movement and Gesture in Cairo." *Journal of the Royal Anthropological Institute* 17, no. 1: 82–99.

———. 2005. *Markets of Dispossession: NGOs, Economic Development, and the State in Cairo.* Durham, NC: Duke University Press.

Evans-Pritchard, E. E. 1958. "The Nuer of the Southern Sudan." In *African Political Systems*, ed. by Meyer Fortes and E. E. Evans-Pritchard, pp. 272–96. London: Oxford University Press.

Ewing, Katherine Pratt. 2008. *Stolen Honor: Stigmatizing Muslim Men in Berlin.* Stanford, CA: Stanford University Press.

Fernea, Elizabeth Warnock, and Basima Qattan Bezirgan, eds. 1977. *Middle Eastern Muslim Women Speak.* Austin: University of Texas Press.

Fernea, Robert. 2000. "A Limited Construction of Masculinity (Gilsenan's Lords of the Lebanese Marches: Violence and Narrative in an Arab Society)." *Current Anthropology* 41, no. 4: 693–94.

Firth, Shirley. 1989. "The Good Death: Approaches to Death, Dying, and Bereavement among British Hindus." In *Perspectives on Death and Dying: Cross-cultural and Multi-disciplinary Views*, ed. by Arthur Berger, Paul Badham, Austin H. Kutscher, Joyce Berger, Michael Perry, and John Beloff, pp. 66–83. Philadelphia: Charles Press.

Forth, Christopher. 2008. *Masculinity in the Modern West: Gender, Civilization, and the Body*. New York: Palgrave Macmillan.

Foucault, Michel. 1982. "The Subject and Power." *Critical Inquiry* 8, no. 4: 777–95.

———. 1979. *Discipline and Punish: The Birth of the Prison*. New York: Vintage.

Gray, John. 2004. *Men Are from Mars, Women Are from Venus: The Classic Guide to Understanding the Opposite Sex*. New York: Harper Paperbacks.

Geertz, Clifford. 1988. *Works and Lives*. Stanford, CA: Stanford University Press.

———. 1979. "Suq: The Bazaar Economy in Sefrou." In *Meaning and Order in Moroccan Society*, ed. by Clifford Geertz, Hildred Geertz, and Lawrence Rosen, pp. 123–225. Cambridge, UK: Cambridge University Press.

———. 1973. *The Interpretation of Cultures*. New York: Basic Books.

Gerholm, Tomas. 1977. *Market, Mosque and Mafraj: Social Inequality in a Yemeni Town*. Stockholm: University of Stockholm.

Ghannam, Farha. (Forthcoming). "Contested Traditions: Gender and Mourning Practices in Egypt." In *Everyday Life in the Muslim Middle East*, 3rd ed., ed. by Donna Lee Bowen, Evelyn A. Early, and Becky Schulthies. Bloomington: Indiana University Press.

———. 2012. "Meanings and Feelings: Local Interpretations of the Use of Violence in the Egyptian Revolution." *American Ethnologist* 39, no. 1: 32–36.

———. 2011. "Mobility, Liminality, and Embodiment in Urban Egypt." *American Ethnologist* 38, no. 4: 790–800.

———. 2008a. "Beauty, Whiteness, and Desire: Media, Consumption, and Embodiment in Egypt." *International Journal of Middle East Studies* 40, no. 4 (Nov.): 544–46.

———. 2008b. "Two Dreams in a Global City: Class and Space in Urban Egypt." In *Other Cities, Other Worlds*, ed. by Andreas Hussain, pp. 267–88. Durham, NC: Duke University Press.

———. 2005. "Women, Gender and the Public/Private Dichotomy." In *Encyclopedia of Women and Islamic Cultures*, vol. 2, pp. 685–88. Leiden, Netherlands: Brill Academic Publishers.

———. 2004. "Quest for Beauty: Globalization, Identity, and the Production of Gendered Bodies in Low-Income Cairo." In *Health and Identity in Egypt*, ed. by Hania Sholkamy and Farha Ghannam, pp. 43–64. Cairo: American University in Cairo Press.

———. 2002. *Remaking the Modern: Space, Relocation, and the Politics of Identity in a Global Cairo*. Berkeley: University of California Press.

Ghonim, Wael. 2012. *Revolution 2.0: The Power of the People Is Greater Than the People in Power*. Boston: Houghton Mifflin Harcourt.

Ghoussoub, Mai, and Emma Sinclair-Webb, eds. 2000. *Imagined Masculinities: Male Identity in the Modern Middle East*. London: Saqi Books.

Giddens, Anthony. 1991. *Modernity and Self-identity: Self and Society in the Late Modern Age*. Stanford, CA: Stanford University Press.

Gilligan, James. 2004. "Culture, Gender, and Violence: 'We Are Not Women.'" In *The Gendered Society Reader*, ed. by Michael S. Kimmel and Amy Aronson, pp. 427–36. New York: Oxford University Press.

Gilman, Sander. 1998. *Making the Body Beautiful: A Cultural History of Aesthetic Surgery*. Princeton, NJ: Princeton University Press.

Gilmore, David. 1990. *Manhood in the Making: Cultural Concepts of Masculinity*. New Haven, CT: Yale University Press.

Gilsenan, Michael. 1996. *Lords of the Lebanese Marches: Violence and Narrative in an Arab Society*. Berkeley: University of California Press.

———. 1982. *Recognizing Islam: Religion and Society in the Modern Arab World*. New York: Pantheon.

Glenn, Evelyn, ed. 2009a. *Shades of Difference: Why Skin Color Matters*. Stanford, CA: Stanford University Press.

———. 2009b. "Consuming Lightness: Segmented Markets and Global Capital in the Skin-Whitening Trade." In Glenn, ed. (2009a), pp. 166–87.

Goffman, Erving. 1959. *The Presentation of the Self in the Everyday Life*. New York: Double Day Archor.

Gregory, Steven. 2007. *The Devil behind the Mirror: Globalization and Politics in the Dominican Republic*. Berkeley: University of California Press.

Gutmann, Matthew. 2007. *The Meaning of Macho: Being a Man in Mexico City*. Berkeley: University of California Press.

Hafez, Sherine. 2012. "No Longer a Bargain: Women, Masculinity, and the Egyptian Uprising." *American Ethnologist* 39, no. 1: 37–42.

Hall, Stuart. 1995. "The Question of Cultural Identity." In *Modernity: An Introduction to Modern Societies*, ed. by Stuart Hall, David Held, Don Hubert, and Kenneth Thompson, pp. 596–634. Cambridge, UK: Polity.

Hamdy, Sherine. 2009. "Islam, Fatalism, and Medical Intervention: Lessons from Egypt on the Cultivation of Forbearance (*Sabr*) and Reliance on God (*Tawakkul*)." *Anthropological Quarterly* 82, no. 1: 173–96.

———. 2008. "When the State and Your Kidneys Fail: Political Etiologies in an Egyptian Dialysis Ward." *American Ethnologist* 35, no. 4: 553–69.

Hearn, Jeff. 2011. "Neglected Intersectionalities in Studying Men: Age(ing), Virtuality, Transnationality." In *Framing Intersectionality: Debates on a Multi-faceted Concept in Gender Studies*, ed. by Helma Lutz, Maria Teresa Herrera Vivar, and Linda Supik, pp. 89–104. Farnham, UK: Ashgate.

———. 2004. "From Hegemonic Masculinity to the Hegemony of Men." *Feminist Theory* 5, no. 1: 49–72.

Herdt, Gilbert. 1994. *Guardians of the Flutes: Idioms of Masculinity*. Chicago: University Of Chicago Press.

Herzfeld, Michael. 1985. *The Poetics of Manhood: Contest and Identity in a Cretan Mountain Village*. Princeton, NJ: Princeton University Press.

Hirschkind, Charles. 2008. "Cultures of Death: Media, Religion, Bioethics." *Social Text* 26, no. 3 96: 39–58.

———. 2006. *The Ethical Soundscape: Cassette Sermons and Islamic Counterpublics*. New York: Columbia University Press.

Hirschkind, Charles, and Saba Mahmood. 2002. "Feminism, the Taliban, and Politics of Counter-Insurgency." *Anthropological Quarterly* 75, no. 2: 339–54.

Hockey, Jennifer Lorna, and Allison James. 2003. *Social Identities across the Life Course*. New York: Palgrave Macmillan.

Holzer, Harry. 2009. "The Employment Problems of Black Men in Segregated Urban Areas." In *Public Housing and the Legacy of Segregation*, ed. by Margery Austin Turner, Susan J. Popkin, and Lynette Rawlings, pp. 237–46. Washington, DC: Urban Institute Press.

Hoodfar, Homa. 1996. "Egyptian Male Migration and Urban Families Left Behind: 'Feminization of the Egyptian Family' or a Reaffirmation of Traditional Gender Roles?" In *Development, Change, and Gender in Cairo: A View from the Household*, ed. by Diane Singerman and Homma Hoodfar, pp. 51–79. Bloomington: Indiana University Press.

hooks, bell. 2004. *The Will to Change: Men, Masculinity, and Love*. New York: Washington Square Press.

Howson, Alexandra. 2004. *The Body in Society: An Introduction*. Malden, MA: Polity.

Inhorn, Marcia. 2012. *The New Arab Man: Emergent Masculinities, Technologies, and Islam in the Middle East*. Princeton, NJ: Princeton University Press.

———. 2009. "Male Genital Cutting: Masculinity, Reproduction, and Male Infertility Surgeries in Egypt and Lebanon." In *Reconceiving the Second Sex: Men, Masculinity, and Reproduction*, ed. by Marcia C. Inhorn, Tine Tjornhoj-Thomsen, Helene Goldberg, and Maruska La Cour Mosegaard, pp. 253–80. New York: Berghahn Books.

———. 2005. "Sexuality, Masculinity, and Infertility in Egypt: Potent Troubles in Marital and Medical Encounters." In *African Masculinities: Men in Africa from the Late Nineteenth Century to the Present*, ed. by Lahoucine Ouzgane and Robert Morell, pp. 289–304. New York: Palgrave Macmillan.

———. 1996. *Infertility and Patriarchy: The Cultural Politics of Gender and Family Life in Egypt*. Philadelphia: University of Pennsylvania Press.

———. 1994. *Quest for Conception: Gender, Infertility, and Egyptian Medical Traditions*. Philadelphia: University of Pennsylvania Press.

Iskandar, Adel. 2011. "The Baltageya: Egypt's Counterrevolution." *Huffington Post*, May 16. www.huffingtonpost.com/adel-iskandar/the-baltageya-egypts-coun_b_862267.html (accessed May 17, 2011).

Ismail, Salwa. 2006. *Political Life in Cairo's New Quarters: Encountering the Everyday State*. Minneapolis: University of Minnesota Press.

Jacob, Wilson Chacko. 2011. *Working Out Egypt: Effendi Masculinity and Subject For-mation in Colonial Modernity, 1870–1940*. Durham, NC: Duke University Press.

Jenkins, Richard. 2008. *Social Identity*. London: Routledge.

Johnson-Hanks, Jennifer. 2002. "On the Limits of Life Stages in Ethnography: Toward a Theory of Vital Conjunctures." *American Anthropologist* 104, no. 3: 865–80.

Joseph, Suad. 2002. "Lebanon/United States." In *Remembering Childhood in the Middle East: Memoirs from a Century of Change*, ed. by Elizabeth Fernea, pp. 302–9. Austin: University of Texas Press.

———. 2001. "Brother/Sister Relationships: Connectivity, Love, and Power in the Re-production of Patriarchy in Lebanon." In *Arab Society: Class, Gender, Power, and Development*, ed. by Nicholas Hopkins and Saad Eddin Ibrahim, pp. 227–62. Cairo: American University in Cairo Press.

———, ed. 1999. *Intimate Selving in Arab Families: Gender, Self, and Identity*. Syracuse, NY: Syracuse University Press.

Kanaaneh, Rhoda. 2005. "Boys or Men? Duped or 'Made'? Palestinian Soldiers in the Israeli Military." *American Ethnologist* 32, no. 2: 260–75.

Kandiyoti, Deniz. 2005. "Bargaining with Patriarchy." In *Gender through the Prism of Difference*, ed. by Maxine Baca Zinn, Pierrette Hondagneu-Sotelo, and Michael A. Messner, pp. 26–35. Oxford: Oxford University Press.

———. 1994. "The Paradoxes of Masculinity: Some Thoughts on Segregated Societies." In *Dislocating Masculinity: Comparative Ethnographies*, ed. by Andrea Cornwall and Nancy Lindisfarne, pp. 197–213. London: Routledge.

Kapchan, Deborah. 1996. *Gender on the Market: Moroccan Women and the Revoicing of Tradition*. Philadelphia: University of Pennsylvania.

Khal, Abdu. 2000. "Circumcision and Making Men." In Ghoussoub and Sinclair-Webb, eds. (2000), pp. 29–32.

Kholoussy, Hanan. 2010. *For Better, For Worse: The Marriage Crisis That Made Modern Egypt*. Stanford, CA: Stanford University Press.

Kimmel, Michael. 2011. *The Gendered Society*. New York: Oxford University Press.

———. 2006. *Manhood in America: A Cultural History*. New York: Oxford University Press.

Lancaster, William. 1997. *The Rwala Bedouin Today*. Cambridge, UK: Cambridge University Press.

Lancy, David F. 2008. *The Anthropology of Childhood: Cherubs, Chattel, Changelings*. Cambridge, UK: Cambridge University Press.

Lane, Edward. 1978. *Manners and Customs of the Modern Egyptians*. The Hague: East-West Publications.

Lehman, Peter, ed. 2001. *Masculinity: Bodies, Movies, Culture*. New York: Routledge.

Lock, Margaret. 2000. "On Dying Twice: Culture, Technology and the Determina-tion of Death." In *Living and Working with the New Medical Technologies*, ed. by Margaret Lock, Allan Young, and Alberto Cambrosio, pp. 233–62. Cambridge, UK: Cambridge University Press.

Lorber, Judith. 2000. *Gender and the Social Construction of Illness*. Walnut Creek, CA: Altamira.

Luciano, Lynne. 2001. *Looking Good: Male Body Image in Modern America*. New York: Hill and Wang.

Lutz, Helma, Maria Teresa Herrera Vivar, and Linda Supik, eds. 2011. *Framing Intersectionality: Debates on a Multi-faceted Concept in Gender Studies*. Farnham, UK: Ashgate.

MacLeod, Arlene Elowe. 1991. *Accommodating Protest: Working Women, the New Veiling, and Change in Cairo*. Cairo: American University in Cairo Press.

Mahmood, Saba. 2005. *Politics of Piety: The Islamic Revival and the Feminist Subject*. Princeton, NJ: Princeton University Press.

Martin, Emily. 1992. *The Woman in the Body: A Cultural Analysis of Reproduction*. Boston: Beacon.

Martino, Wayne, Michael Kehler, and Marcus B. Weaver-Hightower. 2009. *The Problem with Boys' Education: Beyond the Backlash*. New York: Routledge.

Matthews, Hugh. 2003. "The Street as a Liminal Space: The Barbed Spaces of Childhood." In *Children in the City: Home, Neighbourhood and Community*, ed. by Pia Christensen and Margaret O'Brien, pp. 101–17. London: RoutledgeFlamer.

Meneley, Anne. 2007. "Fashions and Fundamentalism in Fin-de-Siècle Yemen: Chador Barbie and Islamic Socks." *Cultural Anthropology* 22, no. 2: 214–43.

———. 1996. *Tournaments of Value: Sociability and Hierarchy in a Yemeni Town*. Toronto: University of Toronto Press.

Mernissi, Fatima. 1989. *Doing Daily Battle: Interviews with Moroccan Women*. New Brunswick, NJ: Rutgers University Press.

———. 1987. *Beyond the Veil: Male-Female Dynamics in Modern Muslim Society*. Bloomington: Indian University Press.

Merry, Sally Engle. 2001. "Spatial Governmentality and the New Urban Social Order: Controlling Gender Violence through Law." *American Anthropologist* 103, no. 1: 16–29.

Messerschmidt, James. 2010. *Hegemonic Masculinities and Camouflaged Politics: Unmasking the Bush Dynasty and Its War against Iraq*. Boulder, CO: Paradigm.

Montgomery, Heather. 2009. *An Introduction to Childhood: Anthropological Perspectives on Children's Lives*. Oxford: Wiley-Blackwell.

Moore, Henrietta L. 2007. *The Subject of Anthropology: Gender, Symbolism and Psychoanalysis*. Cambridge, UK: Polity.

———. 1999. "Whatever Happened to Women and Men? Gender and Other Crises in Anthropology." In *Anthropological Theory Today*, ed. by Henrietta L. Moore, pp. 151–71. Cambridge, UK: Polity.

Morgan, David. 2006. "The Crisis in Masculinity." In *Handbook of Gender and Women's Studies*, ed. by Kathy Davis, Mary Evans, and Judith Lorber, pp. 109–23. London: Sage.

Muwahidi, Ahmad Anisuzzaman. 1989. "Islamic Perspectives on Death and Dying." In *Perspectives on Death and Dying: Cross-cultural and Multi-disciplinary Views*, ed. by

Arthur Berger, Paul Badham, Austin H. Kutscher, Joyce Berger, Michael Perry, and John Beloff, pp. 38–65. Philadelphia: Charles Press.

Najmabadi, Afsaneh. 1998. "Feminism in an Islamic Republic: 'Years of Hardship, Years of Growth.'" In *Islam, Gender, and Social Change*, ed. by Yvonne Y. Haddad and John Esposito, pp. 59–84. New York: Oxford University Press.

Nakamura, Karen, and Hisako Matsuo. 2003. "Female Masculinity and Fantasy Spaces: Transcending Genders in the Takarazuka Theatre and Japanese Popular Culture." In *Men and Masculinities in Contemporary Japan: Dislocating the Salaryman Doxa*, ed. by James Roberson and Nobue Suzuki, pp. 59–76. London: RoutledgeCurzon.

Nakamura, Tadashi. 2003. "Regendering Batterers: Domestic Violence and Men's Movements." In *Men and Masculinities in Contemporary Japan: Dislocating the Salaryman Doxa*, ed. by James Roberson and Nobue Suzuki, pp. 162–79. London: RoutledgeCurzon.

Nash, Jennifer. 2008 "Re-thinking Intersectionality." *Feminist Review*, no. 89: 1–15.

Nelson, Cynthia. 1974. "Public and Private Politics: Women in the Middle Eastern World." *American Ethnologist* 1, no. 3: 551–63.

O'Brien, Rosaleen, Kate Hunt, and Graham Hart. 2005. "It's Caveman Stuff, But That Is to a Certain Extent How Guys Still Operate: Men's Accounts of Masculinity and Help Seeking." *Social Science and Medicine*, no. 61: 503–16.

Ouzgane, Lahoucine, ed. 2006. *Islamic Masculinities*. London: Zed.

Palgi, Phyllis, and Henry Abramovitch. 1984. "Death: A Cross-cultural Perspective." *Annual Review of Anthropology* 13: 385–417.

Peteet, Julie. 2000. "Male Gender and Rituals of Resistance in the Palestinian Intifada: A Cultural Politics of Violence." In Ghoussoub and Sinclair-Webb, eds. (2000), pp. 103–26.

Petersen, Alan. 2009. "Future Research Agenda in Men's Health." In Broom and Tovey, eds. (2009b), pp. 202–14.

Peterson, Mark. 2011. *Connected in Cairo: Growing up Cosmopolitan in the Modern Middle East*. Bloomington: Indiana University Press.

Reeser, Todd W. 2010. *Masculinity in Theory: An Introduction*. Oxford: Wiley-Blackwell.

Reischer, Erica, and Kathryn Koo. 2004. "The Body Beautiful: Symbolism and Agency in the Social World." *Annual Review of Anthropology* 33: 297–317.

Riska, Elianne. 2003. "Gendering the Medicalization Thesis." In *Gender Perspectives on Health and Medicine: Key Themes*, ed. by M. S. Segal and V. Demos, pp. 59–87. Oxford: Elsevier.

Robben, Antonius, ed. 2009. *Death, Mourning, and Burial: A Cross-cultural Reader*. Hoboken, NJ: John Wiley & Sons.

Roberson, James E. 2003. "Japanese Working-Class Masculinities: Marginalized Complicity." In *Men and Masculinities in Contemporary Japan: Dislocating the Salaryman Doxa*, ed. by James Roberson and Nobue Suzuki, pp. 26–43. London: Routledge-Curzon.

Rosenfeld, Dana, and Christopher A. Faircloth. 2006 "Medicalized Masculinities: The

Missing Link?." In *Medicalized Masculinities*, ed. by Dana Rosenfeld and Christopher Faircloth, pp. 1–20. Philadelphia: Temple University Press.

Sabo, Donald, and David Gordon, eds. 1995. *Men's Health and Illness: Gender, Power and the Body*. Thousand Oaks, CA: Sage.

Said, Edward. 1978. *Orientalism*. London: Routledge and Kegan Paul.

Scheper-Hughes, Nancy, and Margaret M. Lock. 1987. "The Mindful Body: A Prolegomenon to Future Work in Medical Anthropology." *Medical Anthropology Quarterly* 1, no. 1: 6–41.

Schielke, Samuli. 2008. "Policing Ambiguity: Muslim Saints-day Festivals and the Moral Geography of Public Space in Egypt." *American Ethnologist* 35, no. 4: 539–52.

Schrock, Douglas, and Michael Schwalbe. 2009. "Men, Masculinity, and Manhood Acts." *Annual Reviews of Sociology* 35: 277–95.

Seal, David Wyatt, and Anke Ehrhardt. 2007. "Masculinity and Urban Men: Perceived Scripts for Courtship, Romantic, and Sexual Interactions with Women." In *Cultures, Society, and Sexuality: A Reader*, ed. by Richard Parker and Peter Aggleton, pp. 375–96. London: Routledge.

Shaheen, Jack G. 2001. *Reel Bad Arabs: How Hollywood Vilifies a People*. New York: Olive Branch Press.

Shehata, Samer. 2009. *Shop Floor Culture and Politics in Egypt*. Albany: State University of New York Press.

Shilling, Chris. 2002. *The Body and Social Theory*. London: Sage.

Singerman, Diane. 1995. *Avenues of Participation: Family, Politics, and Networks in Urban Quarters of Cairo*. Princeton, NJ: Princeton University Press.

Starrett, Gregory. 1995. "The Hexis of Interpretation: Islam and the Body in the Egyptian Popular School." *American Ethnologist* 22, no. 4: 953–69.

Strathern, Marilyn. 2010. "Self-interest and the Social Good: Some Implications of Hagen Gender Imagery." In *Readings for a History of Anthropological Theory*, ed. by Paul A. Erickson and Liam D. Murphy, pp. 370–89. Toronto: University of Toronto Press.

Taussig, Michael. 1992. "Tactility and Distraction." In *Rereading Cultural Anthropology*, ed. by George Marcus, pp. 8–14. Durham, NC: Duke University Press.

Taylor, Yvette, Sally Hines, and Mark E. Casey, eds. 2011. *Theorizing Intersectionality and Sexuality*. New York: Palgrave Macmillan.

Tharwat, Ahmed. 2011. "The Baltagiya and the Post Revolution Egypt." *Insight News*, Sept. 2. http://insightnews.com/commentary/7940-the-baltagiya-and-the-post-revolution-egypt (accessed Sept. 3, 2011).

Thomas, Calvin. 1996. *Male Matters: Masculinity, Anxiety, and the Male Body on the Line*. Urbana: University of Illinois Press.

Thomas, Lynn. 2009. "Skin Lighteners in South Africa: Transnational Entanglements and Technologies of the Self." In Glenn, ed. (2009a), pp. 188–210.

Turner, Bryan. 2009. "The Sociology of the Body." In *The New Blackwell Companion to Social Theory*, ed. by Bryan Turner, pp. 188–210. Oxford: Wiley-Blackwell.

Turner, Terence. 1995. "Social Body and Embodied Subject: Bodiliness, Subjectivity, and Sociality among the Kayapo." *Cultural Anthropology* 10, no. 2: 143–70.

Turner, Victor. 1982. *From Ritual to Theatre: The Human Seriousness of Play*. New York: Performing Arts Journal Publications.

———. 1980. "Social Dramas and Stories about Them." *Critical Inquiry* 7, no. 1: 141–68.

———. 1967. *The Forest of Symbols: Aspects of Ndembu Ritual*. Ithaca, NY: Cornell University Press.

Vaid, Jyotsna. 2009. "Fair Enough? Color and Commodification of Self in Indian Matrimonials." In Glenn, ed. (2009a), pp. 148–165.

Watson, Elwood, and Marc Shaw, eds. 2011. *Performing American Masculinities: The 21st-Century Man in Popular Culture*. Bloomington: Indiana University Press.

Watson, Jonathan. 2000. *Male Bodies: Health, Culture, and Identity*. Philadelphia: Open University Press.

West, Candace, and Don H. Zimmerman. 2010. "Gender Diversity and the Binary." In *Doing Gender Diversity: Readings in Theory and Real-World Experience*, ed. by Rebecca F. Plante and Lis M. Maurer, pp. 3–12. Boulder, CO: Westview.

Whitehead, N. L., ed. 2004. *Violence*. Santa Fe, NM: School of American Research Press.

Whitehead, Stephen. 2002. *Men and Masculinities: Key Themes and New Directions*. Cambridge, UK: Polity.

Wikan, Unni. 1996. *Tomorrow, God Willing: Self-made Destinies in Cairo*. Chicago: University of Chicago Press.

Williams, Raymond. 1977 (1990). *Marxism and Literature*. Oxford: Oxford University Press.

Willis, Paul. 1981. *Learning to Labor: How Working Class Kids Get Working Class Jobs*. New York: Columbia University Press.

Zelizer, Viviana A. 1985. *Pricing the Priceless Child: The Changing Social Value of Children*. New York: Basic Books.

Zuckerhut, Patricia. 2011. "Feminist Anthropological Perspectives on Violence." In *Gender and Violence in the Middle East*, ed. by Moha Ennaji and Fatima Sadiqi, pp. 13–26. London: Routledge.

Index

Made in the USA
Lexington, KY
07 September 2016